HARPERCOLLINS COLLEGE OUTLINE

Introduction to Accounting II

David Minars, J.D., M.B.A., C.P.A.
Brooklyn College

Jae K. Shim, Ph.D.
California State University, Long Beach

Joel G. Siegel, Ph.D., C.P.A.
Queens College

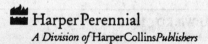
HarperPerennial
A Division of HarperCollins Publishers

An American BookWorks Corporation Production

Project Manager: Mary Mooney
Editor: Robert A. Weinstein

Library of Congress Cataloging-in-Publication Data

Minars, David
  Introduction to accounting II / David Minars, Jae Shim, Joel Siegel.
    p. cm. — (HarperCollins college outline)
  Includes index.
  ISBN: 0-06-467158-5
  1. Corporation—Accounting. 2. Managerial accounting.
I. Shim, Jae K. II. Siegel, Joel G. III. Title. IV. Title.
Introduction to accounting 2. V. Series
HF5686.C7S49 1993
657—dc20   92–53292

93 94 95 96 97 ABW/RRD 10 9 8 7 6 5 4 3 2 1

Introduction to
Accounting II

Contents

Preface

Introduction to Accounting II presents all important advanced accounting topics clearly and concisely, thereby enabling students to significantly enhance their understanding of these topics. The text covers financial accounting, managerial accounting, and taxation. Numerous illustrations and accounting problems with solutions are also integrated, and work synergistically to provide the beginning accounting student with an in-depth understanding of the material under discussion in class.

Although this study guide is primarily intended for students enrolled in the second half of an introductory accounting course at both the undergraduate and graduate levels, it is also highly recommended for individuals seeking college credit by examination and students who need a review of the subject before proceeding to more advanced accounting courses.

The text enables students to map out a realistic approach to studying that includes review and feedback. A good personal study system, conscientiously applied, will endow the student with knowledge and confidence by reducing difficult accounting topics to a series of manageable tasks.

The authors would like to thank Professor John Valenzuela and Tanu Lan for their assistance in this book.

David Minars
Jae K. Shim
Joel G. Siegel

Part 1

Financial Accounting

1

Corporations

The income statement is a financial report that summarizes all revenue and expense items for a period of time and shows the stockholders the factors that resulted in a net income or net loss for a given period. These factors include all revenues and expenses, as well as discontinued operations, extraordinary items, accounting changes, and earnings per share. These items should be disclosed net of taxes after income from continuing operations on the income statement.

INCOME STATEMENT DISCLOSURES

The accounting profession has not mandated a specific format for the income statement; either the single-step or multi-step form is permitted. The accounting profession has also taken the position that income for a period should be reported on an all-inclusive or comprehensive income basis. This rule requires that income or loss for a period should include all revenues, expenses, gains, and losses except for prior period adjustments. Income statement classifications include discontinued operations, extraordinary items, and accounting changes. In addition, earnings per share figures should be disclosed.

Gain or Loss on Discontinued Operations

According to Accounting Principles Board (APB) Statement No. 30, "Reporting the Results of Operations," the gain or loss on discontinued operations (less applicable taxes), together with the loss on disposal of a segment (less applicable taxes), should be shown separately on the income statement. A large corporation may engage in several lines of business. For example, a company may engage in manufacturing and also run a restaurant chain. Each significant part of the company is a segment of the business. If a business sells a segment, it must be reported separately because a company cannot continue to sell segments. Reporting discontinued operations separately enhances the usefulness of the income statement and enables a reader to evaluate the ongoing activities of the enterprise. APB Statement No. 30 provides the following format for the presentation of the income statement:

Income from continuing operations before income taxes	$XXXX	
Provision for income taxes	XXX	
Income from continuing operations		$XXXX
Discontinued operations (Note):		
Income (loss) from operations of discontinued Division X (less applicable income taxes of $_____)		XXXX
Gain (loss) on disposal of Division X, (less applicable income taxes of $_____)		XXXX XXXX
Net income		$XXXX

Solved Problem 1.1. Presentation of Discontinued Operations, Net of Taxes, in the Income Statement

On January 1, 1992, the Board of Directors of the Casterline Medical Supply Corporation decided to discontinue operations of one of its divisions. On September 1, 1992, when the loss from this division's operations for the year was $200,000, the assets of the division were sold for a gain of $500,000. The income from continuing operations, not including the $200,000 loss and $500,000 gain, was $4,000,000 for the year 1992. Assuming a tax rate of 34%, prepare a partial income statement showing gains and losses from the phase-out of discontinued operations.

Solution 1.1

Income from continuing operations before income taxes		$4,000,000
Provision for income taxes ($4,000,000 × 34%)		1,360,000
Income from continuing operations		$2,640,000
Discontinued operations (Note):		
Income (loss) from operations of discontinued Division X (less applicable income taxes of $68,000)	$ (132,000)	
Gain (loss) on disposal of Division X, including provision (less applicable income taxes of $170,000)	330,000	198,000
Net income		$2,838,000

Extraordinary Items

There are two major criteria for extraordinary items: First, they must be unusual in nature; the underlying event or transaction must possess a high degree of abnormality. They must also be of a type clearly unrelated to, or only incidentally related to, the ordinary and typical activities of the entity, taking into account the environment in which the entity operates. Second, they must occur very infrequently. The underlying event or transaction must be of a type that would not reasonably be expected to recur in the foreseeable future, taking into account the environment in which the entity operates.

Extraordinary items should be disclosed in the income statement separately from continuing operations. Extraordinary gains or losses are to be shown net of applicable taxes. Examples of extraordinary items include uninsured losses from earthquakes and floods, expropriation (the taking of property by a foreign government), and gains and losses from the early retirement of debt.

Solved Problem 1.2. Presentation of Extraordinary Gains and Losses, Net of Taxes, in the Income Statement

The Savoy Soap Company showed income from operations of $2,000,000 for the year ended December 31, 1992. The company also suffered the following gains and losses:

Destruction of property due to earthquake	$1,000,000
Expropriation of plant in Peru	500,000
Early retirement of bonds at gain of	400,000

Assuming a corporate tax rate of 34%, what is Savoy's corporate net income for the year ended December 31, 1992?

Solution 1.2

Operating income before taxes		$2,000,000
Income tax expense ($2,000,000 × 34%)		680,000
Income before extraordinary items		$1,320,000
Extraordinary items		
Destruction of property due to earthquake		
($1,000,000 less taxes of $340,000)	$(660,000)	
Expropriation of plant in Peru		
($500,000 less taxes of $170,000)	(330,000)	
Gain on early retirement of bonds		
($400,000 less taxes of $136,000)	264,000	(726,000)
Net income		$594,000

Certain Gains and Losses Not Reportable as Extraordinary Items

According to APB Statement No. 30, certain gains and losses should not be reported as extraordinary items because they are usual in nature or may be expected to recur as a consequence of customary and continuing business activities. Examples include:

(a) Write-down or write-off of receivables, inventories, equipment leased to others, deferred research and development costs, or other intangible amounts.

(b) Gains or losses from exchange or translation of foreign currencies, including those relating to major devaluations and revaluations.

(c) Gains or losses on disposal of a segment of a business. As previously stated, these items must be reported separately as discontinued operations.

(d) Other gains or losses from sale or abandonment of property, plant, or equipment used in the business.

(e) Effects of a strike, including those against competitors and major suppliers.

(f) Adjustment of accruals on long-term contracts.

Solved Problem 1.3. Classification of Ordinary and Extraordinary Items

Classify the following transactions as either ordinary, extraordinary, or other.

	Ordinary Gains and Losses	Extraordinary Gains and Losses	Other
Write-off of an account receivable			
Gains and losses from foreign currency transactions			
Flood damage that has never occurred before			
Employee fraud that has never occurred before			
Losses in the sale of equipment			
Gain on the disposal of a segment of a business			
Losses from the abandonment of equipment			
Expropriation of property			
Gain on the early retirement of debt			
Write-down of obsolete inventory			

Solution 1.3

	Ordinary Gains and Losses	Extraordinary Gains and Losses	Other
Write-off of an account receivable	X		
Gains and losses from foreign currency transactions	X		
Flood damage that has never occurred before		X	
Employee fraud that has never occurred before		X	
Losses in the sale of equipment	X		
Gain on the disposal of a segment of a business			X
Losses from the abandonment of equipment	X		
Expropriation of property		X	
Gain on the early retirement of debt		X	
Write-down of obsolete inventory	X		

CUMULATIVE EFFECT OF AN ACCOUNTING CHANGE

According to APB Statement No. 20, a change in accounting principle results from the adoption of a generally accepted accounting principle different from the generally accepted principle previously used for reporting purposes. The term accounting principle includes not only accounting principles but also the methods of applying them. Adoption of a principle to record transactions for the first time or to record the effects of transactions that were previously immaterial is not considered to be a change in accounting principle. Changes in accounting principle include:

(a) A change in the method of inventory pricing, such as from last-in, first-out (LIFO) to first-in, first-out (FIFO).
(b) A change in depreciation method, such as from the double-declining balance method to the straight-line method.
(c) A change in the method of accounting for long-term construction contracts, such as from the completed-contract method to the percentage-of-completion method.

Pursuant to APB Statement No. 20, the burden for justifying a change in accounting principle rests on the entity proposing the change. However, issuance of a new accounting principle by the Financial Accounting Standards Board (FASB) is considered sufficient justification for a change in accounting principle.

Most changes in accounting principle should be recognized by including the cumulative effect of the change in the net income of the period of the change. The cumulative effect is the effect that the new accounting principle would have had on net income of prior years if it were used instead of the old principle. The amount of the cumulative effect, net of taxes, should be shown in the income statement between the captions "extraordinary items" and "net income." The cumulative effect is not an extraordinary item, but it should be reported in a manner similar to an extraordinary item. The per share information shown on the bottom of the income statement should include the per share amount of the cumulative effect of the accounting change.

Solved Problem 1.4. Cumulative Effect of an Accounting Change

Beginning January 1, 1992, the Henningson Motor Sales Corporation decided to change from the sum-of-the-year's-digits method of depreciation to the straight-line method for financial reporting purposes. The asset being depreciated was bought on January 1, 1991. The data assumed for this problem is as follows:

Year	Sum-of-the-Years' Digits Depreciation	Straight-Line Depreciation	Difference	Tax Rate 34%	Effect on Net Income
1991	$20,000	$10,000	$10,000	$3,400	$ 6,600
1992	18,000	10,000	8,000	2,720	5,280
	$38,000	$20,000	$18,000	$6,120	$11,880

There are 10,000 common shares outstanding. Assume that income before extraordinary items and the cumulative effect of a change in accounting principle is $300,000, and that extraordinary items, net of taxes, shows a $50,000 loss. (a) Make the journal entry to record the change in 1991. (b) Prepare a partial income statement.

Solution 1.4

(a)

Accumulated Depreciation	18,000	
Deferred Tax Effect		6,120
Cumulative Effect of Change in Accounting Principle—Depreciation		11,880
To record cumulative effect of change.		

(b)

Income before extraordinary items and the cumulative effect of a change in accounting principle	$300,000
Extraordinary items, net of taxes	(50,000)
Cumulative effect on prior years of retroactive application of new depreciation method	11,880
Net income	$261,880

Solved Problem 1.5. Preparation of an Income Statement

Prepare an income statement for Glassboro Mirror Inc., which had the following income and expense items for the year ended December 31, 1992:

Sales	$2,500,000
Cost of goods sold	1,875,000
Operating expenses	425,000
Income taxes expense	60,000
Discontinued operations	
Income from operations of discontinued segment (net of taxes, $114,000)	240,000
Gain on disposal of segment (net of taxes, $75,480)	160,000
Extraordinary gain on retirement of bonds (net of taxes, $252,000)	590,000
Cumulative effect of a change in accounting principle (net of taxes, $70,900)	175,000

Solution 1.5

Glassboro Mirror Inc.
Income Statement
for the Year Ended December 31, 1992

Sales		$2,500,000
Cost of goods sold		1,875,000
Gross margin		$ 625,000
Operating expenses		425,000
Income from continuing operations before income taxes		$ 200,000
Income taxes expense		60,000
Income from continuing operations		$ 140,000
Discontinued operations		
Income from operations of discontinued segment (net of taxes, $114,000)	$240,000	
Gain on disposal of segment (net of taxes, $75,480)	160,000	400,000
Income before extraordinary items and cumulative effect of accounting change		$ 540,000
Extraordinary gain on retirement of bonds (net of taxes, $252,000)		590,000
Subtotal		$1,130,000
Cumulative effect of a change in accounting principle (net of taxes, $70,900)		175,000
Net income		$1,305,000

EARNINGS PER SHARE

According to APB Statement No. 15, the earnings per share of common stock should be presented at the bottom of the income statement. The information should be disclosed just below the net income figure. The earnings per share common amounts should be shown for (1) income from continuing operations, (2) income before extraordinary items and cumulative effect of accounting changes, (3) cumulative effect of accounting changes, and (4) net income.

Solved Problem 1.6. Illustration of Earnings Per Share

For the year ended December 31, 1992, the Peabody Coal Corporation drew up the following income statement:

Sales	$7,500,000
Cost of goods sold	4,250,000
Gross margin	$3,250,000
Operating expenses	2,100,000
Income from continuing operations before taxes	$1,150,000
Income tax expense	391,000
Income before extraordinary items and the cumulative effect of a change in accounting principle	$ 759,000
Extraordinary items, net of taxes	(100,000)
Cumulative effect on prior years of retroactive application of new depreciation method	24,000
Net income	$ 683,000

If Peabody had 100,000 shares outstanding on December 31, 1992, what would be the earnings per share on common stock?

Solution 1.6

Per share amounts
Earnings per share (100,000 shares)

Income from continuing operations before taxes	$11.50
Income tax expense	3.91
Income before extraordinary items and the cumulative effect of a change in accounting principle	$ 7.59
Extraordinary items, net of taxes	(1.00)
Cumulative effect on prior years of retroactive application of new depreciation method	0.24
Net income	$ 6.83

Weighted Earnings per Share

If the number of shares outstanding changes during the year, it is necessary to figure the weighted-average number of shares outstanding for the year. For example, if the Dynamic Plastic Corporation had 100,000 shares outstanding at the beginning of the year and issued an additional 50,000 shares on July 1, the weighted-average number of shares would be 125,000 shares, calculated as follows:

Outstanding shares: January 1 through June 30:

100,000 × 6 months =	600,000
July 1 through December 31:	
150,000 × 6 months =	900,000

$$\text{Weighted-average shares} = \frac{1,500,000}{12 \text{ months}} = 125,000$$

Solved Problem 1.7. Computing the Weighted-Average Number of Shares and Earnings per Share

The Continental Tin Company Inc. had the following number of shares outstanding during the year 1992:

January-March	100,000
April-June	200,000
July-September	300,000
October-December	400,000

If Continental had a net income of $500,000 for the year, what were the earnings per share?

Solution 1.7

100,000 × ¼	25,000
200,000 × ¼	50,000
300,000 × ¼	75,000
400,000 × ¼	100,000
Weighted-average shares outstanding	250,000

$$\text{Earnings per share} = \frac{\$500,000}{250,000} = \$2.00 \text{ per share}$$

If a company had nonconvertible preferred stock outstanding, preferred dividends must be subtracted from net income before computing the earnings per share on common stock.

Solved Problem 1.8. Computing the Earnings per Share after Deducting Preferred Dividends

The Weston Burger Chain Inc. had the following number of shares outstanding during the year 1992:

January-June	200,000
July-December	400,000

If Weston had a net income of $400,000 for the year and paid an annual preferred dividend of $100,000, what were the earnings per share?

Solution 1.8

$200,000 \times \frac{1}{2}$	100,000
$400,000 \times \frac{1}{2}$	200,000
Weighted-average shares outstanding	300,000
Net income	$400,000
Preferred dividends	100,000
Net income after payment of preferred dividends	$300,000

$$\text{Earnings per share} = \frac{\$300,000}{300,000} = \$1.00 \text{ per share}$$

Primary and Fully Diluted Earnings per Share

Companies that have no preferred stocks, stock options, or bonds that are convertible into common stock are said to have a simple capital structure. If a company does issue convertible stocks and bonds or stock options, the securities have the potential of diluting the company's earnings per share and the corporation has a complex capital structure. When a company has a complex capital structure, the company must report both primary and fully diluted earnings per share.

Solved Problem 1.9. Presentation of Primary and Fully Diluted Earnings per Share

The Allex Wrench Company Inc. showed a net income of $404,800 for 1992 and $225,000 for 1991. The company had the following primary and potentially diluted shares outstanding for each year:

	1992	1991
Primary	100,000	90,000
Fully diluted	160,000	150,000

Prepare an income statement presentation showing primary and fully diluted earnings per share for 1992 and 1991.

Solution 1.9

	1992	1991
Net Income	$404,800	$225,000
Earnings per share of common stock		
Primary	$4.04	$2.50
Fully diluted	2.53	1.50

RETAINED EARNINGS

Retained earnings represent the accumulation of corporate profits over the years less operating losses and the payment of cash, stock, or property dividends. The retained earnings account must also be adjusted for errors applicable to prior periods. Retained earnings are also subject to appropriations or restrictions pursuant to the approval of a corporation's board of directors.

Prior Period Adjustments

Generally, there are two types of accounting errors:

(1) errors that occur and are discovered in the same accounting period, and

(2) errors that occur in one accounting period and are discovered in a subsequent accounting period.

The first type of error may be corrected by reversing the incorrect entry and recording the correct one or by directly correcting the account balances with a single entry. Correction of the second type of error is more involved. FASB Statement No. 16 requires that the following items shall be accounted for as prior period adjustments and excluded from the computation of net income for the current period:

(a) the correction of an error applicable to a prior period and

(b) adjustments that result from the realization of income tax benefits of pre-acquisition operating loss carry forwards of purchased subsidiaries.

Solved Problem 1.10. Adjusting Retained Earnings for a Prior Period Error

In the year 1992, the Foster Fake Fur Corporation determined that it had overstated its annual depreciation for 1991 by $50,000 ($42,500 net of tax). The starting retained earnings amount at January 1, 1992, was $960,000, and income for the year was $424,000.

(a) Make the journal entry in 1992 recording the prior period adjustment.
(b) Prepare a corrected retained earnings statement for the year 1992.

Solution 1.10

(a)

Accumulated Depreciation	50,000	
Taxes Payable		7,500
Retained Earnings		42,500
To record correction of error in recording depreciation in 1991.		

(b)

Retained earnings, January 1, 1992, as previously reported	$ 960,000
Correction of an error in depreciation in prior period (net of $7,500 tax)	42,500
Adjusted balance of retained earnings on January 1, 1992	$1,002,500
Net income	424,000
Retained earnings, December 31, 1992	$1,426,500

Appropriations or Restrictions of Retained Earnings

Appropriations or restrictions of retained earnings are reclassifications of unappropriated or unrestricted retained earnings. Appropriations are usually established pursuant to legal restrictions, for bonded indebtedness, for contingent or expected losses, and to protect working capital. Appropriated or restricted retained earnings are unavailable for the payment of dividends.

Solved Problem 1.11. Appropriations or Restrictions of Retained Earnings Pursuant to Legal Purposes

The Marzoni Gravel Corporation purchased $100,000 of its own stock. Pursuant to state law, earnings must be retained equal to the corporate stock temporarily acquired as treasury stock. Make the journal entry appropriating the retained earnings.

Solution 1.11

Retained Earnings	100,000	
Appropriation for Purchase of Treasury Stock		100,000
To record restriction due to purchase of treasury stock.		

Solved Problem 1.12. Appropriations or Restrictions of Retained Earnings Pursuant to Contractual Restrictions

The Seabreeze Hotel and Travel Company Inc. sold $10,000,000 in ten-year bonds. The bond indenture requires that a sinking fund be set up and that retained earnings be restricted equal to the amount of the annual contribution to the bond sinking fund. In the year of the bond sale, the board of directors voted to transfer $900,000 to a bond sinking fund. A similar amount was appropriated in retained earnings. Make the entry appropriating the retained earnings.

Solution 1.12

Retained Earnings	900,000	
Appropriation for Bond Sinking Fund		900,000
To record restriction due to terms of the bond indenture agreement.		

Solved Problem 1.13. Appropriations or Restrictions of Retained Earnings Due to Expected Losses

The Radcliffe Computer Corporation is expected to pay $440,000 due to an unfavorable court ruling regarding the infringement of a competitor's computer program. Make the entry appropriating the retained earnings.

Solution 1.13

Retained Earnings	440,000	
Appropriation for Loss Due to Lawsuit		440,000

To record restriction due to possible liability on
  lawsuit.

Solved Problem 1.14. Appropriations or Restrictions of Retained Earnings to Protect Working Capital

The Morris Cable and Wire Corporation expects to undertake a vigorous building program. The board of directors intends to finance the program by internal financing. Pursuant to this goal, the board of directors voted to appropriate $1,000,000 to protect working capital. Make the entry appropriating the retained earnings.

Solution 1.14

Retained Earnings	1,000,000	
Appropriation for Working Capital		1,000,000

To record restriction to protect working capital.

After all appropriations have been recorded in the Retained Earning account, the total retained earnings will consist of both restricted and unrestricted retained earnings.

Solved Problem 1.15. Preparation of a Statement of Retained Earnings

On December 31, 1991, the Bathysphere Exploration Company Inc. had unrestricted retained earnings of $2,000,000. During the day it voted to appropriate retained earnings for the following amounts:

Restrictions

Purchase of treasury stock	$200,000
Bond sinking fund	90,000
Unfavorable contractual obligations	50,000
Plant expansion	500,000

The corporation also declared a cash dividend on its outstanding common stock of $100,000, payable on January 31, 1992. Prepare a Statement of Retained Earnings for the year ended December 31, 1991.

Solution 1.15.

Bathysphere Exploration Company Inc.
Statement of Retained Earnings
for the Year Ended December 31, 1991.

Retained earnings, January 1, 1991		
Appropriated (or restricted)		
Purchase of treasury stock	$200,000	
Bond sinking fund	90,000	
Unfavorable contractual obligations	50,000	
Plant expansion	500,000	
Total appropriated retained earnings		$ 840,000
Unappropriated (or unrestricted)		1,160,000
Subtotal		$2,000,000
Less: Cash dividend, common stock		100,000
Retained earnings, December 31, 1991		$1,900,000

When an appropriation of retained earnings is no longer needed, an entry reversing the appropriation is made.

Solved Problem 1.16. Reversing an Appropriation Entry

In 1991, the Land Development Company Inc. set up an appropriation of retained earnings for $1,500,000, representing the loss of a lawsuit in a lower court. In 1992, on appeal, the lower court's judgment was reversed in favor of Land Development. The board of directors immediately voted to reverse the appropriation of retained earnings. Make the entry recording the reversal.

Solution 1.16

Appropriation for Loss Due to Lawsuit	1,500,000	
Retained Earnings		1,500,000
To record reversal of appropriation for loss		
due to possible liability on lawsuit.		

TREASURY STOCK

Treasury stock is a corporation's own stock, which has been legally issued and subsequently reacquired by the issuing corporation. Treasury stock is not an asset of the corporation. It does not give the corporation the right to receive dividends, or to vote, or the right to exercise preemptive rights.

Recording Treasury Stock

There are two alternatives for recording the acquisition of treasury stock: (1) the cost method and, (2) the par or stated value method. Under the cost method, the treasury stock account is debited for the cost of the shares acquired and is credited upon reissuance for this same cost. Under the par value method, the acquisition cost of the treasury shares is compared with the amount received at the time of their original issue. The treasury stock account is then debited for the par value or stated value of the shares and any excess over par is charged to the related paid-in capital account.

Solved Problem 1.17. Making Journal Entries for the Purchase of Treasury Shares Using Both the Cost and the Par or Stated Value Methods of Accounting

The Cosgrove Peanut Factory Inc. reacquired 200 shares of its own $100 par value stock, at a cost of $110 per share. The shares were sold for $105 per share. Ignoring this second transaction, suppose that the shares were instead sold for $115 per share.

Make the journal entries recording the above transactions using (a) the cost method and (b) the par or stated value method.

Solution 1.17

(a) The cost method

1. Treasury Stock	22,000	
Cash		22,000
To record the purchase of 200 shares at $110 per share.		
2. Cash	21,000	
Paid-in Capital in Excess of Par	1,000	
Treasury Stock		22,000
Sale of 200 shares × $105.		
3. Cash	23,000	
Paid-in Capital in Excess of Par		1,000
Treasury Stock		22,000
Sale of 200 shares × $115.		

(b) The par or stated value method

1. Treasury Stock	20,000	
Paid-in Capital in Excess of Par	2,000	
Cash		22,000
To record the purchase of 200 shares at $110 per share.		
2. Cash	21,000	
Paid-in Capital in Excess of Par		1,000
Treasury Stock		20,000
Sale of 200 shares × $105.		

3. Cash   23,000
    Paid-in Capital in Excess of Par   3,000
    Treasury Stock   20,000
    Sale of 200 shares × $115.

RETIREMENT OF TREASURY STOCK

A company sometimes decides not to reissue its treasury stock. Instead, with the approval of the stockholders, it may elect to retire the stock. If so, it must retire the common stock at its par value, eliminate any applicable paid-in capital in excess of par value, and charge any difference to the retained earnings account.

Solved Problem 1.18. Recording the Retirement of Treasury Stock

National Wine Distillers Inc. decided to retire 5,000 shares of its treasury stock, which it had purchased for $100,000. The common stock had a par value of $10 and was originally issued at $11 a share. Make the journal entry to record the retirement of the 5,000 shares.

Solution 1.18

Common Stock   50,000
Paid-in Capital in Excess of Par   5,000
Retained Earnings   45,000
  Treasury Stock   100,000
To record the retirement of 5,000 shares of $10
    par value common stock that were originally issued
    at $11 per share.

STOCK SUBSCRIPTIONS

A corporation will sometimes sell its stock on a subscription (or install-ment) basis. Under this technique, the purchase price of the stock is paid in installments, and the stock is not issued until it is paid for in full. When the contract is created between the subscriber and the corporation, a current asset called, stock subscriptions receivable, is debited and a credit is made to an account called capital stock subscribed. Any excess purchase price per share over the par value of the stock is credited to the paid-in capital account. When the stock is fully paid for, the capital stock subscribed account is debited and either the preferred or common stock account is credited for the amount of the fully paid for issued stock. The capital stock subscribed account appears as part of contributed capital on the issuing corporation's balance sheet.

Solved Problem 1.19. Recording a Stock Subscription, the Subsequent Installment Payments, and the Final Issuance of the Stock

On February 1, the Musgrave Pen and Pencil Corporation received subscriptions for 30,000 shares of its $10 par value common stock at $12 per share. The agreement called for equal payments on March 1, April 1, and May 1, at which time the fully paid for stock was to be issued. (a) Make the required journal entries to record the stock subscription, the subsequent installment payments, and the issuance of the common stock. (b) Assume that the corporation had 100,000 common shares authorized, of which 70,000 shares were outstanding at the time the corporation entered into the subscription agreement. Prepare the contributed capital section of Musgrave's balance sheet *after* recording the stock subscription agreement.

Solution 1.19

(a)

February 1	Stock Subscriptions Receivable, Common	360,000	
	Common Stock Subscribed		300,000
	Paid-in Capital in Excess of Par Value Common		60,000
	To record receipt of subscription for 30,000 shares of $10 par value common stock for $12 per share.		
March 1	Cash	120,000	
	Stock Subscriptions Receivable, Common		120,000
	To record partial payment for shares.		
April 1	Cash	120,000	
	Stock Subscriptions Receivable, Common		120,000
	To record partial payment for shares.		
May 1	Cash	120,000	
	Stock Subscriptions Receivable, Common		120,000
	To record partial payment for shares.		
May 1	Common Stock Subscribed	300,000	
	Common Stock		300,000
	To record issuance of 30,000 shares of common stock fully paid for.		

(b)

Contributed capital
  Common stock-$10 par value, 100,000
    shares authorized

70,000 shares issued and outstanding	$ 700,000
Subscribed but not issued	300,000
Paid-in capital in excess of par, common	60,000
Total contributed capital	$1,060,000

BOOK VALUE PER SHARE

Book value per share is equal to stockholders' equity available to common stockholders divided by shares outstanding. If a corporation has both preferred and common stock outstanding, it must first calculate the total value of the preferred stock plus any dividends in arrears.

Calculating Book Value per Share

The formula for calculating book value per share is as follows: subtract the total value of the preferred stock from the total stockholders' equity to arrive at the equity pertaining to the common shareholders. The equity applicable to the common stockholders is then divided by the number of common shares outstanding to arrive at book value per share for the common stock. The formula to calculate book value per share of common stock is as follows:

$$\frac{\text{Total Stockholders' Equity} - \text{Preferred Equity}}{\text{Number of Shares of Common Stock Outstanding}}$$

Solved Problem 1.20. Calculating the Book Value per Share of Common Stock

The Lane Paint Corporation has total stockholders' equity of $3,400,000. There are 100,000 common shares outstanding. Calculate the book value per share.

Solution 1.20

$$\frac{\text{Total stockholders' equity}}{\text{Number of common shares outstanding}} = \frac{\$3,400,000}{100,000} = \$34 \text{ per share}$$

Solved Problem 1.21. Calculating the Book Value per Share of Common Stock After Adjusting for Outstanding Preferred Shares

Assume that for 1991 the total stockholders' equity of the Equiblast Construction Corporation is $20,420,000. The corporation has 100,000 shares of its $10 par value 6% preferred stock, which is in arrears for two years, including the current year. The preferred stock is callable at its par value. There are also 1,000,000 shares of $1 par value common stock outstanding. (a) What is the book value per share of common stock? (b) What is the book value per share of common stock if the preferred stock is callable at $11 and is three years in arrears, including the current year?

Solution 1.21

(a)

Total stockholders' equity		$20,420,000
Less: Equity allocated to the preferred shares		
Preferred shares (100,000 × $10)	$1,000,000	
100,000 shares × $0.60 ($10 × 6%) × 2 years	120,000	1,120,000
Equity pertaining to the common shareholders		$19,300,000
Preferred stock: $ 1,120,000 ÷ 100,000 shares		$11.20
Common stock: $19,300,000 ÷ 1,000,000 shares		19.30

(b)

Total stockholders' equity		$20,420,000
Less: Equity allocated to the preferred shares		
Preferred shares (100,000 × $11)	$1,100,000	
100,000 shares × $0.60 ($10 × 6%) × 3 years	180,000	1,280,000
Equity pertaining to the common shareholders		$19,140,000
Preferred stock: $ 1,280,000 ÷ 100,000 shares		$12.80
Common stock: $19,140,000 ÷ 1,000,000 shares		19.14

The income statement is a financial report that summarizes all revenue and expenses for a period of time and shows the stockholders the factors that resulted in a net income or loss for the period. These factors include all revenues and expenses, as well as discontinued operations, extraordinary items, accounting changes, and earnings per share. A corporation's operating profit or loss for the year is closed out into retained earnings at year-end. Retained earnings represent the accumulation of corporate profits over the years less operating losses and the payment of cash, stock, or property dividends. The retained earnings account must also be adjusted for errors applicable to prior periods. Appropriations or restrictions of retained earnings are reclassifications of unappropriated or unrestricted retained earnings. A corporation will sometimes sell its stock on a subscription (or installment) basis. Under this technique, the purchase price of the stock is paid in installments, and the stock is not issued until it is paid for in full. Book value per share equals stockholders' equity available to common stockholders divided by the shares outstanding. In Chapter 2 we will discuss the treatment of long-term investments, stock splits, and stock dividends.

2

Investments in Long-Term Securities

Investments are assets that have been acquired for both growth and future income potential. Investments may be classified as either temporary or long-term. Temporary investments are those that management intends to dispose of within one year and are therefore highly liquid and marketable. Long-term investments are all other investments not meeting these criteria. Long-term investments include common or preferred stock representing an equity interest in another corporation, as well as notes or bonds representing debt.

INVESTMENTS IN EQUITY SECURITIES

An investment in the equity securities of a corporation permits the investor-owner to participate in the earnings of the company. If the investment consists of voting common stock, the investor is also entitled to participate in the election of the purchased (or investee) corporation's board of directors. The percentage of ownership in the investee corporation and the degree of influence that the investor is deemed to have over the investee also determines the method of accounting for the investment.

ACCOUNTING FOR INVESTMENTS IN MARKETABLE EQUITY SECURITIES

FASB Statement No. 12 provides definitive guidance with respect to accounting for investments in marketable equity securities. The term marketable equity securities means both common and preferred stock, stock warrants, stock rights, and call and put options. The term does not include treasury stock, convertible bonds, and preferred stock that is redeemable by the issuing corporation or by the investor.

Use of the Cost Method

FASB Statement No. 12 resolves the issue as to whether securities should be carried at cost or written down to market if the value of the stocks have dropped. Investments in marketable equity securities are recorded at cost. "Cost" also includes broker's fees, commissions, and taxes.

Solved Problem 2.1. Recording Investments at Cost

The Patterson Pulp Corporation bought 10,000 shares of the 100,000 outstanding common shares of the Reed Textile Company Inc. for $440,000. Broker's commissions and other miscellaneous costs were $4,500. Prepare the journal entry recording the purchase at cost.

Solution 2.1.

Investment in Reed Textile Company Inc.	444,500	
Cash		444,500

To record purchase of Reed stock at cost calculated as follows:

Cost of stock	$440,000
Add: Broker's commissions and other costs	4,500
	$444,500

Use of the Lower of Cost or Market Rule

Under FASB Statement No. 12, if the aggregate market value of a portfolio (or group) of marketable equity securities falls below its total or aggregate cost, the difference must be accounted for by use of a valuation or *contra* account. The entry to record the decline in the market value of short-term marketable equity securities is as follows:

Unrealized Loss on Valuation of Marketable Equity Securities	XXXX	
Allowance for Excess of Cost of Marketable Equity Securities over Market Value		XXXX

Any unrealized losses and recoveries on short-term marketable equity securities flow through the income statement. The loss account would appear on the income statement in the other income and expenses section before extraordinary items. Unrealized losses are not tax deductible because the securities have not been sold.

Solved Problem 2.2. Recording Short-Term Marketable Equity Securities at the Lower of Cost or Market

During 1992, the Fahrenheit Thermometer Company owned the following short-term marketable equity securities:

	Cost	Market at Year-End
Georgia-Farrell Lumber Co.	$ 300,000	$ 310,000
Mason-Dixie Cement Corporation	275,000	266,900
Piedmont Vegetable Company Inc.	500,000	470,000
	$1,075,000	$1,046,900

(a) Make the entry to record the decline in the market value of short-term marketable equity securities. (b) Prepare a partial balance sheet at the 1992 year-end showing the carrying value of the investments.

Solution 2.2

(a)

Current assets

	Cost	Market at Year-End	Unrealized Gain (Loss)
Georgia-Farrell Lumber Co.	$ 300,000	$ 310,000	$ 10,000
Mason-Dixie Cement Corporation	275,000	266,900	(8,100)
Piedmont Vegetable Company Inc.	500,000	470,000	(30,000)
	$1,075,000	$1,046,900	($ 28,100)

Unrealized Loss on Valuation of Marketable Equity Securities	28,100	
Allowance for Excess of Cost of Marketable Equity Securities over Market Value		28,100
To record decline in market value of short-term securities at year-end.		

(b)

Cost of short-term marketable equity securities	$1,075,000
Less: Allowance for excess of cost of marketable equity securities over market value	28,100
Securities at lower of cost or market	$1,046,900

Solved Problem 2.3. Recording a Subsequent Increase in the Market Value of Short-Term Marketable Equitable Securities where the Allowance Account in the Prior Year has Reduced the Short-Term Securities Below Cost

During 1993, the securities of the Fahrenheit Thermometer Company (see Solved Problem 2.2) increase in value as follows:

	Cost	Market at Year-End
Georgia-Farrell Lumber Co.	$ 300,000	$ 312,000
Mason-Dixie Cement Corporation	275,000	285,300
Piedmont Vegetable Company Inc.	500,000	475,000
	$1,075,000	$1,072,300

(a) Give the entry to record the reduction in the allowance account thereby increasing the market value of short-term marketable equity securities. (b) Prepare a partial balance sheet at the 1993 year-end showing the carrying value of the investments.

Solution 2.3

(a)

	Cost	Market at Year-End	Unrealized Gain (Loss)
Georgia-Farrell Lumber Co.	$ 300,000	$ 312,000	$ 12,000
Mason-Dixie Cement Corporation	275,000	285,300	10,300
Piedmont Vegetable Company Inc.	500,000	475,000	(25,000)
	$1,075,000	$1,072,300	$ (2,700)

Allowance for Excess of Cost of Marketable Equity Securities over Market Value	25,400	
Recovery of Unrealized Loss on Valuation of Marketable Equity Securities		25,400
To record reduction in allowance account calculated as follows:		
Securities at lower of cost or market 12/31/93	$1,072,300	
Securities at lower of cost or market 12/31/92	1,046,900	
Recovery of unrealized loss	$ 25,400	

(b)

Cost of short-term marketable equity securities	$1,075,000
Less: Allowance for excess of cost of marketable equity securities over market value	2,700
Securities at lower of cost or market	$1,072,300

If the aggregate market value of the portfolio exceeds its aggregate cost, the portfolio is carried at cost and no valuation account is recognized. An unrealized gain that exceeds cost cannot be recognized because to do so would violate the principle of conservatism.

Problem 2.4. Recording an Increase in Short-Term Marketable Equity Securities but not above Original Cost

During 1994, the securities of the Fahrenheit Thermometer Company (see Solved Problem 2.3) increase in value as follows:

	Cost	Market at Year-End
Georgia-Farrell Lumber Co.	$ 300,000	$ 312,200
Mason-Dixie Cement Corporation	275,000	287,400
Piedmont Vegetable Company Inc.	500,000	490,000
	$1,075,000	$1,089,600

(a) Prepare the entry to record the increase in the market value of short-term marketable equity securities. (b) Prepare a partial balance sheet at the 1994 year-end showing the carrying value of the investments.

Solution 2.4

(a)

	Cost	Market at Year-End	Unrealized Gain (Loss)
Georgia-Farrell Lumber Co.	$ 300,000	$ 312,200	$ 12,200
Mason-Dixie Cement Corporation	275,000	287,400	12,400
Piedmont Vegetable Company Inc.	500,000	490,000	(10,000)
	$1,075,000	$1,089,600	$ 14,600

Allowance for Excess of Cost of Marketable Equity Securities over Market Value	2,700	
Recovery of Unrealized Loss on Valuation of Marketable Equity Securities		2,700
To record reduction in allowance account, but not beyond the original cost of the securities.		

(b)

Cost of short-term marketable equity securities	$1,075,000

Solved Problem 2.5. Overview of Lower of Cost or Market Rule

The Sanford Rock and Gravel Corporation holds several investments in common stock. The aggregate cost of all the investments was $200,000. The securities were acquired in 1991 and were held for the period throughout

1991-1994. The market value of the portfolio at year-end balance sheet dates was as follows:

December 31, 1991	$190,000
December 31, 1992	$188,000
December 31, 1993	$197,000
December 31, 1994	$201,000

(a) Based on this data, complete the following schedule:

A	B	C	D	E
			(A – B)	**Increase (Decrease) in Valuation Allowance from Previous Date**
		Carrying Amount at Lower of Cost or Market	**Balance of Valuation Allowance to Reduce Cost or Market**	
Date	**Cost**	**Market**		

(b) What effect would the increase or decrease in the valuation allowance from the previous year have on the income for the years 1991 through 1994?

Solution 2.5

(a)

A	B	C	D	E
			(A – B)	**Increase (Decrease) in Valuation Allowance from Previous Date**
		Carrying Amount at Lower of Cost or Market	**Balance of Valuation Allowance to Reduce Cost or Market**	
Date	**Cost**	**Market**		
12/31/91	$200,000	$190,000	$190,000	$10,000	$10,000
12/31/92	$200,000	$188,000	$188,000	12,000	2,000
12/31/93	$200,000	$197,000	$197,000	3,000	(9,000)
12/31/94	$200,000	$201,000	$200,000	– 0 –	(3,000)

(b) Unrealized losses reported on the income statement will be $10,000 for 1991 and $2,000 in 1992. Unrealized gains reported on the income statement will be $9,000 for 1993 and $3,000 in 1994. Although the securities have increased $4,000 in 1994 and now have a current value above their original cost, the securities cannot be recorded above their original cost of $200,000. Therefore, proper accounting procedure calls for the elimination of the remaining balance in the allowance account of $3,000.

Long-Term Investments

Management may decide to classify marketable equity securities as noncurrent assets rather than current assets because the intent is to hold the securities for more than one year. In an unclassified balance sheet the entire portfolio is considered noncurrent. The accounting treatment for marketable equity securities has both similar and different characteristics. While the changes in the valuation account applicable to current securities is included in the determination of income, the accumulated changes in the valuation account applicable to noncurrent marketable equity securities will be shown as a separate item containing a debit balance in the stockholders' equity section of the balance sheet.

Solved Problem 2.6. Recording Long-Term Marketable Equity Securities at the Lower of Cost or Market

During 1992, the Ingot Steel Company Inc. owned the following long-term marketable equity securities:

	Cost	Market at Year-End
Kasten Glue Factory Inc.	$ 420,750	$ 440,500
Lantern Light Fixtures Corp.	356,000	326,500
Plexiglass Plastics Inc.	600,000	567,000
	$1,376,750	$1,334,000

(a) Make the entry to record the decline in the market value of long-term marketable equity securities. (b) Prepare a partial balance sheet at the 1992 year-end showing the carrying value of the investments in the asset section of the balance sheet and stockholders' equity. Assume common stock outstanding of $3,600,000 and retained earnings of $2,350,000.

Solution 2.6

(a) Long-term investments are as follows:

	Cost	Market at Year-End	Unrealized Gain (Loss)
Kasten Glue Factory Inc.	$ 420,750	$ 440,500	$ 19,750
Lantern Light Fixtures Corp.	356,000	326,500	(29,500)
Plexiglass Plastics Inc.	600,000	567,000	(33,000)
	$1,376,750	$1,334,000	$(42,750)

Unrealized Loss on Noncurrent Marketable
  Equity Securities   42,750
  Allowance for Excess of Cost of Long-Term
    Equity Securities over Market Value   42,750
To record decline in market value of long-term
    securities at year-end.

(b)

Investments and funds (per partial balance sheet)

Cost of long-term marketable equity securities	$1,376,750
Less: Allowance for excess of cost of marketable	
equity securities over market value	42,750
securities at lower of cost or market	$1,334,000

Stockholders' equity

Common stock	$3,600,000
Retained earnings	2,350,000
	$5,950,000
Less: Net unrealized loss on noncurrent marketable	
equity securities	42,750
Total stockholders' equity	$5,907,250

Accounting for a Permanent Decline in the Market Value of a Marketable Security

While an allowance accounting is used to report changes in the market value of long-term marketable equity securities, the accounting treatment for declines that are considered to be permanent rather than temporary is different. The cost basis of the individual security must be written down to its new cost basis. Since the market value becomes the new cost basis, the security cannot later be written up for a recovery. The permanent loss must be recorded as a realized loss in the income statement.

Solved Problem 2.7. Recording the Write-Down of a Long-Term Marketable Equity Security

Using the information contained in Solved Problem 2.6, (a) Give the journal entry recording a $10,000 permanent decline in the market value of the common stock of Plexiglass Plastics Inc. during the year 1993. (b) Assuming the following market values at the end of 1993, prepare a partial balance sheet at the 1993 year-end showing the carrying value of the investments in the asset section of the balance sheet and stockholders' equity. Assume common stock outstanding of $3,600,000 and retained earnings of $2,460,000.

	Cost	Market at Year-End	Unrealized Gain (Loss)
Kasten Glue Factory Inc.	$ 420,750	$ 442,500	$ 21,750
Lantern Light Fixtures Corp.	356,000	323,500	(32,500)
Plexiglass Plastics Inc.	590,000	566,000	(24,000)
	$1,366,750	$1,332,000	$(34,750)

Solution 2.7

(a)

Realized Loss Due to Permanent Decline in Market Value of Noncurrent Marketable Equity Security	10,000	
Long-Term Investment (Plexiglass Plastics Inc.)		10,000

To record permanent decline in market value of
    Plexiglass common stock.

(b)

Allowance for excess of cost of long-term Equity Securities over Market Value	8,000	
Unrealized Gain on Noncurrent Marketable Equity Securities		8,000

To record increase in market value of long-term
    securities at year-end calculated as follows:

Balance December 31, 1992	$42,750
Balance December 31, 1993	34,750
Decrease in balance in allowance account	$ 8,000

Cost of long-term marketable equity securities	$1,366,750
Less: Allowance for excess of cost of marketable equity securities over market value	34,750
Securities at Lower of Cost or Market	$1,332,000

Stockholders' equity

Common stock	$3,600,000
Retained earnings	2,460,000
	$6,060,000
Less: Net unrealized loss on noncurrent marketable equity securities	34,750
Total stockholders' equity	$6,025,250

Accounting for a Change in Marketable Equity Securities

If a marketable equity security is transferred from the current to the noncurrent portfolio, or vice versa, the security must be transferred at the lower of cost or market. If market value is below cost, a new cost basis is recorded, and any realized loss is recorded in net income.

Solved Problem 2.8. Recording the Write-Down of a Marketable Equity Security Pursuant to a Change in Classification

On December 31, 1992, the noncurrent marketable equity portfolio of the Beaver Shipping Service Inc. consisted of the following:

	Cost	Market
Randolph Logging Co. Inc.	$ 85,000	$ 90,000
Rexford Tug Lines Corp.	70,000	60,000
Manor Restaurant Sales Corp.	100,000	94,000
	$255,000	$244,000

In preparing Beaver's year-end financial statements, management elected to transfer Randolph Logging and Rexford Tug Lines to the current portfolio. Make the journal entries at year end reclassifying both investments.

Solution 2.8

December 31, 1992

Short-Term Marketable Equity Securities (Randolph Logging)	85,000	
Long-Term Marketable Equity Securities (Randolph Logging)		85,000
To record transfer of noncurrent security to current portfolio.		

Short-Term Marketable Equity Securities (Rexford Tug Lines)	60,000	
Loss on Reclassification of Marketable Equity Security	10,000	
Long-Term Marketable Equity Securities (Rexford Tug Lines)		70,000
To record transfer of noncurrent security to current portfolio.		

The removal of both Randolph Logging and Rexford Tug Lines will leave Manor Restaurant Sales as the only investment in the noncurrent portfolio.

Recording the Sale of a Marketable Equity Security

When a marketable equity security is sold, the difference between the net proceeds of the sale and the original cost represents a realized gain or loss.

Solved Problem 2.9. Recording the Sale of a Marketable Equity Security

On December 31, 1991, the noncurrent marketable equity portfolio of the Stanton Radio Station Inc. consisted of the following:

	Cost	Market
Wexler Wireless Co. Inc.	$ 75,000	$ 80,000
Granite Telegraph Corp.	60,000	50,000
Vital Signal Corporation Inc.	80,000	74,000
	$215,000	$204,000

During 1992, half of the Granite Telegraph Corp. stock was sold for $28,000, and half of the Vital Signal Corporation stock was sold for $40,500. (a) Make the journal entries recording the stock sales in 1992. (b) Prepare a noncurrent marketable equity portfolio at year-end for 1992 assuming all year-end market values remain unchanged.

Solution 2.9

(a)

Cash	28,000	
Realized Loss on Sale of Marketable Equity		
Securities	2,000	
Long-Term Marketable Equity Securities		
(Granite Telegraph)		30,000
To record sale of half of the stock of Granite		
Telegraph Corp.		
Cash	40,500	
Realized Gain on Sale of Marketable Equity		
Securities		500
Long-Term Marketable Equity Securities		
(Vital Signal Corporation Inc.)		40,000
To record sale of half of the stock of Vital		
Signal Corporation Inc.		

(b)

	Cost	Market
Wexler Wireless Co. Inc.	$ 75,000	$ 80,000
Granite Telegraph Corp.	30,000	25,000
Vital Signal Corporation Inc.	40,000	37,000
	$145,000	$142,000

Stock Dividends

Corporations wishing to "capitalize" retained earnings will issue a stock dividend. A corporation might decide to issue stock dividends, for example, if it needs to retain cash for other purposes. The shares received from either a stock dividend or a stock split are not classified as revenue. The recipient makes no formal entry for the receipt of the stock dividend, but only a memorandum entry indicating that additional shares have been received. This causes the individual cost of the shares to be lowered because the original cost of the shares is now divided by the new total number of shares.

The gains and losses on the sales of investments are reported as other income and expenses, which is part of current operating income; they are not classified as extraordinary items.

Solved Problem 2.10. Recording the Receipt of a Stock Dividend and a Subsequent Sale of Part of the Shares

Foxcroft Designs Limited Inc. bought 100 shares of the Borden Valve Corporation for $18,000. One year later, Borden issued one additional share for every two shares held. (a) Prepare the entry, if any, recording the additional number of shares. (b) Calculate the new cost basis of the shares owned by Foxcroft. (c) Make the entry recording the sale of 70 shares of Borden Valve stock at $130 per share. (d) Calculate the carrying amount of the remaining shares on hand. (e) Where would the gain or loss from the sale of the Borden Valve shares appear on Foxcroft's Income Statement?

Solution 2.10

(a)

There is no formal entry. A memorandum entry is made indicating that 50 additional shares (100 shares ÷ 2) have been received.

(b)

Cost of 100 shares originally purchased	$18,000
Cost of additional 50 shares received as a stock dividend	– 0 –
Total cost (or carrying value) of 150 shares	$18,000
New cost basis of each shares ($18,000 ÷ 150 shares)	$ 120

(c)

Cash	9,100	
Investment in Stocks (Borden Valve)		8,400
Gain on Sale of Investments		700

To record sale of 70 shares of Borden Value calculated as follows:

Sales price: 70 shares × $130	$9,100
Less cost: 70 shares × $120	8,400
Gain on sale	$ 700

(d)

The cost of the remaining shares would be:
150 shares – 70 shares sold = 80 shares.
80 shares × $120 = $9,600.

(e)

The $700 gain on the sale of Borden Valve would be reported under "Other Income and Expenses" on the income statement.

Stock Splits

A corporation may sometimes wish to reduce the par value of its stock to make it more salable to buyers with moderate income. This is accomplished with a stock split whereby the par value of the stock is reduced and the number of outstanding shares is increased. For example, a two-for-one stock split means that both the par value and the market price of the shares would decrease by one-half.

Stock splits are accomplished by either calling in the old shares and issuing new ones, usually on a two-for-one basis, or by issuing additional shares for each old share. A stock split can be recorded on the books of the investor by either a memorandum entry in the stock investment account or by a journal entry recording the receipt of additional shares.

Solved Problem 2.11. Recording a Stock Split on the Books of the Investor

The Higby Dental Supply Corporation owned 100,000 shares of $10 par value common stock of the Bar Office Furniture Corporation. On March 1, 1992, the board of directors of Bar Office Furniture Corporation voted to split the corporation's common stock on a two for one basis. (a) Prepare a memorandum entry in the stock investment account recording the stock split. (b) Make a journal entry in Higby's investment in common stock account recording Bar's stock split.

Solution 2.11

(a) March 1, 1992. On this day the Bar Office Furniture Corporation split their $10 par value common stock on a two for one basis. Higby owned 100,000 shares of Bar's $10 par value common. After the split, Higby now owns 200,000 shares at $5 par value.

(b)

March 1, 1992 Common Stock of Bar ($10 par value)	100,000	
Common-Stock of Bar ($5 par value)		100,000

To record two for one stock split
increasing the number of shares from
100,000 to 200,000 and reducing the par
value from $10 to $5.

Sometimes a company uses a reverse stock split. A reverse stock split reduces the number of shares outstanding and increases the price per share. This method is used when a corporation wishes to raise the price of its stock.

Difference Between a Stock Dividend and a Stock Split

A stock dividend and a stock split are similar in that they both result in an increase in the number of shares outstanding of the issuing corporation. However, pursuant to a stock dividend, the par value of the shares is not decreased. This results in an increase in the total par value of shares outstanding. In a stock split, the number of shares outstanding increase, while there is a corresponding decrease in the par or stated value of each share.

THE EQUITY METHOD OF ACCOUNTING

When a company owns stock in another corporation, the investment may be accounted for under one of three methods: the cost method, the equity method, and the consolidation of statements. The cost method is appropriate where the investor is not deemed to have a significant level of influence over the investee (generally, less than 20% ownership of the outstanding common stock). Under APB Statement No. 18, the equity method of accounting for investments in common stock is used where ownership is 20% to 50% of the outstanding voting stock of the investee. An investor who holds 20% or more of the outstanding stock may have influence over the investee's decision regarding dividend payments or the selection of product lines. Accounting for the investment should therefore reflect, to a limited degree, the success or failure of the investee company.

Accounting under the Equity Method

Under the equity method, the investment is initially recorded at cost. Income is subsequently recognized based on the pro rata share of the investee's earnings, while dividends received reduce the carrying amount of the investment. Extraordinary items and prior period adjustments are recognized separately. Temporary declines in the market price of the investee's stock are *not* recognized. However, a permanent decline in the market price of the investee's stock reduces the investment account.

Solved Problem 2.12. Use of the Equity Method of Recording Investments

On January 2, 1992, the Mulvaney Wood Products Corporation bought 30,000 of the 100,000 outstanding common shares of the Sando Meat Packing Co. Inc. for $650,000. Broker's commissions and other miscellaneous costs were $6,600. Management did not intend to sell the investment within one year, wishing to hold on to the investment for long-term appreciation. On October 1, Mulvaney received a cash dividend of $0.40 per share. Sando's net income for the year ended December 31, 1992 was $200,000. (a) Prepare the journal entry recording the purchase. (b) Prepare the journal entry recording the receipt of the investee's net income and dividend payment for the year ended December 31, 1992. (c) Prepare an analysis of Sando's Investment account showing the final balance at year-end. (d) Assuming that the other assets of Mulvaney at year-end consist of $70,000 in cash, $175,000 in net Accounts Receivable, and inventory of $500,200, prepare the asset section of the balance sheet at year-end, December 31, 1992.

Solution 2.12

(a)

January 2, 1992	Investment in Sando Meat Packing		
	Common Stock	656,600	
	Cash		656,600

To record purchase of Sando
stock at cost calculated
as follows:

Cost of stock	$650,000
Add: Broker's commissions and other costs	6,600
	$656,600

(b)

December 31, 1992	Investment in Sando Meat		
	Common Stock	60,000	
	Investment revenue-equity method		60,000

Net income of $200,000 × 30% =
$60,000.

December 21, 1992	Cash (30,000 × $.40)	12,000	
	Investment in Sando Meat		
	Common Stock		12,000

To record receipt of $.40 per
share on stock of Sando Meat
Packing.

(c)

Investment in Sando Meat Packing Co. Inc. Common Stock

January 2, 1992	656,600	December 21, 1992	12,000
December 31, 1992	60,000		
	716,600		
Balance	704,600		

(d)

Current assets

Cash	$ 70,000	
Accounts receivable, net	175,000	
Inventory	500,200	
Total current assets		$ 745,200

Long-term investments

Investment in Sando Meat common stock	704,600
Total assets	$1,449,800

According to FASB Interpretation No. 35, the presumption that an investor has significant influence over the investee when 20% or more of the voting stock is held is negated under certain conditions. For example, if the investee company files a lawsuit against the investor or complains to a government agency, or the investor cannot become a director of the investee corporation, or the investee withholds information from the investor, then there is strong evidence that the investor has no significant influence over the investee. In this situation, the investor must use the cost method of accounting.

Solved Problem 2.13. Accounting Procedures Required when the Investor Has 20% or More of the Investee's Voting Stock but Has no Significant Influence

On January 2, 1992, the Albatross Seafood Corporation purchased 40,000 of the 100,000 outstanding common voting shares of the Concord Canning Corporation for $5,000,000. Concord immediately complained to the government about possible antitrust violations and has failed to supply vital financial information to Albatross when requested to do so. Albatross has also failed to gain any representation on Concord's board of directors. On December 31, 1992, Concord declared and paid a cash dividend of $1 per share based upon net income of $300,000. (a) Make the journal entry recording the acquisition of Concord. (b) Record the receipt of the dividend.

Solution 2.13

(a)

January 2	Investment in Concord	5,000,000	
	Cash		5,000,000
	To record purchase of 40% of Concord's outstanding stock.		

(b)

December 31	Cash	40,000	
	Dividend Income		40,000
	To record receipt of cash dividend (40,000 shares × $1). Albatross is not using the equity method for recording an increase in the underlying value of Concord because Concord is hostile to the purchase of its shares by Albatross.		

Going from the Cost to the Equity Method

If the investor increases its ownership above 20%, a change must be made from the cost to the equity method for current and future years. In addition, there must be retroactive adjustment for prior years as if the equity method had always been used rather than the cost method. This adjustment will be to the investment in the investee account and to retained earnings for the difference between the amounts reported under the equity method versus the cost method. For example, if the investor owned 15% of an investee in 1992 and 1993 but increased its ownership in 1994 to 30%, a retroactive adjustment would be required.

Consolidated Financial Statements

Consolidated financial statements are generally required by ARB No. 51 where a company owns more than 50% of the voting stock of another firm. APB Statement No. 16, "Accounting for Business Combinations," provides accounting and reporting standards. (See Chapter 3 for further discussion of consolidated financial statements.)

LONG-TERM BONDS

A company with excess cash sometimes buys a bond as a short-term investment to provide a return on idle funds. The purchase price of the bond includes the cost of the bond plus any brokerage commission. Note that there is no account called "premium on investment in bonds." Any premium or discount is included in the investment account. APB Opinion No. 21 requires companies purchasing long-term bonds to amortize the difference between the cost of the bond and its maturity value over the holding period of the bond. The effective interest rate should be used. If a bond is bought between interest dates, the purchaser must also pay the interest that has accrued on the bond since the date of the last interest payment.

Solved Problem 2.14. Recording the Purchase Price of a Bond

On April 1, 1991, the Croton Centrifuge Corporation purchased $1,000,000 of Casey Tube Corporation's ten-year 12% semiannual bonds due in January 1, 2001, for 90¼. The broker's commission was $500. The bonds were subsequently sold on June 1, 1992, at 93. The broker's commission was $500. The bonds pay interest on July 1 and January 1. Assume an effective interest rate of 14%. (a) Make the journal entry to record the purchase of the bonds. (b) Make the journal entries to record interest income earned by the bonds for 1991. (c) Make the journal entry to record the closing of the interest income account for 1991. (d) Make the journal entries to record interest income earned by the bonds for 1992. (e) Prepare the journal entry to record the sale of the bonds on June 1, 1992.

Solution 2.14

(a)

April 1	Investment in Bonds ($902,500 + $500)	903,000	
	Interest Income	30,000	
	Cash		933,000

To record purchase of Casey Tube
Corporation's ten-year bonds at 90¼
plus $500 commission plus accrued
interest ($1,000,000 × 12% × ¼ =
$30,000).

(b)

July 1	Cash	60,000	
	Investment in Bonds	1,605	
	Interest Income		61,605

To record receipt of semiannual
interest and to amortize discount.
Six months' interest received:
    $1,000,000 × 12% × 6/12 = $60,000.
Three months' effective interest:
    $903,000 × 14% × ¼ = $31,605
Three months' face interest:
    $1,000,000 × 12% × ¼ =   30,000
Discount to be amortized $ 1,605
The amortization is based on the three
    month period representing April, May, and June.

December 31	Interest Receivable	60,000	
	Investment in Bonds	3,322	
	Interest Income		63,322

To record receipt of semiannual
interest and to amortize discount.
Six months' effective interest:
    $904,605 × 14% × ½ = $63,322
Six months' face interest:
    $1,000,000 × 12% × ½ =   60,000
Discount to be amortized $ 3,322

(c)

December 31	Interest Income	94,927	
	Income Summary		94,927

To close interest income account
    at year-end.
The interest income amount balance was
    calculated as follows:

Interest Income			
April 1	30,000	July 1	61,605
		December 31	63,322
			124,927
		Balance	94,927

(d)

January 1	Cash	60,000	
	Interest Receivable		60,000
	To record receipt of interest on bonds.		

June 1	Investment in Bonds	2,966	
	Interest Income		2,966
	To record receipt of semiannual interest and to amortize discount.		
	Five months' effective interest:		
	$907,927 \times 14\% \times 5\!/\!12 =$	$52,962	
	Five months' face interest:		
	$1,000,000 \times 12\% \times 5\!/\!12 =$	50,000	
	Discount to be amortized	$ 2,962	

(e)

June 1	Cash	929,500	
	Investment in Bonds		910,893
	Gain on Sale of Bonds		18,607
	To record sale of bonds at $930,000 less a broker's commission of $500.		
	The balance in the bond account was calculated as follows:		

March purchase	$903,000
July 1	1,605
December 31	3,322
June 1	2,966
	$910,893

Solved Problem 2.15. Preparing a Balance Sheet

The trial balance of the Reliance Sheet Metal Corporation appeared as follows at December 31, 1992:

	Debit	Credit
Cash	$ 15,000	
Short-term investments	1,066,000	
Allowance for excess of cost of marketable equity securities over market value		$ 20,000
Accounts receivable (net)	25,000	
Inventory	610,400	
Long-term marketable equity securities	1,300,000	
Unrealized loss on noncurrent marketable equity securities	40,000	
Allowance for excess of cost of marketable equity securities over market value		40,000
Securities at lower of cost or market		
Accounts payable		10,000
Bonds payable		2,000,000
Discount on bonds payable	30,000	
Common stock		600,000
Retained earnings		416,400
	$3,086,400	$3,086,400

Prepare a balance sheet for the Reliance Sheet Metal Corporation as of December 31, 1992.

Solution 2.15

Reliance Sheet Metal Corporation
Balance Sheet
December 31, 1992

ASSETS
Current assets

Cash		$ 15,000
Short-term investments	$1,066,000	
Less: Allowance for excess of cost of marketable equity Securities over market value	20,000	1,046,000
Accounts receivable (net)		25,000
Inventory		610,400
Total current assets		$1,696,400
Long-term investments		
Long-term marketable equity securities	$1,300,000	
Allowance for excess of cost of marketable equity securities over market value	40,000	1,260,000
Total assets		$2,956,400

LIABILITIES
Current liabilities

Accounts payable		$ 10,000
Long-term liabilities		
Bonds payable	$2,000,000	
Less: Discount on bonds payable	30,000	1,970,000
Total liabilities		$1,980,000

STOCKHOLDERS' EQUITY

Common stock	$ 600,000
Retained earnings	416,400
	$1,016,400
Less: Net unrealized loss on noncurrent	
marketable equity securities	40,000
Total stockholders' equity	$ 976,400
Total liabilities and stockholders' equity	$2,956,400

Investments may be classified as either temporary or long-term. Temporary investments are those that management intends to dispose of within one year and are therefore liquid. Long-term investments are intended to be held more than one year. They include common or preferred stock, notes, and bonds. FASB Statement No. 12 requires that securities should be carried at cost or written down to market value if the value of the stocks have dropped.

A stock dividend and a stock split are similar in that they both result in an increase in the number of shares outstanding of the issuing corporation. However, the issuance of a stock dividend does not reduce the par value of the stock. In a stock split, the par value of a share of stock is reduced.

When a company owns stock in another corporation, the investment may be accounted for under one of three methods: the cost method, the equity method, and the consolidation of financial statements. The cost method is appropriate where the investor is not deemed to have significant influence over the investee. Under APB Statement No. 18, the equity method of accounting for investments in common stock is used where ownership is 20% to 50% of the outstanding voting stock of the investee. In the next chapter we will discuss consolidated financial statements.

3

Consolidated Financial Statements

The control of one or more corporations by another corporation through the ownership of voting stock is a phenomenon of modern day business. When a company acquires a controlling interest in the voting shares of another company, unified managerial control is achieved just as if the two companies were a single larger unit. The corporation that owns a majority, or more than 50% of the voting stock, and controls the operations of other companies is known as the parent company. The separate companies controlled by the parent company are called subsidiaries. The portion of the stock of the subsidiaries held by persons outside of the parent company is referred to as the minority interest.

There are many reasons for the trend toward consolidated financial and managerial control. Acquisition of a controlling interest in a subsidiary is an economical way for one company to acquire another, expand its operations, gain a more prominent competitive position, and reduce the risk of an operating loss through diversification of product lines and services.

BUSINESS COMBINATIONS

Business combinations occur when a corporation and one or more other businesses are brought together as a single entity, to carry on the activities of the previously separate enterprises. A business combination will be accounted for under one of two methods: the pooling of interests (or pooling) method or the purchase method.

The Pooling Method

Under the *pooling* method no sale or purchase is deemed to have occurred, and the assets and liabilities of the combining firms continue to be carried at their original recorded costs. The income of the constituents is combined and restated for each period presented. Finally, consolidated financial statements for the year the combination takes place should be presented as if the combination had taken place at the *beginning* of the period.

The Purchase Method

Under the *purchase* method the acquiring corporation records the net assets acquired at the price paid by the acquiring corporation. A purchasing company may voluntarily pay more than the book value for an investment in a subsidiary because the subsidiary's assets have increased in value or because the subsidiary possesses an attribute or asset important to the parent. Any excess of purchase price over the fair market value of the net identifiable assets is recorded as goodwill. Net income of the acquired company is brought forth from the date of acquisition. Further discussion of both the purchase and pooling methods of accounting is not necessary in an introductory accounting book. A more detailed discussion of the purchase and pooling methods of accounting can be found in any advanced accounting text.

PREPARATION OF A CONSOLIDATED FINANCIAL STATEMENT

When to Prepare a Consolidated Financial Statement

A consolidated financial statement is more meaningful than the separate financial statements of several companies. It is usually prepared when one of the companies in the group directly or indirectly has a controlling financial interest in the other companies. More specifically, a consolidated financial statement is generally required when (1) the "parent" owns over 50% of the voting stock of another company or "subsidiary" and (2) the operations of the parent and subsidiaries are sufficiently homogenous in nature so that a consolidated statement is deemed more relevant than the separate financial statements of each company involved.

A consolidated financial statement may not be appropriate when any one of the following conditions is present: (1) control over a subsidiary is temporary, such as when the subsidiary is in receivership, (2) the parent has sold or contracted to sell the subsidiary shortly after the year-end, or (3) the presence of a large minority interest makes separate statements more meaningful.

Preparation of Consolidated Statements after Acquisition

When financial and managerial control exists, the parent company may prepare a consolidated financial statement. A consolidated statement presents the financial affairs of the parent company and its subsidiaries as if they were a single economic unit.

Solved Problem 3.1. Recording the Acquisition of a Subsidiary and the Preparation of a Consolidated Financial Statement

On January 2, 1992, Parent Corporation purchased from stockholders 100% of the voting common shares of Subsidiary Corporation at their book value of $300,000. At the date of acquisition, the balance sheets of the Parent and Subsidiary corporations appeared as follows:

	Parent	Subsidiary
Cash	$ 430,000	$ 80,000
Accounts receivable (net)	200,000	120,000
Property, plant, and equipment (net)	870,000	400,000
Total assets	$1,500,000	$600,000
Accounts and notes payable	$1,000,000	$300,000
Common stock	300,000	200,000
Retained earnings	200,000	100,000
Total liabilities and shareholders' equity	$1,500,000	$600,000

(a) Make the journal entry recording the purchase on January 2, 1992. (b) Prepare the balance sheets of both Parent and Subsidiary on January 3, 1992, immediately after the acquisition. (c) Prepare a consolidated worksheet on January 3, 1992, showing the journal entry eliminating the investment in the subsidiary. (d) Prepare a consolidated balance sheet as of January 3, 1992.

Solution 3.1

(a)

January 2, 1992	Investment in Subsidiary	300,000	
	Cash		300,000

To record the purchase of 100%
of the common stock of
Subsidiary Corporation.

(b)

	Parent	Subsidiary
Cash	$ 130,000	$ 80,000
Investment in Subsidiary Corporation	300,000	– 0 –
Accounts receivable (net)	200,000	120,000
Property, plant, and equipment (net)	870,000	400,000
Total assets	$1,500,000	$600,000
Accounts and notes payable	$1,000,000	$300,000
Common stock	300,000	200,000
Retained earnings	200,000	100,000
Total liabilities and shareholders' equity	$1,500,000	$600,000

(c)

	Parent	Subsidiary	Elimination Entries Debit	Elimination Entries Credit	Consolidated Balance Sheet
Cash	130,000	80,000			210,000
Investment in Subsidiary Corp.	300,000	– 0 –		(a) 300,000	
Accounts receivable (net)	200,000	120,000			320,000
Property, plant, and equipment	870,000	400,000			1,270,000
	1,500,000	600,000			1,800,000
Accounts and notes payable	1,000,000	300,000			1,300,000
Common stock	300,000	200,000	(a) 200,000		300,000
Retained earnings	200,000	100,000	(a) 100,000		200,000
	1,500,000	600,000	300,000	300,000	1,800,000

(d)

Parent Corporation and Subsidiary
Consolidated Balance Sheet
January 3, 1992

ASSETS

Cash	$ 210,000
Accounts receivable (net)	320,000
Property, plant, and equipment (net)	1,270,000
Total assets	$1,800,000

LIABILITIES

Accounts and notes payable		$1,300,000

STOCKHOLDERS' EQUITY

Common stock	$300,000	
Retained earnings	200,000	
Total stockholders' equity		500,000
Total liabilities and stockholders' equity		$1,800,000

Procedure for
Preparation of
Consolidated
Statements

Affiliated companies often have transactions with each other. These transactions may include intercompany sales and purchases, receivables and payables, and dividends. To eliminate a double counting of these transactions, a worksheet must be prepared at the end of the accounting period eliminating these types of intercompany transactions.

Solved Problem 3.2. Using a Worksheet to Eliminate Intercompany Transactions and the Preparation of Consolidated Financial Statements

Referring to Solved Problem 3.1, assume that the year-end financial statements of Parent and Subsidiary, before the books were closed, showed the following amounts:

	Parent	Subsidiary
Cash	$ 115,000	$100,000
Investment in Subsidiary Corporation	300,000	– 0 –
Accounts receivable (net)	260,000	140,000
Dividends receivable	10,000	– 0 –
Property, plant, and equipment (net)	900,000	480,000
Cost of goods sold	235,000	135,000
Other operating expenses	75,600	45,000
Interest expense	3,500	2,400
Total	$1,899,100	$902,400
Accounts and notes payable	$1,000,000	$350,000
Cash dividends payable	15,000	10,000
Common stock	300,000	200,000
Retained earnings	200,000	100,000
Sales	381,700	242,000
Interest earned	2,400	400
Total	$1,899,100	$902,400

Cash dividends payable by Subsidiary Corporation at year-end are $10,000. Subsidiary Corporation paid $2,400 in interest expense during the year to Parent Corporation. An intercompany profit of $20,000 included in the ending inventory sold by Parent Corporation to Subsidiary must be eliminated. (a) Prepare a consolidated trial balance as of December 31, 1992. (b) Using the figures obtained from the consolidated trial balance, prepare a worksheet showing income, expenses, and a final trial balance as of December 31, 1992. (c) Using the worksheet formulated in (b) prepare a consolidated balance sheet as of December 31, 1992. (d) Using the worksheet formulated in (b), prepare a consolidated income statement as of December 31, 1992.

Solution 3.2

(a)

	Parent	Subsidiary	Elimination Entries Debit	Elimination Entries Credit	Consolidated Balance Sheet
Cash	115,000	100,000			215,000
Investment in Subsidiary Corp.	300,000	– 0 –		(a) 300,000	
Accounts receivable (net)	260,000	140,000			400,000
Dividends receivable	10,000	– 0 –		(b) 10,000	
Property, plant, and equip. (net)	900,000	480,000			1,380,000
Cost of goods sold	235,000	135,000		(c) 20,000	350,000
Other operating expenses	75,600	45,000			120,600
Interest expense	3,500	2,400		(d) 2,400	3,500
	1,899,100	902,400			2,469,100
Accounts and notes payable	1,000,000	350,000			1,350,000
Cash dividends payable	15,000	10,000	(b) 10,000		15,000
Common stock	300,000	200,000	(a) 200,000		300,000
Retained earnings	200,000	100,000	(a) 100,000		200,000
Sales	381,700	242,000	(c) 20,000		603,700
Interest earned	2,400	400	(d) 2,400		400
	1,899,100	902,400	332,400	332,400	2,469,100

(b)

	Consolidated Trial Balance	Income Statement Debit	Income Statement Credit	Balance Sheet Debit	Balance Sheet Credit
Cash	215,000			215,000	
Accounts receivable (net)	400,000			400,000	
Property, plant, and equip. (net)	1,380,000			1,380,000	
Cost of goods sold	350,000	350,000			
Other operating expenses	120,600	120,600			
Interest expense	3,500	3,500			
	2,469,100				
Accounts and notes payable	1,350,000				1,350,000
Cash dividends payable	15,000				15,000
Common stock	300,000				300,000
Retained earnings	200,000				200,000
Sales	603,700		603,700		
Interest earned	400		400		
	2,469,100	474,100	604,100	1,995,000	1,865,000
Net income		130,000			130,000
		604,100	604,100	1,995,000	1,995,000

(c)

Parent Corporation and Subsidiary
Consolidated Balance Sheet
December 31, 1992

ASSETS

Cash	$ 215,000
Accounts receivable (net)	400,000
Property, plant, and equipment (net)	1,380,000
Total assets	$1,995,000

LIABILITIES

Accounts and notes payable	$1,350,000	
Cash dividends payable	15,000	
Total liabilities		$1,365,000

SHAREHOLDERS' EQUITY

Common stock	$ 300,000	
Retained earnings	330,000	
Total shareholders' equity		630,000
Total liabilities and shareholders' equity		$1,995,000

(d)

Parent Corporation and Subsidiary
Consolidated Income Statement
December 31, 1992

Income		
Sales	$603,700	
Interest earned	400	
Total income		$604,100
Less: expenses		
Cost of goods sold	$350,000	
Other operating expenses	120,600	
Interest expense	3,500	474,100
Net income		$130,000

PURCHASES OTHER THAN FOR BOOK VALUE

Purchase of Less than 100% of the Book Value of a Subsidiary

When a parent purchases less than 100% of the book value of a subsidiary, a minority interest arises. The minority interest must appear on the consolidated balance sheet at an amount equal to their percentage of ownership multiplied by the net assets (total assets less total liabilities) of the subsidiary. The minority appears as the first account in the stockholders' equity section of the consolidated balance sheet.

Solved Problem 3.3. Recording the Acquisition of Less than 100% of a Subsidiary, Thereby Creating a Minority Interest

On January 2, 1992, Parent Corporation purchased from stockholders 90% of the common shares of Subsidiary Corporation for $180,000. At the date of acquisition, the balance sheets of the Parent and Subsidiary corporations appeared as follows:

	Parent	Subsidiary
Cash	$ 375,000	$ 90,000
Accounts receivable (net)	450,000	110,000
Property, plant, and equipment (net)	775,000	450,000
Total assets	$1,600,000	$650,000
Accounts and notes payable	$ 500,000	$350,000
Bonds payable	600,000	100,000
Common stock	300,000	150,000
Retained earnings	200,000	50,000
Total liabilities and shareholders' equity	$1,600,000	$650,000

(a) Prepare the journal entry recording the purchase on January 2, 1992, of 90% of the outstanding common stock of Subsidiary Corporation for $180,000. (b) Prepare the balance sheets of both Parent and Subsidiary as of January 3, 1992 immediately after the acquisition. (c) Prepare a consolidated worksheet as of January 3, 1992, showing the journal entry eliminating the investment in the subsidiary and the minority interest. (d) Prepare a consolidated balance sheet as of January 3, 1992.

Solution 3.3

(a)

January 2, 1992	Investment in Subsidiary	180,000	
	Cash		180,000
	To record the purchase of 90% of the common stock of Subsidiary Corporation.		

(b)

	Parent	Subsidiary
Cash	$ 195,000	$ 90,000
Investment in Subsidiary Corporation	180,000	– 0 –
Accounts receivable (net)	450,000	110,000
Property, plant, and equipment (net)	775,000	450,000
Total assets	$1,600,000	$650,000
Accounts and notes payable	$ 500,000	$350,000
Bonds payable	600,000	100,000
Common stock	300,000	150,000
Retained earnings	200,000	50,000
Total liabilities and shareholders' equity	$1,600,000	$650,000

(c)

	Parent	Subsidiary	Elimination Entries Debit	Elimination Entries Credit	Consolidated Balance Sheet
Cash	195,000	90,000			285,000
Investment in Subsidiary Corp.	180,000	– 0 –		(a) 180,000	
Accounts receivable (net)	450,000	110,000			560,000
Property, plant, and equip. (net)	775,000	450,000			1,225,000
	1,600,000	650,000			2,070,000
Accounts and notes payable	500,000	350,000			850,000
Bonds payable	600,000	100,000			700,000
Common stock	300,000	150,000	(a) 135,000		300,000
					15,000M
Retained earnings	200,000	50,000	(a) 45,000		200,000
					5,000M
	1,600,000	650,000	180,000	180,000	2,070,000

M = Minority Interest

(d)

Parent Corporation and Subsidiary
Consolidated Balance Sheet
January 3, 1992

ASSETS		
Cash		$ 285,000
Accounts receivable (net)		560,000
Property, plant, and equipment (net)		1,225,000
Total assets		$2,070,000
LIABILITIES		
Accounts and notes payable	$850,000	
Bonds payable	700,000	
Total liabilities		$1,550,000
STOCKHOLDERS' EQUITY		
Minority interest	$ 20,000	
Common stock	300,000	
Retained earnings	200,000	
Total shareholders' equity		520,000
Total liabilities and shareholders' equity		$2,070,000

Recording the Purchase of a Subsidiary at More than Book Value

Sometimes a purchasing company may voluntarily pay more than the book value for an investment in a subsidiary because (1) the subsidiary's assets have increased in value, (2) the subsidiary possesses special technology, or (3) the parent wishes to gain access to certain sales markets. Any excess of the purchase price over the fair market value of the net identifiable assets is recorded as goodwill.

Solved Problem 3.4. Recording the Acquisition of a Subsidiary at more than Its Book Value

On January 2, 1992, Parent Corporation purchased from stockholders 100% of the common shares of Subsidiary Corporation for $240,000. At the date of acquisition, the balance sheets of the Parent and Subsidiary corporations appeared as follows:

	Parent	Subsidiary
Cash	$ 400,000	$ 75,000
Accounts receivable (net)	435,000	85,000
Property, plant, and equipment (net)	900,000	425,000
Total assets	$1,735,000	$585,000
Accounts and notes payable	$ 535,000	$385,000
Bonds payable	700,000	– 0 –
Common stock	300,000	150,000
Retained earnings	200,000	50,000
Total liabilities and shareholders' equity	$1,735,000	$585,000

Subsidiary's property, plant, and equipment has a fair market value of $440,000. Any excess of the purchase price over the fair market value of the assets will be attributable to goodwill.

(a) Make the journal entry recording the purchase on January 2, 1992. (b) Prepare the balance sheets of both Parent and Subsidiary on January 3, 1992 immediately after the acquisition. (c) Prepare a consolidated worksheet on January 3, 1992 showing the journal entry eliminating the investment in the subsidiary and the minority interest. (d) Prepare a consolidated balance sheet as of January 3, 1992.

Solution 3.4

(a)

January 2, 1992	Investment in Subsidiary	240,000	
	Cash		240,000
	To record the purchase of 100% of the common stock of Subsidiary Corporation.		

(b)

	Parent	Subsidiary
Cash	$ 160,000	$ 75,000
Investment in Subsidiary Corporation	240,000	– 0 –
Accounts receivable (net)	435,000	85,000
Property, plant and equipment (net)	900,000	425,000
Total assets	$1,735,000	$585,000
Accounts and notes payable	$ 535,000	$385,000
Bonds payable	700,000	– 0 –
Common stock	300,000	150,000
Retained earnings	200,000	50,000
Total liabilities and shareholders' equity	$1,735,000	$585,000

(c)

	Parent	Subsidiary	Elimination Entries Debit	Elimination Entries Credit	Consolidated Balance Sheet
Cash	160,000	75,000			235,000
Investment in Subsidiary Corp.	240,000	– 0 –		(a) 240,000	
Accounts receivable (net)	435,000	85,000			520,000
Property, plant, and equip. (net)	900,000	425,000	(a) 15,000		1,340,000
Goodwill			(a) 25,000		25,000
	1,735,000	585,000			2,120,000
Accounts and notes payable	535,000	385,000			920,000
Bonds payable	700,000	– 0 –			700,000
Common stock	300,000	150,000	(a) 150,000		300,000
Retained earnings	200,000	50,000	(a) 50,000		200,000
	1,735,000	585,000	240,000	240,000	2,120,000

(d)

Parent Corporation and Subsidiary
Consolidated Balance Sheet
January 3, 1992

ASSETS

Cash	$ 235,000
Accounts receivable (net)	520,000
Property, plant, and equipment (net)	1,340,000
Goodwill	25,000
Total assets	$2,120,000

LIABILITIES

Accounts and notes payable	$920,000	
Bonds payable	700,000	
Total liabilities		$1,620,000

STOCKHOLDERS' EQUITY

Common stock	$300,000	
Retained earnings	200,000	
Total shareholders' equity		500,000
Total liabilities and shareholders' equity		$2,120,000

A consolidated statement presents the financial affairs of the parent company and its subsidiaries as if they were a single economic unit. When a consolidated statement is prepared, the parent company and each subsidiary also prepares financial statements for their individual entities. A consolidation does not destroy the individual identity or legal obligations of each subsidiary; each unit, as a separate legal entity, remains liable to its creditors. Bonds, which may be sold by any type of legal entity, including both a parent and its subsidiaries, will be discussed in Chapter 4.

Part 2

Liabilities

4

Bonds Payable: Advanced Topics

A corporation may, in order to raise funds, issue bonds. Bonds payable represents a long-term contractual obligation to make periodic interest payments on the amount borrowed and to repay the principal, or face amount of the bond, upon maturity. The actual issuance of the bonds may be made directly by the borrowing corporation, or they may be issued or transferred to banks or brokers who, in turn, market the bonds through their own channels. It is not unusual for bond issues to mature in 10 years, 20 years, or longer. Bonds are used in long-term financing, whereas promissory notes are used in short-term financing.

The contract between the issuing corporation and the bondholders is called the bond indenture agreement. It contains such provisions as the rate of interest that the bonds shall pay, whether the bonds are secured or unsecured, the designation of the trustee, and whether a sinking fund is to be established for the benefit of the bondholders. A trustee, generally a large bank, is usually appointed by the issuer to represent the bondholders. Most corporate bond issuers utilize the services of a trustee instead of attempting to deal with thousands of bondholders. A sinking fund provides that a corporation make periodic payments of cash into an interest earning fund to be used for the ultimate retirement of the bonds at their maturity date.

ACCOUNTING FOR BONDS

Classifications of Bonds

There are many types of bonds, each tailored to meet the particular financial requirements of the issuing corporation. The standard denomination (par or face value) of a bond is $1,000; but bonds with par values of $5,000 or $10,000 may also be issued. Some common types of bonds include the following:

Debenture bonds represent unsecured loans. Unsecured bondholders rank as general or ordinary creditors of the corporation and rely upon the general credit of the corporation. Debenture bonds may only be issued by financially strong companies.

Bearer or coupon bonds. These bonds are not registered in the name of the buyer. The holder must take initiative in collecting the interest. Title to bearer bonds passes upon transfer to the new purchaser.

Registered bonds. The names of the owners of these bonds are in the records of the corporation. Interest payments are mailed to owners of record.

Serial bonds are bond issues that mature in installments, usually in increments of a full year.

Secured bonds. Debt is accompanied by a pledge of property, such as land and buildings, by the issuing corporation. Several loans may be made using the same property for collateral. This gives rise to first mortgage bonds, second mortgage bonds, and so on. Second and third mortgage bonds usually carry a higher interest rate than first mortgage bonds because, in the event of default (nonpayment), payment is made to each group of creditors in their order of priority.

Convertible bonds are exchangeable into other securities at the option of the bondholder.

Callable bonds. The issuing corporation has the option of retiring bonds before maturity at a preestablished price.

Recording the Sale of a Bond

The sale of a bond requires that the issuing corporation make a one time entry debiting cash and crediting bonds payable. Subsequent interest payments are recorded by a debit to interest expense and a credit to cash. The credit to bonds payable is at the par or face value of the bond. Bond market price quotations are generally expressed as percentages. Thus a quoted price of 102 means that a $1,000 bond will sell for $1,020; quotation of 99 means that a $1,000 bond will sell for $990.

Solved Problem 4.1. Recording the Sale of a Bond and Paying Interest

Mattock Molding Corporation issued at par $1,000,000 in 9%, ten-year bonds on January 1, 1990. The bonds pay interest semiannually, every July 1 and January 1. (a) Make the entry to record the issuance of the bonds on

January 1. (b) Make the entry recording the first interest payment on July 1. (c) Make the entry recording the retirement of the bonds at the end of the ten-year period on December 31, 1999.

Solution 4.1

(a)

January 1, 1990	Cash	1,000,000	
	Bonds Payable		1,000,000

To record issuance of 9%, 10-year bonds.

(b)

July 1, 1990	Interest Expense	45,000	
	Cash		45,000

To record payment of semiannual interest on bonds ($1,000,000 × 9% × ½).

(c)

December 31, 1999	Bonds Payable	1,000,000	
	Cash		1,000,000

To record retirement of bonds at their maturity date.

Solved Problem 4.2. Record the Exchange of Property for a Bond

On May 1, 1992, the Mechano Tool Corporation gave Paul Ullman $100,000 in 10%, ten-year bonds in exchange for land with a fair market value of $100,000. Prepare the journal entry to record the acquisition of the land.

Solution 4.2

May 1, 1992	Land	100,000	
	Bonds Payable		100,000

To record exchange of land for bonds.

Solved Problem 4.3. Record the Exchange of Land and Buildings for Bonds

On June 1, 1992, the Sheldon Color and Dye Corporation gave Maxine Prentice $1,000,000 in 10%, ten-year bonds in exchange for land and buildings. The land had a value of $500,000 and the buildings $600,000. Prepare the journal entry to record the acquisition of the land and buildings.

Solution 4.3

June 1, 1992	Land	500,000	
	Buildings	600,000	
	Bonds Payable		1,000,000
	Premium on Bonds Payable		100,000

To record exchange of land and buildings for bonds.

Solved Problem 4.4. Record the Exchange of Services for Bonds

On July 1, 1992, the Walthers Pattern Corporation gave Paul Booth a $10,000 10%, ten-year bond in exchange for legal services valued at $9,000. Make the journal entry to record the issuance of the bond.

Solution 4.4

July 1, 1992	Legal Services	9,000	
	Discount on Bonds Payable	1,000	
	Bonds Payable		10,000
	To record payment of bond for legal services.		

ISSUING BONDS BETWEEN INTEREST PAYMENT DATES

Bonds are generally sold at a date other than their interest payment date. Thus they are sold at their market value plus accrued interest.

Solved Problem 4.5. Recording the Sale of a Bond Plus Accrued Interest

Referring to Solved Problem 4.1, suppose that the $1,000,000 in bonds were sold on April 1, 1990, plus accrued interest. (a) Make the entry to record the sale of the bonds on April 1. (b) Make the entry recording the first interest payment on July 1. (c) Make the entry recording bond interest payable at the end of the first year that the bonds are outstanding.

Solution 4.5

(a)

April 1, 1990	Cash	1,022,500	
	Bonds Payable		1,000,000
	Interest Expense		22,500
	To record issuance of 9%, ten-year bonds plus accrued interest ($1,000,000 × 9% × ¼).		

(b)

July 1, 1990	Interest Expense	45,000	
	Cash		45,000
	To record payment of semiannual interest on bonds ($1,000,000 × 9% × ½).		

(c)

December 31, 1990	Interest Expense	45,000	
	Interest Payable		45,000
	To record liability for interest payable on January 1, 1991.		

BOND VALUATION

Present Value Determination

Bonds payable represent a contractual obligation to make periodic interest payments on the amount borrowed and to repay the principal amount of the bond at its maturity. A company always sells a bond at its present value. Present value is composed of two elements: (1) the present value of the bond principal at its maturity and (2) the present value of periodic interest payments. Present value is always less than the future value of a bond. The period interest rate paid by the bond is called the contract interest rate, coupon rate, or stated rate. The market interest rate, or effective rate, is the rate that investors demand on their investment purchases. The calculation for the price of the bond includes the use of two tables: (1) the present value of a single payment received at the end of a given number of time periods and (2) the present value of periodic payments at a given percentage multiplied by a given number of time periods. It must also be noted that if a $100,000 bond due in five years pays $5,000 every six months (or 10% annually), the present value will be based on ten periods (five years × two). Thus if an issuing corporation wants to estimate the proceeds it would realize from the sale of an issue, it must compute the present value of these two cash flows using the market yield rate (effective interest rate).

Solved Problem 4.6. Using Present Values to Calculate the Market Price of a Bond Issue

Cannon Tire and Rubber Inc. issued $1,000,000 of 8% bonds, interest payable semiannually, when the yield rate was 6%. The bond issue will mature in five years. The interest factor for a single payment in ten periods at 3% is 0.744. For periodic payments, the factor is 8.530. What is the present value of the bond?

Solution 4.6

Present value of one
($1,000,000 × 0.744) $ 744,000

Present value of interest payments:
($1,000,000 × 4% × 8.530)   341,200
                                                                                     $1,085,200

Issuing Bonds at a Discount or Premium

When bonds are issued, only the par value of the bonds is recorded in the bonds payable account. Bonds are sold at par when the stated rate of interest equals the market rate. Bonds are sold at a discount (less than par) when the stated rate of interest is less than the market rate. Bonds are sold at a premium (more than par) when the stated rate of interest is greater than the market rate for similar debt. The bond discount or premium, if any, will be recorded in a separate account and reported in the balance sheet as a direct deduction from or addition to the face amount of the bond. The discount or premium must be amortized over the outstanding period of the bond.

Solved Problem 4.7. Using Present Values to Calculate the Price of a Bond Issue Sold at a Discount

On January 1, 1992, the Amalgamated Pretzel Company Inc. issued $1,000,000 of 10% bonds, interest payable semiannually, when the yield rate was 12%. The bond issue will mature in five years. The interest factor for a single payment in ten periods at 6% is 0.558. For periodic payments at 6%, the factor is 7.360. (a) What is the present value of the bond? (b) Make the journal entry recording the sale of the bond. (c) Show how bonds payable would appear under the Long-Term Liabilities section of Amalgamated's Balance Sheet immediately after the sale.

Solution 4.7

(a)

Present value of one for ten periods at 6%:
($1,000,000 × 0.558) $ 558,000

Present value of interest payments:
($1,000,000 × 5% × 7.360)   368,000
Present value of bond issue $ 926,000

(b)

January 1, 1992	Cash	926,000	
	Discount on Bonds Payable	74,000	
	Bonds Payable		1,000,000
	To record sale of bonds at a discount.		

(c)

Long-term Liabilities
    10% Bonds Payable $1,000,000
    Less: Unamortized Bond Discount   74,000 $ 926,000

Solved Problem 4.8. Using Present Values to Calculate the Price of a Bond Issue Sold at a Premium

On January 1, 1992, Standard Robotics Ltd. Inc. issued $1,000,000 of 10% bonds, interest payable semiannually, when the yield rate was 8%. The bond issue will mature in five years. The interest factor for a single payment in 10 periods at 4% is 0.676. For periodic payments at 4%, the factor is 8.111. (a) What is the present value of the bond? (b) Make the journal entry recording the sale of the bond. (c) Show how bonds payable would appear under the Long-Term Liabilities section of Standard's Balance Sheet immediately after the sale.

Solution 4.8

(a)

Present value of one for ten periods at 4%:
($1,000,000 × 0.676) $ 676,000

Present value of interest payments:
($1,000,000 × 5% × 8.111)   405,550
Present value of bond issue $1,081,550

(b)

January 1, 1992	Cash	1,081,550	
	Bonds Payable		1,000,000
	Premium on Bonds Payable		81,550
	To record sale of bonds at a premium.		

(c)

Long-Term Liabilities
10% Bonds Payable $1,000,000
Add: Unamortized Bond Premium   81,550 $1,081,550

Discount and Premium Amortization

There are two ways of amortizing, or writing off, bond discount or premium: (1) *the straight-line* method, and (2) *the effective interest* method.

STRAIGHT-LINE AMORTIZATION

The straight-line method calls for writing off, in equal amounts, the bond premium or discount each period for the life of the bonds. For example, if a corporation issued ten-year bonds paying interest semiannually at a $10,000 discount, the discount amortization per interest period would be $500 ($10,000 ÷ 20 periods). The straight-line method is acceptable only when the discount or premium is immaterial.

Solved Problem 4.9. Issuing Bonds Payable, Paying and Accruing Interest, and Amortizing Discount Using the Straight-Line Method

On January 1, 1992, Ralston Wholesale Druggists Inc. issued 10%, 20-year bonds with a face amount of $10,000,000. The bonds sold at 97½ and pay interest on July 1 and January 1. Ralston elects to amortize bond discount using the straight-line method.

(a) Give the journal entry recording the sale of the bonds on January 1, 1992. (b) Make the journal entry recording the semiannual interest payment on July 1, 1992, and (c) the interest accrual on December 31, 1992.

Solution 4.9

(a)

January 1, 1992	Cash ($10,000,000 × 97½)	9,750,000	
	Discount on Bonds Payable	250,000	
	Bonds Payable		10,000,000
	To record 10%, 20-year bonds at a discount.		

(b)

July 1, 1992	Interest Expense	506,250	
	Cash ($10,000,000 × 10% × ½)		500,000
	Discount on Bonds Payable		6,250
	($250,000 ÷ 40 periods)		
	To record semiannual interest and amortization of bond discount.		

(c)

December 31, 1992	Interest Expense	506,250	
	Interest Payable		500,000
	($10,000,000 × 10% × ½)		
	Discount on Bonds Payable		6,250
	($250,000 ÷ 40 periods)		
	To accrue six months' interest and amortization of bond discount.		

Solved Problem 4.10. Issuing Bonds Payable, Paying and Accruing Interest, and Amortizing Premium Using the Straight-Line Method

On February 1, 1992, Hanover Mattress and Bedding Corporation issued 10%, 20-year bonds with a face amount of $10,000,000. The bonds sold at 103 and pay interest on January 1 and July 1. Hanover elects to amortize bond premium using the straight-line method.

(a) Give the journal entry recording the sale of the bonds on February 1, 1992. (b) Make the journal entry recording the semiannual interest payment on July 31, 1992, and (c) the interest accrual on December 31, 1992.

Solution 4.10

(a)

February 1, 1992	Cash	10,383,333	
	Bonds Payable		10,000,000
	Premium on Bonds Payable		300,000
	Interest Expense		83,333
	To record 10%, 20-year bonds at a premium plus interest expense of $83,333 ($10,000,000 × 10% × 1⁄12).		

(b)

July 1, 1992	Interest Expense ($500,000–$7,500)	492,500	
	Premium on Bonds Payable		
	($300,000 ÷ 40 periods)	7,500	
	Cash ($10,000,000 × 10% × ½)		500,000
	To record semiannual interest and		
	amortization of bond premium.		

(c)

December 31, 1992	Interest Expense	410,417	
	Premium on Bonds Payable	6,250	
	($300,000 ÷ 40 periods × ⅚)		
	Interest Payable		416,667
	($10,000,000 × 10% × 5/12)		
	To accrue five months' interest and		
	amortization of bond premium.		

Effective Interest Amortization

The effective (compound) interest method is preferred over the straight-line method because it offers a more accurate measurement of interest expense. To calculate the interest and amortization of bond discount for each interest period under the effective interest method, a constant interest rate must be applied to the carrying value of the bonds at the beginning of the interest period. A standard interest and amortization table utilizing the effective interest method has the following headings:

B (Semiannual Interest Expense Yield) × (Carrying Value Column F)	C (Semiannual Interest Paid to Bondholders Nominal) × Face	D Amortization of Discount (B – C)	E Unamortized Discount at End of the Period (E – D)	F Carrying Value at End of the Period (F – D)

Solved Problem 4.11. Preparing an Effective Interest Amortization Table; Recording Interest Payments and the Related Discount Amortization

On January 1, 1990, Supreme Sales Department Stores Inc. sold $500,000 of its 11%, ten-year bonds for $471,325. The yield rate is 12%. Supreme amortizes bond discount using the effective interest method. Interest payments are to be made on July 1 and January 1. (a) Prepare a discount amortization table for the first four semiannual interest periods. (b) Record the sale of the bonds. (c) Record the first four semiannual interest payments, including the payment of the bond interest on January 1, 1991. (d) What is the bond interest expense for 1990 and 1991?

Solution 4.11

(a)

B (Semiannual Interest Expense, 6%) × (Column F)	C Semiannual Interest Paid to Bondholders 5.5% × $500,000	D Amortization of Discount (B – C)	E Unamortized Discount at End of the Period (E – D)	F Carrying Value at End of the Period (F – D)
			$28,675	$471,325
$28,280	$27,500	$780	27,895	472,105
28,326	27,500	826	27,069	472,931
28,376	27,500	876	26,193	473,807
28,428	27,500	928	25,265	474,735

(b)

January 1, 1990	Cash	471,325	
	Discount on Bonds Payable	28,675	
	Bonds Payable		500,000
	To record 11%, ten-year bonds at a discount.		

(c)

July 1, 1990	Interest expense	28,280	
	Cash		27,500
	Discount on Bonds Payable		780
	To record semiannual interest and amortization of bond discount.		

December 31, 1990	Interest Expense	28,326	
	Interest Payable		27,500
	Discount on Bonds Payable		826
	To record semiannual interest and amortization of bond discount.		

January 1, 1991	Interest Payable	27,500	
	Cash		27,500
	To record payment of bond interest.		

July 1, 1991	Interest Expense	28,376	
	Cash		27,500
	Discount on Bonds Payable		876
	To record semiannual interest and amortization of bond discount.		

December 31, 1991	Interest Expense	28,428	
	Interest Payable		27,500
	Discount on Bonds Payable		928
	To record semiannual interest and		
	amortization of bond discount.		
January 1, 1992	Interest Payable	27,500	
	Cash		27,500
	To record payment of bond interest.		

(d)

1990

July 1, 1990	Interest Expense	$28,280
December 31, 1990	Interest Expense	28,326
	Total Interest Expense	$56,606

1991

July 1, 1991	Interest Expense	$28,376
December 31, 1991	Interest Expense	28,428
	Total Interest Expense	$56,804

Adjusting Entries

An adjusting entry is required when interest dates do not coincide with the end of the accounting period, to record accrued interest or revenue and any premium or discount amortization.

Solved Problem 4.12. Preparing an Effective Interest Amortization Table; Recording Interest Payments and the Related Premium Amortization

On August 30, 1990, The Acardia Oil Company Inc. sold $300,000 of its 12%, 20-year bonds for $324,000. Acardia amortizes bond premium using the effective interest method. The yield rate is 11%. Interest payments are to be made on February 28 and August 31. (a) Prepare a premium amortization table for the first two semiannual interest periods. (b) Record the sale of the bonds. (c) Record adjusting entries and semiannual interest payments, up to August 31, 1992.

Solution 4.12

(a)

Semiannual Interest Dates	B (Semiannual Interest Expense, 5½%) × (Column F)	C (Semiannual Interest Paid to Bondholders 6%) × Face	D Amortization of Premium (B – C)	E Unamortized Premium at End of the Period (E – D)	F Carrying Value at End of the Period (F – D)
8–30–90				$24,000	$324,000
2–28–91	$17,820	$18,000	$180	23,820	323,820
8–31–91	17,810	18,000	190	23,630	323,630
2–28–92	17,800	18,000	200	23,430	323,430
8–31–92	17,789	18,000	211	23,219	323,219

(b)

August 30, 1990	Cash	324,000	
	Bonds Payable		300,000
	Premium on Bonds Payable		24,000
	To record 12%, 20-year bonds at a premium.		

(c)

December 31, 1990	Interest Expense ($17,820 × 4/6)	11,880	
	Premium on Bonds Payable ($180 × 4/6)	120	
	Interest Payable ($18,000 × 4/6)		12,000
	To accrue four months' interest and amortization of bond premium for four months.		
February 28, 1991	Interest Expense ($17,820 × 2/6)	5,940	
	Premium on Bonds Payable ($180 × 2/6)	60	
	Interest Payable	12,000	
	Cash		18,000
	To record semiannual interest payment and amortization of bond premium for two months.		
August 31, 1991	Interest Expense	17,810	
	Premium on Bonds Payable	190	
	Cash		18,000
	To record payment of six months interest.		
December 31, 1991	Interest Expense ($17,800 × 4/6)	11,867	
	Premium on Bonds Payable ($200 × 4/6)	133	
	Interest Payable ($18,000 × 4/6)		12,000
	To accrue four months' interest and amortization of bond premium for four months.		

February 28, 1992	Interest Expense ($17,800 × 2/6)	5,933	
	Premium on Bonds Payable ($200 × 2/6)	67	
	Interest Payable	12,000	
	Cash		18,000
	To record semiannual interest		
	payment and amortization of		
	bond premium for two months.		

August 31, 1992	Interest Expense	17,789	
	Premium on Bonds Payable	211	
	Cash		18,000
	To record payment of six months interest.		

Solved Problem 4.13. Journal Entry to Record the Sale of the Bonds at a Discount, the Presentation of the Long-Term Liabilities Section of the Balance Sheet Immediately Following the Sale of the Bonds, and the Entries to Record the Semiannual Payment of Interest on the Bonds

On January 1, 1990, the Wappinger Lawnmower Company Ltd. sold $1,000,000 of 12%, ten-year bonds for 98. The bonds pay interest semiannually on June 30 and December 31. (a) Make the journal entry to record the sale of the bonds. (b) Prepare the Long-Term Liabilities section of the Balance Sheet immediately following the sale of the bonds. (c) Give the entries to record the semiannual payment of interest on the bonds at June 30 and December 31. (d) Make the entry to record the amortization of discount on a straight-line basis at December 31. (e) How would the Interest Expense and Discount on Bonds Payable ledger accounts appear at the end of the year? (f) Prepare the Long-Term Liabilities section of the Balance Sheet at year end after the amortization of interest has been recorded. (g) Make the journal entry at the end of the tenth year recording the redemption of the bonds at their maturity date.

Solution 4.13

(a)

January 1, 1990	Cash	980,000	
	Discount on Bonds Payable	20,000	
	Bonds Payable		1,000,000

(b)

Long-Term Liabilities

| 12% Bonds Payable, due in ten years | $1,000,000 | |
| Less: Discount on Bonds Payable | 20,000 | $ 980,000 |

(c)

June 30	Interest Expense	60,000	
	Cash		60,000
	($1,000,000 × 12% × 6/12).		

December 31	Interest Expense	60,000	
	Cash		60,000
	($1,000,000 × 12% × 6⁄12).		

(d)

December 31	Interest Expense	2,000	
	Discount on Bonds Payable		2,000
	Discount of $20,000 ÷ 10 years = $2,000.		

(e)

Interest Expense				Discount on Bonds Payable			
June 30	60,000			January 1	20,000	Dec. 31	2,000
Dec. 31	60,000			Balance	18,000		
	2,000						
	122,000						

(f)

Long-Term Liabilities
    12% Bonds Payable, due in ten years $1,000,000
    Less: Discount on Bonds Payable   18,000 $ 982,000

(g)

December 31	Bonds Payable	1,000,000	
	Cash		1,000,000
	To record redemption of bonds at		
	their maturity date.		

Solved Problem 4.14. Journal Entry to Record the Sale of the Bonds at a Premium, the Presentation of the Long-Term Liabilities Section of the Balance Sheet Immediately Following the Sale of the Bonds, and the Entries to Record the Semiannual Payment of Interest on the Bonds

On January 1, 1990, the Melon Clothing Corporation sold $1,000,000 of 12%, ten-year bonds for 102. The bonds pay interest semiannually on June 30 and December 31. (a) Prepare the journal entry to record the sale of the bonds. (b) Prepare the Long-Term Liabilities section of the Balance Sheet immediately following the sale of the bonds. (c) Make the entries to record the semiannual payment of interest on the bonds at June 30 and December 31. (d) Give the entry to record the amortization of premium on a straight-line basis at December 31. (e) How would the Interest Expense and Premium on Bonds Payable ledger accounts appear at the end of the year? (f) Prepare the Long-Term Liabilities section of the Balance Sheet at year end after the amortization of interest has been recorded. (g) Make the journal entry at the end of the tenth year recording the redemption of the bonds at their maturity date.

Solution 4.14

(a)

January 1, 1990	Cash	1,020,000	
	Bonds Payable		1,000,000
	Premium on Bonds Payable		20,000

(b)

Long-Term Liabilities

12% Bonds Payable, due in ten years	$1,000,000	
Add: Premium on Bonds Payable	20,000	$1,020,000

(c)

June 30	Interest Expense	60,000	
	Cash		60,000
	($1,000,000 × 12% × 6/12).		

December 31	Interest Expense	60,000	
	Cash		60,000
	($1,000,000 × 12% × 6/12).		

(d)

December 31	Premium on Bonds Payable	2,000	
	Interest Expense		2,000
	Premium of $20,000 ÷ 10 years = $2,000.		

(e)

Interest Expense				Discount on Bonds Payable			
June 30	60,000	Dec. 31	2,000	Dec. 31	2,000	January 1	20,000
Dec. 31	60,000					Balance	18,000
	120,000						
Balance	118,000						

(f)

Long-Term Liabilities

12% Bonds Payable, due in ten years	$1,000,000	
Add: Premium on Bonds Payable	18,000	$1,018,000

(g)

December 31	Bonds Payable	1,000,000	
	Cash		1,000,000
	To record redemption of bonds at their maturity date.		

RETIREMENT OF BONDS

Retirement of Bonds Before Maturity

A corporation that has issued callable bonds may decide to retire the issue before their maturity date. The entry to record the payment is a debit to Bonds Payable and a credit to Cash. If the bonds were issued at a discount or premium, it will also be necessary to write off both the principal and the pro-rata portion of the unamortized discount or premium on the bonds retired. The gain or loss from the early retirement of bonds is treated as an extraordinary item.

Bonds may be retired in a series. Such bonds are called serial bonds. Assume, for example, a $500,000, ten-year serial bond issue, $50,000 to be retired at par at the end of each year. The annual retirement entry is a debit to bonds payable and a credit to cash or to bond sinking fund cash for $50,000.

Retirement of Bonds Originally Sold at a Discount

Solved Problem 4.15. Journal Entry to Record the Retirement of Bonds Originally Sold at a Discount

On January 1, 1990, the Vision Rubber Corporation issued $1,000,000 in ten-year bonds paying interest at 10% annually. The bonds were sold at a discount of $20,000. At the end of five years, all of the bonds were repurchased by the corporation on the open market at 100½. Make the entry recording the retirement of the bonds at the end of the five years.

Solution 4.15

Bonds Payable	1,000,000	
Extraordinary Loss on Retirement of Bonds	15,000	
Discount on Bonds Payable		10,000
Cash ($1,000,000 × 100½)		1,005,000

To record the retirement of the bonds at the end of five years.

Solved Problem 4.16. Journal Entry to Record the Repurchase of Half of the Bonds Originally Sold at a Discount

Assume the same facts as in Solved Problem 4.15, except that the corporation repurchased half of the bonds on the open market at 100¾. Make the entry to record the retirement of half the bonds at the end of the five-year period.

Solution 4.16

Bonds Payable	500,000	
Extraordinary Loss on Retirement of Bonds	8,750	
Discount on Bonds Payable		5,000
Cash		503,750

The computation is as follows:

Original amount of bonds issued		$1,000,000
Discount to be amortized	$20,000	
Amortization over five years		
($20,000 ÷ 10 years = $2,000 × 5 years)	10,000	
Less: Unamortized discount		10,000
Carrying value at retirement		$ 990,000
Retirement of half of the bonds:		$ 495,000
Less: Purchase price ($500,000 × 100¾)		503,750
Extraordinary loss on retirement of bonds		$ 8,750

Retirement of Bonds Originally Sold at a Premium

Solved Problem 4.17. Journal Entry to Record the Retirement of Bonds Originally Sold at a Premium

On January 1, 1990, the Klaxton Gas and Chemical Corporation issued $1,000,000 in ten-year bonds paying interest at 10% annually. The bonds were sold at a premium of $20,000. At the end of five years, all of the bonds were repurchased by the corporation on the open market at 98. Make the entry to record the retirement of the bonds at the end of five years.

Solution 4.17

Bonds Payable	1,000,000	
Premium on Bonds Payable	10,000	
Cash		980,000
Extraordinary Gain on Retirement of Bonds		30,000

To record the retirement of the bonds at the end of five years.

Solved Problem 4.18. Journal Entry to Record the Retirement of Half of the Bonds Originally Sold at a Premium

Assume the same facts as in Solved Problem 4.17, except that the corporation repurchased only half of the bonds on the open market at 98. Make the entry recording the retirement of half the bonds at the end of five years.

Solution 4.18

Bonds Payable	500,000	
Premium on Bonds Payable	5,000	
Cash		490,000
Extraordinary Gain on Retirement of Bonds		15,000

The computation is as follows:

Face amount of bonds issued		$1,000,000
Premium to be amortized	$20,000	
Amortization over five years		
($20,000 ÷ 10 years = $2,000 × 5 years)	10,000	
Add: Unamortized premium		10,000
Carrying value at retirement		$1,010,000
Retirement of half of the bonds:		$ 505,000
Less: Purchase price ($500,000 × 98)		490,000
Extraordinary gain on retirement of bonds		$ 15,000

OTHER PROBLEMS RELATING TO BONDS

Converting Bonds into Stocks

A convertible bond gives the bondholder the option to convert the bond into stock at a later date. The conversion formula usually stipulates how many shares of stock can be received for each $1,000 of face value. Most bondholders tend to convert bonds when the market price of the stock is rising.

Solved Problem 4.19. Journal Entry Converting Bonds into Common Stock

Henry Alstyne, an owner of $100,000 of convertible bonds issued by the Recall Printing Corporation, has elected to convert the bonds into common stock because he believes that the common stock is currently a better investment than the bonds. The books of the corporation indicate that the unamortized discount applicable to these bonds is $2,000. The bond indenture permits each $1,000 bond to be converted into thirty shares of the corporation's $25 par value common stock. Make the journal entry to record Alstyne's election to convert the bonds into common stock.

Solution 4.19

Bonds Payable	100,000	
Discount on Bonds Payable		2,000
Common Stock		75,000
Premium on Common Stock		23,000

$100,000 ÷ $1,000 (par value) = 100 bonds.
100 bonds × 30 shares = 3,000 shares.
3,000 shares × $25 par value = $75,000.

Bond Sinking Fund

In order to make the bond offering attractive to potential investors, a corporation might agree to create a bond sinking fund to accumulate funds for the repayment of the bond at its maturity date. When the sinking fund is created, periodic cash payments are made to the fund. The trustee of the fund takes the cash and invests it in income-producing securities. When the bonds approach maturity, the trustee converts the securities into cash by selling them, then uses the proceeds to pay off the bondholders. Any excess cash is returned to the corporation. If there is a shortage, the corporation would be required to make an additional deficiency payment at the bond retirement date. The cash and securities that constitute the bond sinking fund are usually shown as a single amount on the balance under a caption called Long-Term Investments, which is just below the Current Assets section of the Balance Sheet.

Solved Problem 4.20. Journal Entries to Record the Payment to the Bondholders out of the Sinking Fund, and the Subsequent Closing of the Fund

Ten years ago, the Algonquin Speedboat Corporation sold $1,000,000 in bonds. The bond indenture specifically required that the corporation set up a bond sinking fund to repay the bondholders when the bonds mature. If the sinking fund now contains $1,004,000, make the journal entry to record the payment to the bondholders and the closing out of the sinking fund.

Solution 4.20

Bonds Payable	1,000,000	
Cash	4,000	
Bond Sinking Fund Cash		1,004,000

To record payment of bonds out of sinking fund.

Appropriation on Retained Earnings for Bond Redemption

In addition to the requirement for sinking fund deposits, the bond indenture may provide for an appropriation (or restriction) on retained earnings, requiring the corporation to retain earnings equal to the balance in the sinking fund. The bondholders are thus provided with double protection. The sinking fund insures the availability of adequate cash for the redemption of the bonds. The appropriation of retained earnings reduces the amount of dividend payments that may be distributed to the stockholders. This enhances the company's ability to meet its bond interest and sinking fund payments and also enables the company to meet its regular operating cash needs as well.

To illustrate, assume that the bond indenture of Empire Equipment Inc. provided for an annual appropriation of retained earnings of $50,000. The entry at the end of each year as follows:

December 31 Retained Earnings	50,000	
Retained Earnings-Appropriation for Bond Redemption		50,000

To record appropriation of retained earnings.

Retained Earnings Appropriation for Bond Redemption is shown in the Stockholders' Equity Section of the Balance Sheet as part of retained earnings. When the bonds are paid at maturity, the contractual restriction on retained earnings will be removed. The journal entry to remove the total appropriation is

December 31 Retained Earnings Appropriated for		
Bond Redemption	500,000	
Retained Earnings		500,000

How Bonds Differ from Stocks

Bonds differ from a corporation's outstanding stock in several ways: (1) Bonds are a liability of the corporation, and bondholders are classified as creditors of the corporation. On the other hand, shareholders are both investors and owners of the corporation. (2) In case of a corporate liquidation, bondholders must be paid before the stockholders. (3) Bonds pay interest, which is a tax-deductible expense. Stockholders are paid dividends, which is not tax deductible because they represent a distribution of corporate profits. (4) Bonds have a maturity date, which means that at some time in the future, the bonds must be redeemed (paid) by the corporation. Capital stock, which may consist of both common and preferred stock, has no maturity date and may remain outstanding indefinitely.

Since bond interest is a tax-deductible expense, it reduces taxable income, thereby reducing the corporation's tax liability.

Solved Problem 4.21. Calculating the After-Tax Cost of Bond Interest

The Judson Radio and Television Corporation pays bond interest of $1,000,000 a year. If Judson is subject to a tax rate of 34%, calculate the after-tax cost of the bond interest.

Solution 4.21

Interest Expense	$1,000,000
Less: Tax Savings ($1,000,000 × 34%)	340,000
After-Tax Cost of Interest	$ 660,000

Solved Problem 4.22. Analyzing Alternative Methods for Raising Capital

The management of the Dakota Land Development Corporation is trying to determine whether to issue bonds or preferred stock. At the present time, there is only common stock outstanding on which the corporation has never paid a cash dividend. Under Plan A, Dakota would issue $1,000,000 in bonds paying interest of 8% annually and no preferred stock. Under Plan B, the company would not sell bonds but would issue preferred stock that would automatically pay $60,000 a year in cash dividends. The company's income statement for the year beginning January 1, 1990, is expected to be as follows:

Sales	$1,000,000
Cost of Goods Sold	600,000
Gross Profit	$ 400,000
Operating Expenses	200,000
Net Income	$ 200,000

Dakota is subject to a tax rate of 34%. Prepare a schedule of cash available under Plan A and Plan B after payment of all taxes and dividends to the preferred stockholders.

Solution 4.22

	Plan A	Plan B
Sales	$1,000,000	$1,000,000
Less: Cost of Goods Sold	600,000	600,000
Gross Profit	$ 400,000	$ 400,000
Less: Operating Expenses	200,000	200,000
Income before Interest	$ 200,000	$ 200,000
Bond Interest $1,000,000 × 8%	80,000	– 0 –
Income before Taxes	$ 120,000	$ 200,000
Less: Federal Taxes @ 34%	40,800	68,000
Net Income	$ 79,200	$ 132,000
Less: Preferred Dividends	– 0 –	60,000
Cash Available	$ 79,200	$ 72,000

A bond arises from a contract known as an indenture and represents a promise to pay a sum of money at a designated maturity date, plus periodic payments of interest at a specified rate on the face value of the bond. A corporation may issue several types of bonds. Bonds pay interest that is tax deductible to the corporation. In order to make the bond offering attractive to potential investors, a corporation might agree to create a bond sinking fund to accumulate funds for the repayment of the bond at its maturity date. Bonds differ from a corporation's outstanding stock in several ways. For example, bonds are a liability of the corporation and bondholders are classified as creditors of the corporation. Bonds also pay interest, which is a tax-deductible expense.

5

Notes, Mortgages, Leases, and Pensions

A business typically has both current and long-term liabilities. Current liabilities are obligations that must be paid using existing current assets or the creation of other current liabilities. Current liabilities include accounts payable, short-term notes payable, payroll and other taxes payable, and accrued liabilities. Long-term liabilities include obligations that will not require the use of existing current assets because they do not mature within one year or within the current operating cycle. They include long-term notes, mortgages, leases, and pensions.

LONG-TERM NOTES PAYABLE

Long-term notes payable are usually used to purchase plant or operating assets. These notes contain both a dollar amount equivalent to the cash price of the asset and an interest factor to compensate the sellers for the use of their funds that they would have received had they sold them for cash.

Recording the Exchange of an Interest-Bearing Long-Term Note for a Plant Asset

A company may sometimes purchase an asset in exchange for a long-term note. If the purchase price of the asset is approximately equal to the cash price of the asset, and the interest is approximately equal to the prevailing market rate for interest, an entry must be made debiting an asset account for the purchase price of the asset and crediting Notes Payable.

Solved Problem 5.1. Recording the Purchase of a Plant Asset Using an Interest-Bearing Note

On January 1, 1990, Catcher Fish Hatcheries Inc. purchased a holding tank for trout. The company used a $100,000, three-year, 10% note, with interest compounded annually. The note, plus accumulated interest, must be paid at the end of the three years. (a) Prepare the journal entry recording the purchase on January 1, 1990. (b) Prepare the journal entry recording interest at the end of the first year. (c) Prepare the journal entry recording interest at the end of the second year. (d) Prepare the journal entry recording the interest expense and payment of the note at the end of the third year. (e) Prepare a schedule showing the accumulation of interest over the three-year period of the note.

Solution 5.1

(a)

January 1, 1990	Equipment	100,000	
	Notes Payable		100,000
	To record purchase of equipment in return for a $100,000, three-year, 10% note.		

(b)

December 31, 1990	Interest Expense	10,000	
	Notes Payable		10,000
	To record interest due on note: $100,000 × 10%.		

(c)

December 31, 1991	Interest Expense	11,000	
	Notes Payable		11,000
	To record interest due on note: $110,000 × 10%.		

(d)

December 31, 1992	Interest Expense	12,100	
	Notes Payable		12,100
	To record interest due on note: $121,000 × 10%.		

December 31, 1992 Notes Payable   133,100
                   Cash   133,100
                   To record payment of note at
                   maturity date.

(e)

Year	Amount of Note	Interest Earned for Year (10%)	Total of Interest + Note
12/31/90	$100,000	$10,000	$110,000
12/31/91	$110,000	$11,000	$121,000
12/31/92	$121,000	$12,100	$133,100

Recording the Exchange of a Note Having Either an Unreasonable Rate or No Rate of Interest for a Plant Asset

In some cases, a noninterest note, or a note containing an unreasonable rate of interest, may be given in exchange for assets. In this situation, the purchaser must record the note at its present value using the prevailing rate of interest on the date of the exchange. Any difference between the present value of the note and its maturity value must be recorded in an account called Discount on Notes Payable.

Solved Problem 5.2. Recording the Purchase of a Plant Asset Using a Noninterest-Bearing Note

Planet Newspapers Inc. purchased equipment for $100,000. The company gave a $100,000 noninterest bearing note. The prevailing market rate on January 1, 1990, the day the note was given, was 12%. The note, plus accumulated interest, must be paid at the end of three years. (a) Prepare the journal entry recording the purchase of the assets on January 1, 1990. The present value of a note due in three years at 12% is 0.7118. (b) Prepare a balance sheet presentation showing the long-term note payable immediately after the exchange. (c) Prepare a schedule showing the accumulation of interest over the three-year period of the note. (d) Prepare the journal entry recording the interest at the end of the first year. (e) Prepare the journal entry recording the interest at the end of the second year. (f) Prepare the journal entry recording the interest expense and payment of the note at the end of the third year.

Solution 5.2

(a)

January 1, 1990   Equipment   71,180
                   Discount on Notes Payable   28,820
                     Notes Payable   100,000
                   To record purchase of equipment in
                     return for $100,000 noninterest
                     bearing three-year note. Present
                     value $100,000 × 0.7118.

(b)

Long-term liabilities

Long-term notes payable	$100,000	
Less: Unamortized discount based on 12% interest rate at date of issue	28,820	$71,180

(c)

Year	Beginning-of-Year Carrying Amount	Discount To Be Amortized Each Year	Unamortized Discount at the End of Year	End-of-Year Carrying Amount
12/31/90	$71,180	$8,542*	$20,278**	$ 79,722
12/31/91	79,722	9,565	10,713***	89,287
12/31/92	89,287	10,713	– 0 –	100,000

* $71,180 × 12%.
** $28,820 (Discount) – $8,542.
*** $20,278 (Discount) – $9,565.

(d) Note: All numbers are slightly rounded.

December 31, 1990 Interest Expense	8,542	
Notes Payable		8,542
To record interest due on note ($71,180 × 12%).		

(e)

December 31, 1991 Interest Expense	9,565	
Notes Payable		9,565
To record interest due on note ($79,722 × 12%).		

(f)

December 31, 1992 Interest Expense	10,713	
Notes Payable		10,713
To record interest due on note ($89,287 × 12%).		

December 31, 1992 Notes Payable	100,000	
Cash		100,000
To record payment of note at maturity date.		

MORTGAGE NOTES PAYABLE

The purchase of certain large assets such as real estate and equipment is often financed by the issuance of mortgage notes payable. Upon issuance of the notes, the assets purchased are pledged as collateral for the loan. The mortgage notes are usually repaid in monthly installments consisting of principal and interest. The mortgage payable is reduced by the amount of principal contained in the payment.

Solved Problem 5.3. Payment of a Mortgage Note Payable

On January 1, 1990, the Jefferson Entertainment Corporation purchased equipment for $100,000, which was financed by the issuance of a $100,000 mortgage note payable bearing interest at 12% annually. The equipment is to be used as collateral for the mortgage note. Monthly payments are $2,500. (a) Prepare the journal entry showing the purchase of the equipment on January 1, 1990. (b) Prepare a monthly payment schedule for payments for the payment dates of February 1, March 1, and April 1. (c) Prepare journal entries showing mortgage payments on February 1, March 1, and April 1.

Solution 5.3

(a)

January 1, 1990	Equipment	100,000	
	Mortgage Note Payable		100,000
	To record purchase of equipment in exchange for $100,000, 12% mortgage.		

(b)

A	B	C	D	E
				Balance of Mortgage
		Interest 1%	Reduction	Note
Payment	Monthly	per Month	in Mortgage	Note
Date	Payment	Column E	Note	Payable
1/1/90				$100,000
2/1/90	$2,500	$1,000	$1,500	98,500
3/1/90	2,500	985	1,515	96,985
4/1/90	2,500	970	1,530	95,455

(c)

February 1, 1990	Mortgage Note Payable	1,000	
	Interest Expense	1,500	
	Cash		2,500
	To record monthly mortgage payment.		

March 1, 1990	Mortgage Note Payable	1,515	
	Interest Expense	985	
	Cash		2,500
	To record monthly mortgage payment.		

April 1, 1990	Mortgage Note Payable	1,530	
	Interest Expense	970	
	Cash		2,500
	To record monthly mortgage payment.		

LEASES

Instead of owning the asset, a company often elects to lease it. A lease is a contractual agreement that conveys the right to use a leased asset for a given period of time. The two parties to a lease are the lessor and the lessee. The lessor conveys the right to use the asset for a stated period of time to the lessee.

Capital Leases

All long-term leases are either capital leases or operating leases. A long-term capital lease, in effect, consists of installment payments. To be classified as a capital lease, at least any one of the following criteria must be met:

(1) The period of the lease is 75% or more of the estimated service life of the leased asset.

(2) The present value of the minimum lease payments is 90% or more of the fair value of the leased asset.

(3) Ownership of the leased asset is transferred to the lessee at the end of the lease period.

(4) The lease gives the lessee the option of purchasing the leased asset at less than fair market value at some point during or at the end of the lease period.

The accounting treatment of leases is governed by FASB Statement No. 13.

If any one of those requirements for a capital lease are met, the asset must be recorded by debiting an asset called Leased Equipment under Capital Leases and crediting a liability account called Obligations Under Capital Leases. The liability will be reduced by all subsequent lease payments made by the lessee. The account called obligations under capital leases is classified as a Long-Term Liability on the Balance Sheet. The leased asset is also subject to annual depreciation. The accounting treatment of leases is governed by FASB Statement No. 13.

Solved Problem 5.4. Journal Entry Recording a Lease Using the Present Value of the Total Lease Payments

On January 1, 1990, the Goodline Tire and Belt Corporation leased an asset from Allentown Leasing Inc. The lease term calls for an annual payment of $5,000 for five years, which is the approximate useful life of the asset. At the end of the lease term, title to the equipment is to pass to Goodline. All of the factors necessary for recording the transaction as a capital lease are present. Assume that Goodline's annual interest cost is 12%, which has a present value factor for five years of 3.605. (a) Calculate the present value of the asset. (b) Prepare the journal entry recording the lease at its present value. (c) Prepare the lease payment schedule using the following headings:

Year	A Lease Payment	B Interest 12% on Unpaid Obligation $(D \times 12\%)$	C Reduction of Lease Obligation $(A - B)$	D Balance of Lease Obligation

(d) Prepare the journal entries recording the payment of the lease obligations for Years 1 and 2. (e) Prepare the journal entries recording the depreciation expense for Years 1 and 2.

Solution 5.4

(a)

Periodic payment of $5,000 \times 3.605 = \$18,025$.

(b)

January 1, 1990   Leased Equipment Under Capital Leases 18,025
                         Obligations Under Capital Leases   18,025
                         To record lease contract.

(c)

Year	A Lease Payment	B Interest 12% on Unpaid Obligation (D × 12%)	C Reduction of Lease Obligation (A − B)	D Balance of Lease Obligation
				$18,025
1	$5,000	$2,163	$2,837	15,188
2	5,000	1,823	3,177	12,011
3	5,000	1,441	3,559	8,452
4	5,000	1,014	3,986	4,466
5	5,000	534*	4,466	– 0 –

* Rounded.

(d)

Year 1 Interest Expense (Column B)   2,163
       Obligations Under Capital Leases (Column C)   2,837
        Cash   5,000
       To record lease payment for Year 1.

Year 2 Interest Expense (Column B)   1,823
       Obligations Under Capital Leases (Column C)   3,177
        Cash   5,000
       To record lease payment for Year 2.

(e)

Year 1 Depreciation Expense   3,605
        Accumulated Depreciation — Leased
          Equipment Under Capital Leases   3,605
       To record annual depreciation
       ($18,025 ÷ 5 years = $3,605).

Year 2 Depreciation Expense   3,605
        Accumulated Depreciation — Leased
          Equipment Under Capital Leases   3,605
       To record annual depreciation
       ($18,025 ÷ 5 years = $3,605).

Operating Leases

Leases that do not meet any of the four criteria listed above required for classification as a capital lease are designated as operating leases. Under this type of arrangement, each payment is recorded by a debit to a rental expense account and a credit to cash.

Solved Problem 5.5. Recording an Operating Lease

On January 1, 1990, the American Piston Corporation entered into a rental agreement whereby it will make a $10,000 annual payment to the Unger Tool Company Inc., in return for the use of a stamping machine for a five-year period. The payment is to be made at the beginning of the year. The arrangement does not meet the criteria that requires recording as a capital lease. Prepare the journal entry recording the rental payment for the first year.

Solution 5.5

January 1, 1990	Machinery Rental Expense	10,000	
	Cash		10,000
	To record annual rental payment for machine.		

PENSIONS

Employers use pension plans to provide benefits to employees upon retirement. The main advantages of pension plans are that they help to attract and keep highly skilled and valuable employees, while payments to the plan are tax deductible. The two most common types of pension plans are defined contribution and defined benefit plans. FASB Statement No. 87 governs the accounting for pensions and establishes standards for financial reporting. In accounting for pensions plans, the employer usually makes an annual contribution to a funding agency such as an insurance company that is responsible for accumulating the fund's assets and for making pension payments to the participants when they retire. Under both defined contribution and defined benefit plans, the pension expense for a given year is equal to the employer's contribution to the fund for that year. The entry for a pension contribution would appear as follows:

Pension Expense	XXXXX	
Cash		XXXXX

Defined Contribution Plans

A defined contribution plan provides pension benefits to an employee in return for services rendered. An individual account is established for each participant. The plan specifies how contributions that are to be credited to the individual's account are to be calculated. In effect, the contribution is fixed, but the ultimate benefits to be paid to the employee-participant may vary.

Defined Benefit Plans

A defined benefit plan specifies the amount of benefits to be provided to the employee-participant when he or she retires. The benefit is a function of one or more factors, such as age, years of service, or compensation paid.

Accounting for Pension Costs

The accounting for a defined contribution plan is relatively simple. The employer makes a contribution to the plan, and gain or loss attributable to the earnings of the pension fund are shared by the pension plan's participants. On the other hand, the accounting for a defined benefit plan is more complex. The accounting for the plan involves the recognition of (1) the net periodic pension cost, and (2) liabilities and assets.

The Net Periodic Pension Cost

The basic components of the pension cost for the accounting period is the total of the service plus interest costs, reduced by an amount earned on pension assets. The service cost component of the pension expense is the actuarial present value of benefits calculated by the pension formula based on the employee's service for the period covered. The interest component is the increase in the projected benefit obligation due to the passage of time. The actual return on pension assets is the difference between the fair value of the pension plan's assets at the beginning and end of the period.

Solved Problem 5.6. Determining the Actual Return on Pension Assets

The following facts pertain to the pension plan of Arrow Gas and Chemicals for 1991:

Expected return on pension assets	12%
Fair market value of assets January 1, 1991	$100,000
Fair market value of assets December 31, 1991	$128,000
Contributions to pension plan	$ 15,000
Benefits paid to retired employees	$ 10,000

Assuming that contribution and benefits payments were made at year end, calculate the actual return on pension assets for 1991.

Solution 5.6

Fair market value of assets December 31, 1991	$128,000
Less: Fair market value of assets January 1, 1991	100,000
Difference	$ 28,000
Add: Benefits paid to employees	10,000
Less: Contributions to pension plan	(15,000)
Actual return on pension assets	$ 23,000

If the amount of cash contributed to the pension fund is less than the pension expense, a liability results, which must be recorded on the balance sheet.

Solved Problem 5.7. Recording the Pension Expense where the Actual Cash Payment is Less Than the Expense

On December 31, 1992, the Soloway Light and Fixture Corporation determined that its pension expense for the year was $35,000. The company then made a $25,000 payment into the fund. Prepare the journal entry recording the payment.

Solution 5.7

December 31, 1992	Pension expense	35,000	
	Cash		25,000
	Accrued Pension Cost Payable		10,000
	To record partial payment into pension fund.		

Minimum Pension Liability

FASB Statement No. 87 requires that a minimum liability be recorded when the accumulated benefits obligation exceeds the total fair value of the pension plan's assets. Recording the minimum liability requires a debit to an intangible asset account called intangible asset-deferred pension cost and a credit to an account called additional pension liability. FASB Statement No. 87 states that an asset should not be recorded if the fair value of the pension plan assets exceeds the accumulated benefit obligation. Recording an asset would violate the principle of conservatism.

Solved Problem 5.8. Recording the Minimum Pension Liability for an Accounting Period

On December 31, 1992, the Fairmont Foundry Corporation determined that its accumulated benefits obligation was $2,500,000, when the fair value of its pension plan assets was $2,000,000. Prepare the journal entry recording the minimum pension liability for the year.

Solution 5.8

December 31, 1992	Intangible Asset-Deferred Pension Cost	500,000	
	Additional Pension Liability Accumulated Benefits Obligation		500,000
	$2,500,000 – $2,000,000 (fair value of assets).		

If the amount paid into the pension plan exceeds the correct actuarially computed pension cost, any excess payment is charged to an account called prepaid pension cost.

Solved Problem 5.9. Recording the Pension Payment in Excess of the Actuarially Computed Pension Cost

On December 31, 1992, the Dundee Airplane Corporation determined that its pension obligation for the year was $2,000,000. Management subsequently made a $2,100,000 payment into the pension plan at year-end. Give the journal entry recording the pension payment.

Solution 5.9

December 31, 1992	Pension Expense	2,000,000	
	Prepaid Pension Cost	100,000	
	Cash		2,100,000
	To record payment into pension fund.		

Solved Problem 5.10. True and False Questions

Determine whether the following statements are true (T) or false (F).

_____ 1. If the purchase price of the asset is equal to a note that is given in exchange, an entry must be made debiting an asset account for the purchase price of the asset and crediting notes payable.

_____ 2. All notes given in exchange for assets must be recorded at their discounted present value.

_____ 3. A mortgage payment consists of both a partial payment for both principal and for interest.

_____ 4. The two parties to a lease are the vendor and vendee.

_____ 5. To be classified as a capital lease, the period of the lease must be 90% or more of the estimated service life of the leased asset.

_____ 6. Leases that do not meet any of the four criteria listed for a capitalized lease are designated as operating leases.

_____ 7. The main advantages of a pension plan are that they help to attract and keep highly skilled and valuable employees and that the payments to the plan are tax deductible.

_____ 8. In a defined contribution plan, the contribution is fixed but the ultimate benefits to be paid to the employee-participant may vary.

_____ 9. If the amount of cash contributed to the pension fund is less than the pension expense, an asset results, which must be recorded on the balance sheet.

_____ 10. Recognition of the minimum liability requires a debit to an intangible asset called intangible asset-deferred pension cost and a credit to an account called additional pension liability.

Solution 5.10

1. T	6. T
2. F	7. T
3. T	8. T
4. F	9. F
5. F	10. T

A business typically has both current and long-term liabilities. Long-term notes payable are usually used to purchase high cost assets such as plant and equipment. The purchase of assets such as real estate and equipment is often financed by the issuance of mortgage notes payable. All long-term leases are either capital leases or operating leases. A long-term capital lease, in effect, consists of installment payments. Employers use a pension plan to provide benefits to employees when they retire. The two most common types of pensions plans are defined contribution and defined benefit plans. In Chapter 6, we will discuss the preparation of a cash flow statement.

Part 3

Cash Flow and Financial Analysis

6

Statement of Cash Flows

*C*ash is vital to the operation of every business. How management utilizes the flow of cash can determine a firm's success or failure. Financial managers must control their company's cash flow so that bills can be paid on time and extra dollars can be put into the purchase of inventory and new equipment or invested to generate additional earnings.

FASB REQUIREMENTS

Management and investors have always recognized the need for a cash flow statement. Therefore, in recognition of the fact that cash flow information is an integral part of both investment and credit decisions, the Financial Accounting Standards Board has issued Statement No. 95, "Statement of Cash Flows." This pronouncement requires that enterprises include a statement of cash flows as part of the financial statements. A statement of cash flows reports the cash receipts, payments, and net change in cash on hand resulting from the operating, investing, and financing activities of an enterprise during a given period. The presentation reconciles beginning and ending cash balances.

Accrual Basis of Accounting

Under generally accepted accounting principles, most companies use the accrual basis of accounting. This method requires that revenue be recorded when earned and that expenses be recorded when incurred. Revenue may include credit sales that have not yet been collected in cash and expenses incurred that may not have been paid in cash. Thus, under the accrual basis of accounting, net income will generally not indicate the net cash flow from operating activities. To arrive at net cash flow from operating activities, it is necessary to report revenues and expenses on a cash basis. This is accomplished by eliminating those transactions that did not result in a corresponding increase or decrease in cash on hand.

Solved Problem 6.1. Calculating Correct Cash Inflows

During 1992, the Waterston Electric Supply Corporation earned $2,100,000 in credit sales, of which $100,000 remained uncollected as of the end of the calendar year. How much cash was actually collected by the corporation in 1992?

Solution 6.1

Credit sales	$2,100,000
Less: Credit sales uncollected at year end	100,000
Actual cash collected	$2,000,000

Cash and Cash Equivalents

FASB Statement No. 95 also requires that the cash flow statement explain the changes during the period in cash and cash equivalents. The latter are defined as short-term, highly liquid investments both readily convertible to known amounts of cash and so near maturity that it is appropriate to refer to them as being the equivalent of cash. Investments may or may not meet the definition of a cash equivalent. The statement indicates that only those investments with remaining maturities of three months or less at the date of their acquisition can qualify as cash equivalents.

For example, if a company bought a three-month United States Treasury bill two months ago, it would be treated as cash equivalent because it was purchased within three months of its maturity date. However, a one-year bill purchased a year ago does not become a cash equivalent when its remaining maturity becomes three months or less. Other items commonly considered to be cash equivalents include commercial paper and money market funds.

Presentation of Noncash Investing and Financing Transactions

A statement of cash flows focuses only on transactions involving the cash receipts and disbursements of a company. Noncash investing and financing transactions, such as the acquisition of land in return for the issuance of either bonds, preferred, or common stock, should not be presented in the body of the statement. These noncash transactions must, however, be disclosed elsewhere in the cash flow statement.

OPERATING ACTIVITIES

As previously stated, the statement of cash flows classifies cash receipts and cash payments into operating, investing, and financing activities. Operating activities include all transactions that are not investing or financing activities. They only relate to income statement items. Thus cash received from the sale of goods or services, including the collection or sale of trade accounts and notes receivable from customers, interest received on loans, and dividend income are to be treated as cash from operating activities. Cash paid to acquire materials for the manufacture of goods for resale, rental payments to landlords, payments to employees as compensation, and interest paid to creditors are classified as cash outflows for operating activities.

Solved Problem 6.2. Determining Cash Inflows or Outflows from Operating Activities

During 1992, the Fullmore Sugar and Beet Corporation had $3,400,000 in cash receipts from the sale of goods, collections worth $790,000 from accounts receivable, and $330,000 in interest and dividend income from debt and equity securities. Cash payments to acquire materials for the manufacture of goods totaled $1,650,000, its payments on accounts and notes payable amounted to $275,000, and it paid $810,000 in federal and state taxes and fines. Calculate net cash provided by operations for the year 1992.

Solution 6.2

Cash received:	
Sale of goods	$3,400,000
Collection of accounts receivable	790,000
Interest and dividends	330,000
Total	$4,520,000

Cash paid:	
Acquisition of materials	$1,650,000
For accounts and notes payable	275,000
For taxes, duties and fines	810,000
Total	$2,735,000
Net cash provided by operating activities	$1,785,000

Solved Problem 6.3. Determining Cash Inflows or Outflows from Operating Activities using Changes in the Individual Account Balances

For the year ended December 31, 1992, the net income of the Forbes Picture Frame Corporation was $60,000. Depreciation on plant assets for the year was $25,000. The balances of the current assets and current liability accounts at the beginning and end of 1992 are as follows:

	Beginning	End
Cash	$ 70,000	$ 65,000
Short-term investments	– 0 –	9,000
Accounts receivables	90,000	100,000
Inventories	155,000	145,000
Prepaid expenses	9,500	7,500
Accounts payable	59,000	51,000

What is the amount to be reported for cash flows from operating activities for 1992?

Solution 6.3

Net income		$60,000
Add: Depreciation	$25,000	
Decrease in inventories	10,000	
Decrease in prepaid expenses	2,000	37,000
		$97,000
Deduct:		
Increase in short-term investments	$ 9,000	
Increase in accounts receivable	10,000	
Decrease in accounts payable	8,000	27,000
Cash inflows from operating activities		$70,000

INVESTING ACTIVITIES

Investing activities include cash inflows from the sale of property, plant, and equipment used in the production of goods and services, debt instruments or equity of other entities, and the collection of principal on loans made to other enterprises. Cash outflows under this category may result from the purchase of plant and equipment and other productive assets, debt instruments or equity of other entities, and the making of loans to other enterprises.

Solved Problem 6.4. Determining Cash Inflows or Outflows from Investing Activities

During 1992, the Zandex Altimeter Corporation sold its plant and equipment for $9,000,000 and sold all of its stock investment in Trunk Realty Corporation, an unrelated entity, for $8,000,000. It then bought a new plant for $7,000,000 and made a loan of $5,500,000 to another company. Calculate net cash provided by the corporation's investing operations for the year 1992.

Solution 6.4

Cash received:		
Sale of plant and equipment	$9,000,000	
Sale of stock investment	8,000,000	
Total		$17,000,000
Cash paid:		
Purchase of new plant	$7,000,000	
Loan to another entity	5,500,000	
Total		12,500,000
Net cash provided by investing activities		$ 4,500,000

FINANCING ACTIVITIES

The financing activities of an enterprise involve the sale of a company's own preferred and common stock, bonds, mortgages, notes, and other short- or long-term borrowings. Cash outflows classified as financing activities include the repayment of short- and long-term debt, the reacquisition of treasury stock, and the payment of cash dividends.

Solved Problem 6.5. Determining Cash Inflows or Outflows from Financing Activities

In 1992, the Hanniford Ore Processing Corporation sold 2,000 shares of its own common stock for $2,000,000 cash and $10,000,000 of its 10%, ten-year bonds. It also issued another $50,000,000 in preferred stock in return for land and buildings. Hanniford then reacquired 10,000 shares of its own common stock for $8,800,000 and paid a cash dividend of $4,000,000. Calculate net cash provided by the corporation's investing operations for the year 1992.

Solution 6.5

Cash received:

Sale of common stock	$ 2,000,000	
Sale of bonds	10,000,000	
Total		$12,000,000

Cash paid:

Reacquisition of common stock	$ 8,800,000	
Cash dividend paid	$ 4,000,000	
Total		12,800,000
Net cash used in financing activities		$ 800,000

The issuance of the preferred stock in exchange for the land and buildings is a noncash transaction that would be disclosed in supplementary form at the end of the statement elsewhere of cash flows.

Solved Problem 6.6. Identifying Each Type of Cash Flow Activity

Classify each transaction in the first three columns by its correct cash flow activity.

	Operating	Investing	Financing	Not Applicable*
		Type of Activity		
Payments to acquire materials for manufacturing				
Payments to acquire stock of other companies				
Proceeds from the issuance of equity instruments				
Acquisition of land for the corporation's common stock				
Receipt of interest and dividends				
Payment of dividends				
Issuance of corporate bonds				
Issuance of corporate mortgage				
Receipts from sale of corporate plant				
Exchange of corporate bonds for the corporation's preferred stock				

* Shown as supplementary disclosure.

Solution 6.6

	Type of Activity			
	Operating	Investing	Financing	Not Applicable*
Payments to acquire materials for manufacturing	X			
Payments to acquire stock of other companies		X		
Proceeds from the issuance of equity instruments			X	
Acquisition of land for the corporation's common stock				X
Receipt of interest and dividends	X			
Payment of dividends			X	
Issuance of corporate bonds			X	
Issuance of corporate mortgage			X	
Receipts from sale of corporate plant		X		
Exchange of corporate bonds for the corporation's preferred stock				X

* Shown as supplementary disclosure.

Solved Problem 6.7. Calculating Net Cash Used in Investing and Financing Activities

O'Hara Bus and Terminal Lines Inc.'s transactions for the year ended December 31, 1992, included the following:

(1) Purchased real estate for $500,000, which was borrowed from a bank.
(2) Sold investment securities worth $600,000.
(3) Paid dividends of $300,000.
(4) Issued 500 shares of common stock for $350,000.
(5) Purchased machinery and equipment for $175,000.
(6) Paid $750,000 toward a bank loan.
(7) Accounts receivable outstanding of $100,000 were paid.
(8) Accounts payable were increased by $190,000.

Calculate O'Hara's net cash used in its (a) investing activities and (b) financing activities.

Solution 6.7

(a) Investing activities:

Cash inflows:		
Sale of investment securities		$ 600,000
Less cash outflows:		
Purchase of real estate	$500,000	
Purchase of machinery and equipment	175,000	675,000
Net cash used in investing activities		$ (75,000)

(b) Financing activities:

Cash inflows:		
Borrowed from bank to purchase real estate		$ 500,000
Issued common stock		350,000
		$ 850,000
Less cash outflows:		
Paid dividends	$(300,000)	
Paid bank loan	(750,000)	1,050,000
Net cash used in investing activities		$ (200,000)

Solved Problem 6.8. Calculating Net Cash Inflows and Outflows for Operating, Investing and Financing Activities

Ace Pipeline and Transmission Corporation's transactions for the year ended December 31, 1992, included the following:

(1) Cash sales of $2,300,000.
(2) Taxes, fines, and penalties of $80,000.
(3) Sold investment securities for $980,000.
(4) $330,000 in cash was borrowed from a bank.
(5) Cash paid for inventory totaled $940,000.
(6) Issued 10,000 shares of its preferred stock for land with a fair market value of $750,000.
(7) Purchased a secret formula for $100,000.
(8) Purchased land for $230,000.
(9) Paid $225,000 toward a bank loan.
(10) Sold 600 of its 10% debenture bonds due in the year 2000 for $600,000.

Calculate Ace's net cash inflows or outflows for (a) operating, (b) investing, and (c) financing activities. (d) Which of the transactions are not reported as part of the operating, investing, or financing activities of the corporation but, rather, are reported separately on the statement of cash flows?

Solution 6.8

(a) Operating activities:

Cash inflows:		
Cash sales		$2,300,000
Less: Cash outflows:		
Cash paid for inventory	$(940,000)	
Taxes, fines, and penalties	(80,000)	1,020,000
Net cash inflows from operating activities		$1,280,000

(b) Investing activities:

Cash inflows:		
Sold investment securities		$ 980,000
Less: Cash outflows:		
Purchased secret formula	$(100,000)	
Purchase of land	(230,000)	330,000
Net cash inflows from investing activities		$ (650,000)

(c) Financing activities:

Cash inflows:		
Borrowing from bank		$ 330,000
Sold debenture bonds		600,000
		$ 930,000
Less: Cash outflows:		
Paid bank loan		(225,000)
Net cash inflows from investing activities		$ (705,000)

(d) The issuance of 10,000 shares of Ace's preferred stock for land with a fair market value of $750,000 does not involve an exchange of cash and must be reported separately on the statement of cash flows.

Solved Problem 6.9. Calculating Net Cash Inflows and Outflows for Operating, Investing, and Financing Activities; Journal Entries for the Sale of Equipment; and the Preparation of a Reconciliation of Beginning and Ending Cash

Newport Steam Corporation's balance sheet accounts as of December 31, 1991, and December 1992, and the information relating to the 1991 activities are presented below:

	December 31	
	1992	1991
ASSETS		
Cash	$ 230,000	$ 100,000
Short-term investments	300,000	– 0 –
Accounts receivable (net)	550,000	550,000
Inventory	680,000	600,000
Long-term investments	200,000	300,000
Plant assets	1,700,000	1,000,000
Accumulated depreciation	(450,000)	(450,000)
Goodwill	90,000	100,000
Total assets	$3,300,000	$2,200,000
LIABILITIES AND STOCKHOLDERS' EQUITY		
Accounts payable	$ 825,000	$ 720,000
Long-term debt	325,000	– 0 –
Common stock, $1 par	800,000	700,000
Additional paid-in capital	370,000	250,000
Retained earnings	980,000	530,000
Total liabilities and stockholders' equity	$3,300,000	$2,200,000

Information relating to 1992 activities is as follows:

(1) Net income for 1992 was $700,000.
(2) Purchase of short-term investments for $300,000, which will mature on June 30, 1993.
(3) Cash dividends declared and paid in 1992 worth $250,000.
(4) Equipment costing $400,000, having accumulated depreciation of $250,000, was sold in 1992 for $150,000.
(5) Plant assets worth $1,100,000 were purchased for cash.
(6) A long-term investment costing $100,000 was sold for $135,000.
(7) 100,000 shares of $1 par value common stock were sold for $2.20 a share.
(8) Amortization of goodwill for 1992 was $10,000.

Calculate Newport's net cash inflows or outflows for (a) operating, (b) investing, and (c) financing activities. (d) Prepare the journal entry reflecting the sale of the equipment. (e) Prepare the journal entry reflecting the sale of the long-term investment. (f) Prepare a reconciliation of beginning and ending cash. (g) Prepare a reconciliation of beginning and ending plant assets. (h) Discuss whether or not the short-term investments are cash equivalents.

Solution 6.9

(a) Operating activities:

Net income	$ 700,000
Depreciation	250,000
Increase in inventory	(80,000)
Increase in accounts payable	105,000
Gain on sale of investment	(35,000)
Amortization of goodwill	10,000
Total cash provided from operating activities	$ 950,000

(b) Investing activities:

Sale of equipment	$ 150,000
Sale of investment	135,000
Purchase of short-term investments	(300,000)
Purchase of plant assets	(1,100,000)
Total cash used for investing activities	$(1,115,000)

(c) Financing activities:

Dividends paid	$ (250,000)
Long-term debt	325,000
Common stock issued	220,000
Total cash provided from financing activities	$ 295,000

(d)

Cash	150,000	
Accumulated Depreciation	250,000	
Equipment		400,000

(e)

Cash	135,000	
Long-Term Investment		100,000
Gain on Sale of Long-Term Investment		35,000

(f) Reconciliation of cash:

January 1, 1992	$ 100,000
Add: Cash provided from operating activities	950,000
Cash provided from financing activities	295,000
Less: Cash used for investing activities	(1,115,000)
December 31, 1992	$ 230,000

(g) Reconciliation of beginning and ending plant assets.

January 1, 1992	$ 1,000,000
Add: Plant assets purchased	1,100,000
Less: Plant assets sold	(400,000)
December 31, 1992	$ 1,700,000

(h) Only short-term investments acquired within three months of their maturity date may be treated as cash equivalents. The short-term investments acquired by Newport are due at the end of six months and are therefore not cash equivalents.

PRESENTATION OF THE CASH FLOW STATEMENT

A cash flow statement, can be presented in either the direct or indirect format. The investing and financing sections will be the same under either format. However, the operating section will be different.

The Direct Method

Enterprises that utilize the direct method should report separately the following classes of operating cash receipts and payments:

(1) cash collected from customers, including lessees, licensee, and other similar items;
(2) interest and dividends received;
(3) other operating cash receipts, if any;
(4) cash paid to employees and other suppliers of goods or services, including suppliers of insurance, advertising and other similar expenses;
(5) interest paid;
(6) income taxes paid; and
(7) other operating cash payments, if any.

Companies using the direct method must provide a reconciliation of net income to net cash flow from operating activities in a separate schedule in the financial statements.

The Indirect Method

The indirect method starts with net income and reconciles it to net cash flow from operating activities. Adjustments are made for items that affected net income but did not affect cash. For example, if a corporation has credit sales of $600,000 during 1992, but collected only $575,000 in cash, accounts receivable at year end would show an increase of $25,000. Thus, while an enterprise may have had $600,000 in revenue, not all of these sales resulted in an inflow of cash. Therefore, to reconcile net income to net cash flow from operating activities, the increase of $25,000 in accounts receivable would have to be subtracted from net income.

Likewise, where a company incurs expenses of $100,000 but makes actual cash payments of only $90,000, the $10,000 increase in accounts payable must be added back to net income in order to arrive at the net cash flow from operating activities.

Solved Problem 6.10. Preparation of a Statement Of Cash Flows

A comparative balance sheet and income statement of Banner Cord Corporation for the year ended December 31, 1991, was presented as follows:

Banner Cord Corporation
Comparative Balance Sheet
December 31, 1992

	1992	1991	Change Increase/Decrease	
ASSETS				
Cash	$ 74,000	$ 98,000	$ 24,000	Decrease
Accounts receivable	52,000	72,000	20,000	Decrease
Prepaid expenses	12,000	– 0 –	12,000	Increase
Long-term investments	1,000	2,000	1,000	Decrease
Land	140,000	– 0 –	140,000	Increase
Building	400,000	– 0 –	400,000	Increase
Accumulated depreciation-building	(22,000)	– 0 –	22,000	Increase
Equipment	136,000	– 0 –	136,000	Increase
Accumulated depreciation-equipment	(20,000)	– 0 –	20,000	Increase
Total	$773,000	$172,000		
LIABILITIES AND STOCKHOLDERS' EQUITY				
Accounts payable	$ 81,000	$ 12,000	$ 69,000	Increase
Bonds payable	300,000	– 0 –	300,000	Increase
Common stock	120,000	120,000	– 0 –	
Retained earnings	272,000	40,000	232,000	Increase
Total	$773,000	$172,000		

Banner Cord Corporation
Income Statement
for the Year Ended December 31, 1992

Revenues		$ 984,000
Operating expenses (excluding depreciation)	$538,000	
Depreciation expense	42,000	580,000
Income from operations		$ 404,000
Income tax expense		136,000
Net income		$ 268,000

During 1992, Banner Cord paid $36,000 in cash dividends.

Prepare a statement of cash flows using (a) the direct method and (b) the indirect method.

Solution 6.10

(a) The statement of cash flows, using the *direct method*, would be presented as follows:

Banner Cord Corporation
Statement of Cash Flows
for the Year Ended December 31, 1992

Cash flows from operating activities:		
Cash received from customers	$ 1,004,000	
Cash payments for operating expenses	(469,000)	
Cash payments for prepaid expenses	(12,000)	
Cash payments for taxes	(136,000)	
Net cash provided by operating activities		$387,000
Cash flows from investing activities:		
Cash paid to purchase land	$ (140,000)	
Cash paid to purchase building	(400,000)	
Cash paid to purchase equipment	(136,000)	
Sale of long-term investment	1,000	
Net cash used in investing activities		(675,000)
Cash flows from financing activities:		
Cash received from the issuance of bonds	$ 300,000	
Cash paid for dividends	(36,000)	
Net cash provided by financing activities		264,000
Net decrease in cash and cash equivalents		(24,000)
Cash and cash equivalents at the beginning of the year		98,000
Cash and cash equivalents at the end of the year		$ 74,000

Under this method, the $1,004,000 in cash received from customers represents $984,000 in sales increased by a reduction in accounts receivable of $20,000. Accounts receivable was reduced due to a conversion into cash. The cash outflow of $469,000 was determined by reducing the $538,000 in expenses by the increase to accounts payable of $69,000. This increase is due to the fact that an expense was incurred for the period that will not be paid until a future period. All other amounts were obtained either directly from the balance sheet or the income statement.

Under the direct method, a separate schedule reconciling net income to net cash would be presented as follows:

Banner Cord Corporation
Statement of Cash Flows
for the Year Ended December 31, 1992

Cash flows from operating activities:		
Net income		$268,000
Add: Adjustments to reconcile net income to net cash:		
Depreciation expense	$ 42,000	
Decrease in accounts receivable	20,000	
Increase in prepaid expenses	(12,000)	
Increase in accounts payable	69,000	119,000
Net cash provided by operating activities		$387,000

(b) If the indirect method were utilized, the cash flow statement would be presented as follows:

Banner Cord Corporation
Statement of Cash Flows
for the Year Ended December 31, 1992

Cash flows from operating activities:		
Net income		$268,000
Add: Adjustments to reconcile net income to net cash:		
Depreciation expense	$ 42,000	
Decrease in accounts receivable	20,000	
Increase in prepaid expenses	(12,000)	
Increase in accounts payable	69,000	119,000
Net cash flow provided by operating activities		$ 387,000
Cash flows from investing activities:		
Cash paid to purchase land	$(140,000)	
Cash paid to purchase building	(400,000)	
Cash paid to purchase equipment	(136,000)	
Sale of long-term investments	1,000	
Net cash used in investing activities		(675,000)
Cash flows from financing activities		
Cash received from the issuance of bonds	$ 300,000	
Cash paid for dividends	(36,000)	
Net cash provided by financing activities		264,000
Net decrease in and cash equivalents		$ (24,000)
Cash and cash equivalents at the beginning of the year		$ 98,000
Cash and cash equivalents at the end of the year		$ 74,000

*T*he statement of cash flows is useful to management in helping to assessing an entity's ability to generate future cash flows and to meet its financial obligations as they become due. These obligations include the demands of vendors for payments on accounts and for employee wages. Cash provides the best measure of short-term liquidity since it represents the asset generally used to meet short-term liquidity needs. Also, cash is easily understood since virtually all users of financial statements are familiar with it. In Chapter 7, we will discuss financial statement analysis.

7

Financial Statement Analysis

*A*ccounting can be thought of as the art of creating scorecards for business operations. It translates raw data into a set of objective numbers integrated into financial statements that provide information about the firm's profits, performance, problems, and future prospects. Financial analysis is the study of the relationships among these financial numbers; it helps users to identify the major strengths and weaknesses of a business enterprise.

WHO USES FINANCIAL ANALYSIS

The techniques of financial analysis are important to two groups: *internal management* and *external users,* such as investors and banks.

Internal Managers

Internal managers analyze the financial statements to determine whether the company is earning an adequate return on its assets. They also use financial ratios as "flags" to indicate potential areas of strength or weakness. Many financial analysts use rule-of-thumb measurements for key financial ratios. For example, most analysts feel that a current ratio (current assets divided by current liabilities) of two to one is acceptable for most businesses. However, while a company may meet or even surpass this ratio, the financial statements might indicate that an increasing proportion of the current assets consists of accounts receivable that have been outstanding for more than 30 days. Slow payment might require management to change its credit policy by shortening the credit period or by implementing a more effective cash-collection policy. Internal management also uses this "number-crunching" process to decide how much inventory is to be held at any one time or whether to merge with or acquire another company.

External Users

External users include investors, creditors, unions, and prospective employees. Investors might use the financial statements to study whether there is an adequate profit margin or a favorable return on assets. The financial health of the company, as perceived by investors, will affect the market price of the company's stock, cost of financing, and bond rating. For creditors, financial statements indicate a company's ability to repay a loan. A union will study the financial statements to evaluate their wage and pension demands when their old contract with management expires. Finally, students and other job hunters might analyze a company's financial statements to determine career opportunities.

Horizontal and Vertical Analysis

Financial statement analysis includes horizontal analysis (percentage change over the years) and vertical analysis (percentage relationship within one year). Sources of financial information include a company's annual financial report, SEC filings, financial reference books put out by such firms as Dun & Bradstreet, trade publications, and financial newspapers such as the *Wall Street Journal*.

An analyst also studies industry norms. This measurement indicates how a company is performing in comparison with other companies in the same industry. Unfortunately, there are limitations to the use of this method. First, one company in the same industry might be involved in manufacturing and selling a product in large quantities at the wholesale level, while another enterprise might only sell at the retail level to the public. Second, each enterprise might use a different accounting method for financial reporting purposes. For example, one company might value its ending inventory according to the FIFO method, while a competitor might use LIFO. In addition, the two companies might use a different accounting method for recording depreciation. The cumulative effect of the use of different accounting methods might make a comparison of net income and fixed-asset valuation of little importance.

FINANCIAL STATEMENT ANALYSIS

The financial community uses several methods for evaluating the financial health of an enterprise. These methods include trend analysis, horizontal and vertical analysis, and ratio analysis.

Trend Analysis

Trend analysis indicates in which direction a company is headed. Trend percentages are computed by taking a base year and assigning its figures as a value of 100. Figures generated in subsequent years are expressed as percentages of base-year numbers.

Solved Problem 7.1. Illustration of Trend Analysis Showing Changes Between a Base Year and All Subsequent Years

The Hotspot Appliance Corporation showed the following figures for a five-year period:

	1995	1994	1993	1992	1991
		(Thousands of Dollars)			
Net sales	$910	$875	$830	$760	$775
Cost of goods sold	573	510	483	441	460
Gross profit	$337	$365	$347	$319	$315

(a) Prepare a schedule showing trend percentages. (b) What trends are shown for net sales, cost of goods sold, and gross profit?

Solution 7.1

(a)

	1995	1994	1993	1992	1991
Net sales	117	113	107	98	100
Cost of goods sold	125	111	105	96	100
Gross profit	107	116	110	101	100

With 1991 taken as the base year, its numbers are divided into those from subsequent years to yield comparative percentages. For example, net sales in 1991 ($775,000) is divided into 1995's net-sales figure ($910,000).

(b) Net sales shows an upward trend after a downturn in 1992. Cost of goods sold shows a sharp increase between 1994 and 1995 after a small drop in costs between 1991 and 1992. There appears to be a substantial drop in gross profit between 1994 and 1995 which is attributable to the increased cost of goods sold.

Trend percentages show horizontally the degree of increase or decrease, but they do not indicate the reason for the changes. They do serve to indicate unfavorable developments that will require further investigation and analysis. A significant change may have been caused by a change in the application of an accounting principle or by controllable internal conditions, such as a decrease in operating efficiency.

Horizontal Analysis

Horizontal analysis improves an analyst's ability to use dollar amounts when evaluating financial statements. It is more useful to know that sales have increased 25% than to know that sales increased by $50,000. Horizontal analysis requires that you: (1) compute the change in dollars from the earlier base year, and (2) divide the dollar amount of the change by the base period amount.

Solved Problem 7.2. Comparative Income Statement—Horizontal Analysis

The comparative income statement of the Ogel Supply Corporation as of December 31, 1992, appears as follows:

	1992	1991
Net sales	$990,000	$884,000
Cost of goods sold	574,000	503,000
Gross profit	$416,000	$381,000
Operating expenses:		
Selling expenses	$130,000	$117,500
General expenses	122,500	120,500
Total operating expenses	$252,500	$238,000
Income from operations	163,500	143,000
Interest expense	24,000	26,000
Income before income taxes	$139,500	$117,000
Income tax expense	36,360	28,030
Net income	$103,140	$ 88,970

Prepare a detailed horizontal analysis statement.

Solution 7.2

	1992	1991	Increase (Decrease) Amount	Percent
Net sales	$990,000	$884,000	$106,000	12.0
Cost of goods sold	574,000	503,000	71,000	14.1
Gross profit	416,000	381,000	35,000	9.2
Operating expenses:				
Selling expenses	130,000	117,500	12,500	10.6
General expenses	122,500	120,500	2,000	1.7
Total operating expenses	252,500	238,000	14,500	6.1
Income from operations	163,500	143,000	20,500	14.3
Interest expense	24,000	26,000	(2,000)	(7.7)
Income before income taxes	139,500	117,000	22,500	19.2
Income tax expense	36,360	28,030	8,330	29.7
Net income	$103,140	$ 88,970	$ 14,170	15.9

Solved Problem 7.3. Comparative Balance Sheet—Horizontal Analysis

The comparative balance sheet of the Ogel Supply Corporation as of December 31, 1992, appears as follows:

	1992	1991
ASSETS		
Current assets:		
Cash	$ 60,000	$ 30,000
Accounts receivable, net	113,000	79,000
Inventories	107,100	106,900
Prepaid expenses	5,700	6,100
Total current assets	$285,800	$222,000
Property, plant, and equipment, net	660,000	665,000
Total assets	$945,800	$887,000
LIABILITIES		
Current liabilities:		
Notes payable	$ 40,000	$ 33,000
Accounts payable	100,600	57,500
Total current liabilities	$140,600	$ 90,500
Long-term debt	400,000	410,000
Total liabilities	$540,600	$500,500
STOCKHOLDERS' EQUITY		
Common stock, no-par	$200,000	$200,000
Retained earnings	205,200	186,500
Total stockholders' equity	$405,200	$386,500
Total liabilities and stockholders' equity	$945,800	$887,000

Prepare a detailed horizontal analysis statement.

Solution 7.3

	1992	1991	Increase (Decrease) Amount	Percent
ASSETS				
Current assets:				
Cash	$ 60,000	$ 30,000	$ 30,000	100.0
Accounts receivable, net	113,000	79,000	34,000	43.0
Inventories	107,100	106,900	200	0.0
Prepaid expenses	5,700	6,100	(400)	(7.0)
Total current assets	$285,800	$222,000	$ 63,800	28.7
Property, plant, and				
equipment, net	660,000	665,000	(5,000)	.1
Total assets	$945,800	$887,000	$ 58,800	6.6
LIABILITIES				
Current liabilities:				
Notes payable	$ 40,000	$ 33,000	$ 7,000	21.2
Accounts payable	100,600	57,500	43,100	75.0
Total current liabilities	$140,600	$ 90,500	$ 50,100	55.4
Long-term debt	400,000	410,000	(10,000)	(2.4)
Total liabilities	$540,600	$500,500	40,100	8.1
STOCKHOLDERS' EQUITY				
Common stock, no-par	200,000	$200,000.	$ –	0.0
Retained earnings	205,200	186,500	18,700	10.0
Total stockholders' equity	$405,200	$386,500	$ 18,700	5.0
Total liabilities and				
stockholders' equity	$945,800	$887,000	$ 58,800	6.6

Vertical Analysis

Vertical analysis shows the percentage relationship of each item on the financial statement to a total figure representing 100 percent. Each income-statement account is compared to net sales. For example, if net sales is $100,000 and net income after taxes is $8,000, then the company's net income is $8,000 divided by $100,000, or 8% of the net sales figure.

Vertical analysis also reveals the internal structure of the business. This means that if total assets are $750,000 and cash shows a year-end balance of $75,000, then cash represents 10% of the total assets of the business at year-end. Vertical analysis shows the mix of assets that generate the income as well as the sources of capital provided by either current or noncurrent liabilities, or by the sale of preferred and common stock.

A company's vertical percentages should be compared to those of its competitors or to industry averages to determine the company's relative position in the marketplace. Like horizontal analysis, vertical analysis is not the end of the process. The analyst must be prepared to examine problem areas indicated by horizontal and vertical analysis.

Solved Problem 7.4. Comparative Income Statement—Vertical Analysis

The comparative income statement of the Ogel Supply Corporation at December 31, 1992, appears as follows:

	1992	1991
Net sales	$990,000	$884,000
Cost of goods sold	574,000	503,000
Gross profit	$416,000	$381,000
Operating expenses:		
Selling expenses	$130,000	$117,500
General expenses	122,500	120,500
Total operating expenses	$252,500	$238,000
Income from operations	$163,500	$143,000
Interest expense	24,000	26,000
Income before income taxes	$139,500	$117,000
Income tax expense	36,360	28,030
Net income	$103,140	$ 88,970

Prepare a detailed vertical analysis statement.

Solution 7.4

	1992		1991	
	Amount	Percent	Amount	Percent
Net sales	$990,000	100.0	$884,000	100.0
Cost of goods sold	574,000	58.0	503,000	57.0
Gross profit	$416,000	42.0	$381,000	43.0
Operating expenses:				
Selling expenses	$130,000	13.1	$117,500	13.3
General expenses	122,500	12.4	120,500	13.6
Total operating expenses	$252,500	25.5	$238,000	26.9
Income from operations	$163,500	16.5	$143,000	16.1
Interest expense	24,000	2.4	26,000	2.9
Income before income taxes	$139,500	14.1	$117,000	13.2
Income tax expense	36,360	3.7	28,030	3.2
Net income	$103,140	10.4	$ 88,970	10.0

Solved Problem 7.5. Comparative Balance Sheet—Vertical Analysis

The comparative balance sheet of the Ogel Supply Corporation at December 31, 1992, appears as follows:

	1992	1991
ASSETS		
Current assets:		
Cash	$ 60,000	$ 30,000
Accounts receivable, net	113,000	79,000
Inventories	107,100	106,900
Prepaid expenses	5,700	6,100
Total current assets	$285,800	$222,000
Property, plant, and equipment, net	660,000	665,000
Total assets	$945,800	$887,000
LIABILITIES		
Current liabilities:		
Notes payable	$ 40,000	$ 33,000
Accounts payable	100,600	57,500
Total current liabilities	$140,600	$ 90,500
Long-term debt	400,000	410,000
Total liabilities	$540,600	$500,500
STOCKHOLDERS' EQUITY		
Common stock, no-par	$200,000	$200,000
Retained earnings	205,200	186,500
Total stockholders' equity	$405,200	$386,500
Total liabilities and stockholders' equity	$945,800	$887,000

Prepare a detailed vertical analysis statement.

Solution 7.5

	1992		1991	
	Amount	Percent	Amount	Percent
ASSETS				
Current assets:				
Cash	$ 60,000	6.3	$ 30,000	3.4
Accounts receivable, net	113,000	11.9	79,000	8.9
Inventories	107,100	11.3	106,900	12.1
Prepaid expenses	5,700	0.6	6,100	.7
Total current assets	$285,800	30.1	$222,000	25.3
Property, plant, and equipment, net	660,000	69.9	665,000	74.9
Total assets	$945,800	100.0	$887,000	100.0

LIABILITIES

Current liabilities:				
Notes payable	$ 40,000	4.2	$ 33,000	3.7
Accounts payable	100,600	10.6	57,500	6.5
Total current liabilities	$140,600	14.8	$ 90,500	10.2
Long-term debt	400,000	42.3	410,000	46.2
Total liabilities	$540,600	57.1	$500,500	56.4
STOCKHOLDERS' EQUITY				
Common stock, no-par	$200,000	21.1	$200,000	22.6
Retained earnings	205,200	21.7	186,500	21.0
Total stockholders' equity	$405,200	42.8	$386,500	43.6
Total liabilities and				
stockholders' equity	$945,800	100.0	$887,000	100.0

After completing the statement analysis, the financial analyst will consult with management to discuss problem areas, possible solutions, and the company's prospects for the future.

RATIO ANALYSIS

Ratios provide a convenient and useful way of expressing a relationship between numbers. For example, management is always interested in its ability to pay its current liabilities as they become due.

Liquidity Analysis

Ratios used to determine the debt-paying ability of the company include the *current ratio* and the *acid-test* or *quick ratio*. A term also frequently used in financial statement analysis is *working capital*.

Current Ratio

The current ratio is a valuable indicator of a company's ability to meet its current obligations as they become due. The ratio is computed by using the following formula:

$$\frac{\text{Current Assets}}{\text{Current Liabilities}}$$

Solved Problem 7.6. Calculating the Current Ratio

Assume that in Solved Problem 7.3 the Ogel Supply Corporation showed the following current assets and current liabilities for the years ended December 31, 1992, and December 31, 1991:

	1992	1991
ASSETS		
Current assets:		
Cash	$ 60,000	$ 30,000
Accounts receivable, net	113,000	79,000
Inventories	107,100	106,900
Prepaid expenses	5,700	6,100
Total current assets	$285,800	$222,000
LIABILITIES		
Current liabilities:		
Notes payable	$ 40,000	$ 33,000
Accounts payable	100,600	57,500
Total current liabilities	$140,600	$ 90,500

(a) Calculate the current ratio for 1992 and 1991. (b) What does the change in the ratio indicate?

Solution 7.6

(a)

	1992	1991
$\dfrac{\text{Total current assets}}{\text{Total current liabilities}}$	$\dfrac{\$285,800}{\$140,600} = 2.0$	$\dfrac{\$222,000}{\$90,500} = 2.5$

(b) The change from 2.5 to 2.0 indicates that Ogel has a diminished ability to pay its current liabilities as they mature. However, a current ratio of 2.0 to 1 is still considered a "secure" indicator of a company's ability to meet its current obligations incurred in operating the business.

Acid-Test or Quick Ratio

Unlike the current ratio, the acid-test or quick ratio places emphasis on the relative convertibility of the current assets into cash. The ratio places greater emphasis on receivables than on inventory, since the inventory may not be readily convertible into cash. This method also assumes that prepaid expenses have minimal resale value. The ratio is computed by using the following formula:

$$\frac{\textbf{Cash + Short-Term Investments + Accounts Receivable, Net}}{\textbf{Current Liabilities}}$$

Solved Problem 7.7. Calculating the Acid-Test or Quick Ratio

Assume that in Problem 7.3 the Ogel Supply Corporation showed the following current assets and current liabilities for the years ended December 31, 1992, and December 31, 1991:

	1992	1991
Current assets:		
Cash	$ 60,000	$ 30,000
Accounts receivable, net	113,000	79,000
Inventories	107,100	106,900
Prepaid expenses	5,700	6,100
Total current assets	$285,800	$222,000
Current liabilities:		
Notes payable	$ 40,000	$ 33,000
Accounts payable	100,600	57,500
Total current liabilities	$140,600	$ 90,500

(a) Calculate the acid-test or quick ratio for 1992 and 1991. (b) What do the ratios indicate?

Solution 7.7

(a)

	1992	1991
Current assets:		
Cash	$ 60,000	$ 30,000
Accounts receivable, net	113,000	79,000
Total Current Assets	$173,000	$109,000
Current liabilities:		
Notes payable	$ 40,000	$ 33,000
Accounts payable	100,600	57,500
Total current liabilities	$140,600	$ 90,500

	1992	1991
$\dfrac{\text{Total acid–test assets}}{\text{Total current liabilities}}$	$\dfrac{\$173,000}{\$140,600} = 1.2$	$\dfrac{\$109,000}{\$90,500} = 1.2$

(b) The ratios are unchanged. This shows that, despite a significant increase in both the acid-test or quick assets and current liabilities, Ogel still maintains the same ability to meet its current obligations as they mature.

Working Capital

Working capital is the *excess* of current assets over current liabilities.

Working capital item are those that are flowing through the business in a regular pattern and may be diagrammed as follows:

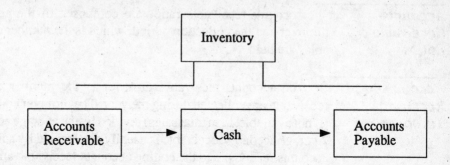

Solved Problem 7.8. Calculating Working Capital

Assume that in Solved Problem 7.3 the Ogel Supply Corporation showed the following current assets and current liabilities for the years ended December 31, 1992 and 1991:

	1992	1991
Current assets:		
Cash	$ 60,000	$ 30,000
Accounts receivable, net	113,000	79,000
Inventories	107,100	106,900
Prepaid expenses	5,700	6,100
Total current assets	$285,800	$222,000
Current liabilities:		
Notes payable	$ 40,000	$ 33,000
Accounts payable	100,600	57,500
Total current liabilities	$140,600	$ 90,500

(a) Calculate working capital for 1992 and 1991. (b) What issue must Ogel resolve due to the change?

Solution 7.8

(a)

	1992	1991
Total current assets	$285,800	$222,000
Total current liabilities	140,600	90,500
Working capital	$145,200	$131,500

(b) The change from $131,500 to $145,200 indicates that Ogel has increased its working capital, which Ogel must now decide whether it is making effective use of. For example, should any excess working capital be used to purchase short-term income-producing investments?

Accounts-Receivable Ratios

Accounts-receivable ratios are composed of the accounts receivable turnover and the collection period, which is the number of days the receivables are held.

Accounts-Receivable Turnover

The accounts-receivable turnover is the number of times accounts receivable are collected during the year. The turnover equals net credit sales (if not available, then total sales) divided by the average accounts receivable. Average accounts receivable is usually determined by adding the beginning accounts receivable to the ending accounts receivable and dividing by two. However, average accounts receivable may be arrived at with greater accuracy on a quarterly or monthly basis, particularly for a seasonal business. Unfortunately, this information is typically known only to management. Using data for the shortest time period will provide the most reliable ratio.

The higher the accounts-receivable turnover, the more successfully the business collects cash. However, an excessively high ratio may signal an excessively stringent credit policy, with management not taking advantage of the potential profit by selling to customers with greater risk. Note that here, too, before changing its credit policy, management has to consider the profit potential versus the inherent risk in selling to more marginal customers. For example, bad debt losses will increase when credit policies are liberalized to include riskier customers.

The formula for determining the accounts-receivable turnover is expressed as follows:

$$\frac{\text{Net Credit Sales}}{\text{Average Net Accounts Receivable}}$$

Solved Problem 7.9. Calculating the Accounts Receivable Turnover

Assume that in Solved Problem 7.3 the Ogel Supply Corporation showed the following accounts-receivable totals for the years ended December 31, 1992, and December 31, 1991:

	1992	1991
Current assets:		
Accounts receivable, net	$113,000	$79,000

Assuming sales of $990,000 for 1992, calculate the accounts-receivable turnover for 1992.

Solution 7.9

Average accounts receivable = ($113,000 + $79,000) ÷ 2 = $96,000

$$\frac{\text{Sales}}{\text{Average accounts receivable}} = \frac{\$990,000}{\$96,000} = 10.3$$

Days-Sales-in-Receivables

The days-sales-in-receivables determines how many days' sales remain in accounts receivable. The determination is a two-step process. First, divide the net sales by 365 days to determine the sales amount for an average day. Then divide this figure into the average net accounts receivable.

Solved Problem 7.10. Calculating the Days-Sales-in-Receivables

In Solved Problem 7.9 it was determined that the Ogel Supply Corporation's accounts receivable turnover was 10.3. Use this figure to calculate the days-sales-in-receivables for 1992.

Solution 7.10

Step one:

$$\frac{\text{Net sales}}{365 \text{ days}} = \frac{\$990,000}{365} = \$2,712$$

Step two:

$$\frac{\text{Average net accounts receivable}}{\text{One day's sales}} = \frac{\$96,000}{\$2,712} = 35.4 \text{ days}$$

Inventory Ratios

A company with excess inventory is tying up funds that could be invested elsewhere for a return. Inventory turnover is a measure of the number of times a company sells its average level of inventory during the year. A high turnover indicates an ability to sell the inventory, while a low number indicates an inability. A low inventory turnover may lead to inventory obsolescence and high storage and insurance costs. The formula for determining inventory turnover is:

$$\frac{\textbf{Cost of Goods Sold}}{\textbf{Average Inventory}}$$

Solved Problem 7.11. Calculating the Inventory Turnover

Assume that in Solved Problem 7.3 the Ogel Supply Corporation showed the following inventory amounts for the years ended December 31, 1992, and December 31, 1991:

	1992	1991
Current assets:		
Inventories	107,100	106,900

If cost of goods sold is $574,000 for 1992, calculate the inventory turnover for 1992.

Solution 7.11

Average inventories = ($107,100 + $106,900) ÷ 2 = $107,000

$$\frac{\text{Cost of goods sold}}{\text{Average inventories}} = \frac{\$574,000}{\$107,000} = 5.4$$

Interrelationship of Liquidity and Activity to Earnings

There is a trade-off between liquidity risk and return. Liquidity risk is reduced by holding more current assets than noncurrent assets. There will be less of a return, however, because the return rate on current assets (i.e., marketable securities) is usually less than the return rate on productive fixed assets. Further, excessive liquidity may mean that management has not been aggressive enough in finding attractive capital-investment opportunities. There should be a balance between liquidity and return.

High profitability does not automatically mean a strong cash flow. Cash problems may exist even with a high net income due to maturing debt and the need for asset replacement, among other reasons. For instance, it is possible that a growth business may have a decline in liquidity because cash is needed to finance an expanded sales base.

Measuring a Company's Ability to Pay Its Long-Term Debt

A corporation with a large amount of debt runs a greater risk of insolvency than one with a large amount of preferred or common stock outstanding. The reason is that payment of interest is mandatory, while the payment of dividends is discretionary with the corporation's board of directors. Individuals and banks that purchase the long-term notes and bonds issued by an enterprise take a special interest in a business's ability to repay its debt plus interest. Two key methods used to measure a company's ability to pay its legal obligations as they become due are the debt ratio and the times-interest-earned ratio.

DEBT RATIO

The debt ratio indicates how much of the company's assets were obtained by the issuance of debt. If the ratio is 1, it means that all of the firm's assets were financed by the issuance of debt. If the ratio is 0.6, it means that 60% of the company's assets were financed by debt. The formula for the debt ratio is:

$$\frac{\text{Total Liabilities}}{\text{Total Assets}}$$

Solved Problem 7.12. Calculating the Debt Ratio

Assume that in Solved Problem 7.3 the Ogel Supply Corporation showed the following assets and liabilities for the years ended December 31, 1992, and December 31, 1991:

	1992	1991
ASSETS		
Current assets:		
Cash	$ 60,000	$ 30,000
Accounts receivable, net	113,000	79,000
Inventories	107,100	106,900
Prepaid expenses	5,700	6,100
Total current assets	$285,800	$222,000
Property, plant, and equipment, net	660,000	665,000
Total assets	$945,800	$887,000
LIABILITIES		
Current liabilities:		
Notes payable	$ 40,000	$ 33,000
Accounts payable	100,600	57,500
Total current liabilities	$140,600	$ 90,500
Long-term debt	400,000	410,000
Total liabilities	$540,600	$500,500

Calculate the debt ratio for 1992 and 1991.

Solution 7.12

	1992	1991
$\dfrac{\text{Total liabilities}}{\text{Total assets}}$	$\dfrac{\$540,600}{\$945,800} = 0.57$	$\dfrac{\$500,500}{\$887,000} = 0.56$

TIMES-INTEREST-EARNED RATIO

The times-interest-earned ratio measures a company's ability to pay its interest obligations. For example, a times-interest-earned ratio of 5 means that the company earned enough to pay its annual interest obligation five times.

Solved Problem 7.13. Calculating the Interest-Coverage Ratio

Assume that in Solved Problem 7.2 the Ogel Supply Corporation showed the following income from operations and interest expense for the years ended December 31, 1992, and December 31, 1991:

	1992	1991
Interest expense	$ 24,000	$ 26,000
Income from operations	163,500	143,000

(a) Calculate the times-interest-earned ratio for 1992 and 1991. (b) What do the ratios indicate?

Solution 7.13

(a)

	1992	1991
$\dfrac{\text{Income from operations}}{\text{Interest expense}}$	$\dfrac{\$163,500}{\$24,000} = 6.8$	$\dfrac{\$143,000}{\$26,000} = 5.5$

(b)   The ratios indicate that Ogel will have little difficulty paying its interest obligations. Ogel might even consider borrowing more money.

Profitability Ratios

These ratios measure the profitability of the company. The primary ratios are *rate of return on net sales, rate of return on total assets,* and *rate of return on total stockholders' equity.*

RATE OF RETURN ON NET SALES

The formula for calculating the rate of return on net sales is as follows:

$$\frac{\text{Net Income}}{\text{Net Sales}}$$

This ratio reveals the profit margin of the business. It tells how much earnings are associated with each sales dollar.

Solved Problem 7.14. Calculating the Rate of Return on Net Sales

Assume that in Solved Problem 7.2 the Ogel Supply Corporation showed the following net income and net sales figures for the years ended December 31, 1992, and December 31, 1991:

	1992	1991
Net sales	$990,000	$884,000
Net income	103,140	88,970

(a) Calculate the rate of return on net sales for 1992 and 1991. (b) What do the ratios indicate?

Solution 7.14

(a)

	1992	1991
$\dfrac{\text{Net sales}}{\text{Net income}}$	$\dfrac{\$103,140}{\$990,000} = 10.4\%$	$\dfrac{\$88,970}{\$884,000} = 10.1\%$

(b)   The increase in the rate of return indicates that the company is more profitable on each sales dollar obtained.

RATE OF RETURN ON TOTAL ASSETS

The rate of return measures the ability of the company to earn a profit on its total assets. In making the calculation, interest expense must be added back to the net income, since both creditors and investors have financed the company's operations. The formula is:

$$\frac{\textbf{Net Income + Interest Expense}}{\textbf{Average Total Assets}}$$

where average total assets $= \dfrac{\text{total assets (beginning) + total assets (ending)}}{2}$

Solved Problem 7.15. Calculating the Rate of Return on Net Sales

Assume that in Solved Problems 7.2 and 7.3 the Ogel Supply Corporation showed the following net income, interest expense, and total assets for the years ended December 31, 1992, and December 31, 1991:

	1992	1991
Net income	$103,140	$ 88,970
Interest expense	24,000	26,000
Total assets	945,800	887,000

Calculate the rate of return on total assets for 1992.

Solution 7.15

$$\text{Average total assetss} = \frac{\$103,140 + \$24,000}{(\$945,800 + \$887,000) \div 2} = \frac{\$127,140}{\$916,400} = 13.9\%$$

RATE OF RETURN ON COMMON STOCKHOLDERS' EQUITY

The rate of return on common stock shows the relationship between net income and the common stockholders' investment in the company. To compute this rate, preferred dividends must be subtracted from net income. This leaves net income available to the common shareholders. The formula for computing the rate of return on common stock is:

$$\frac{\textbf{Net Income – Preferred Dividends}}{\textbf{Average Common Stockholders' Equity}}$$

Solved Problem 7.16. Calculating the Rate of Return on Common Stockholders' Equity

Assume that in Solved Problems 7.2 and 7.3 the Ogel Supply Corporation showed the following net income for 1992, and total stockholders' equity for the years ended December 31, 1992, and December 31, 1991:

	1992	1991
Net income	$103,140	$ 88,970
Total stockholders' equity	405,200	386,500

Calculate the rate of return on total common stockholders' equity for 1992.

Solution 7.16.

Average common stockholders' equity = ($405,200 + $386,500) ÷ 2 = $395,850

$$\frac{\text{Net income}}{\text{Average common stockholders' equity}} = \frac{\$103,140 - 0}{\$395,850} = 26.1\%$$

The return on the common stockholders' equity is 26.1%, which is 12.2% higher than the return on assets, which is 13.9%. The company is borrowing at a lower rate to earn a higher rate. The practice is called trading on equity, or leverage, and is directly related to the debt ratio. However, should revenues drop, the interest on debt must still be paid. Thus, in times of operating losses, excessive debt can hurt profitability.

Earnings per Share

Earnings per share (EPS) is computed by dividing net income less the preferred dividends by the number of common shares outstanding. The preferred-share dividend must be subtracted because it represents a prior claim to dividends that must be paid before any payment of dividends can be made to the common shareholders. If there is no preferred stock, earnings per share equals net income divided by common shares outstanding.

Solved Problem 7.17. Calculating Earnings per Share

Assume that in Solved Problems 7.2 and 7.3 the Ogel Supply Corporation showed the following net income for 1992 and 1991, and that 10,000 common shares were outstanding for the years ended December 31, 1992, and December 31, 1991:

	1992	1991
Net income	$103,140	$88,970

Calculate the earnings per share for 1992 and 1991.

Solution 7.17

$$\frac{\text{Net income}}{\text{Common shares outstanding}} \qquad \underset{1992}{\frac{\$103,140 - 0}{10,000}} = \$10.31 \qquad \underset{1991}{\frac{\$88,970 - 0}{10,000}} = \$8.90$$

Evaluating Stock as an Investment

Investors purchase stock to earn a return on their investment. This return consists of both gains from the sale of appreciated stock and from dividends. Two ratios used to analyze the value of a stock include the *price-earnings ratio* and the *book value per share* of stock.

PRICE-EARNINGS RATIO

The price-earnings ratio equals the market price per share divided by the earnings per share. A high price-earnings ratio is generally favorable because it indicates that the investing public looks at the company in a positive light. However, too high a price-earnings ratio could mean a poor investment because the stock may be overvalued, while a low price-earnings ratio stock could be a good investment if it's a case of the stock being undervalued.

Solved Problem 7.18. Calculating the Price-Earnings Ratio

Assume that for the years 1992 and 1991 the market price per share of common stock for Ogel Corporation was as follows:

	1992	1991
Market price per share	$130.00	$95.00

(a) Using the earnings per share of $10.31 for 1992 (from Solved Problem 7.17) and $8.90 for 1991, calculate the price/earnings ratio for each year.

(b) What evaluation might be derived from the change in the price of the stock?

Solution 7.18

(a)

	1992	1991
$\dfrac{\text{Market price per share}}{\text{Earnings per share of common stock}}$	$\dfrac{\$130.00}{\$10.31} = 12.6$	$\dfrac{\$95.00}{\$8.90} = 10.7$

(b) The increase in the price-earnings multiple indicates that the stock market had a higher opinion of the business in 1992, possibly due to the company's increased profitability.

BOOK VALUE PER SHARE

The book value per share equals the net assets available to common stockholders divided by the shares outstanding. Net assets equals stockholders' equity minus preferred stock. The comparison of book value per share to market price per share provides a clue as to how investors regard the firm. The formula for calculating book value per share is as follows:

$$\frac{\text{Total Stockholders Equity} - \text{Preferred Equity}}{\text{Number of Shares of Common Stock Outstanding}}$$

Solved Problem 7.19. Calculating the Book Value Per Share of Common Stock

Assume that for the years 1992 and 1991 the stockholders' equity of Ogel Corporation was as follows:

	1992	1991
Total stockholders' equity	$405,200	$386,500

If there are 10,000 shares of common stock outstanding at December 31 of each year, what is book value per share for each year?

Solution 7.19

	1992	1991
$\dfrac{\text{Total stockholders' equity}}{\text{Common shares outstanding}}$	$\dfrac{\$405,200}{10,000} = \$40.52$	$\dfrac{\$386,500}{10,000} = \$38.65$

LIMITATIONS OF RATIO ANALYSIS

Some of the limitations of ratio analysis are as follows:

(1) Many large businesses are involved with multiple lines of business, so that it is difficult to identify the industry to which a specific company belongs. A comparison of its ratios with other corporations may thus be meaningless.

(2) Accounting and operating practices differ among companies, which can distort the ratios and make comparisons meaningless. For example, the use of different inventory-valuation methods would affect inventory and asset-turnover ratios.

(3) Industry averages published by financial advisory services are only approximations. Therefore the company may have to look at the ratios of its major competitors if such ratios are available.

(4) Financial statements are based on historical costs and do not consider inflation.

(5) Management may hedge or exaggerate its financial figures. Hence certain ratios will not be accurate indicators.

(6) A ratio does not describe the quality of its components. For example, the current ratio may be high but inventory may consist of obsolete merchandise.

(7) Ratios are static and do not take into account future trends.

Solved Problem 7.20. Horizontal Analysis

Jayson Rag and Cloth Corporation provides the following comparative income statements for the years ended December 31, 1992, and December 31, 1991.

	1992	1991	Percentage of Increase (Decrease)
Sales	$600,000	$700,000	
Cost of goods sold	220,000	180,000	
Gross profit	$380,000	$520,000	
Operating expenses	130,000	200,000	
Net income	$250,000	$320,000	

(a) Using horizontal analysis, fill in the percentage changes. (b) Appraise the results.

Solution 7.20

(a)

	1992	1991	Percentage of Increase (Decrease)
Sales	$600,000	$700,000	(14.0)
Cost of goods sold	220,000	180,000	22.0
Gross profit	$380,000	$520,000	(27.0)
Operating expenses	130,000	200,000	(35.0)
Net income	$250,000	$320,000	(22.0)

(b) Gross profit declined 27.0% because of the combined effects of lower revenue and higher cost of goods sold. However, there was a significant cut in operating expenses. This kept the decline in net income to only 22%.

Solved Problem 7.21. Index Numbers

The Travis Refrigerant Company reports the following information for the period 1991–1993:

	1993	1992	1991
Current liabilities	$15,000	$14,000	$10,000
Long-term liabilities	80,000	66,000	60,000

If the base year is 1991, compute the index numbers using trend analysis.

Solution 7.21

	1993	1992	1991
Current liabilities	150	140	100
Long-term liabilities	133	110	100

Solved Problem 7.22. Vertical Analysis

The Blake Knife and Tool Corporation reported the following income-statement information:

	1992	1991
Net sales	$350,000	$200,000
Cost of goods sold	200,000	100,000
Operating expenses	70,000	50,000

(a) Prepare a comparative income statement for 1992 and 1991 by using vertical (common size) analysis. (b) Evaluate the results.

Solution 7.22

(a)

	1992 Amount	1992 Percent	1991 Amount	1991 Percent
Net sales	$350,000	100.0	$200,000	100.0
Cost of goods sold	200,000	57.0	100,000	50.0
Gross profit	$150,000	43.0	$100,000	50.0
Operating expenses	70,000	20.0	50,000	25.0
Net income	$ 80,000	23.0	$ 50,000	25.0

(b) Cost of goods sold has risen, possibly because of a higher cost in buying merchandise. Operating expenses have dropped, possibly from improved cost control. Overall, profitability has declined.

Solved Problem 7.23. Liquidity Ratios

Nelson Safe Company's selected balance-sheet accounts as of December 31, 1993 appears below:

Current Assets	
Cash	$ 5,000
Marketable securities	10,000
Accounts receivable	80,000
Inventories	100,000
Prepaid expenses	2,000
Total current assets	$197,000
Current Liabilities	
Notes payable	$ 9,000
Accounts payable	160,000
Accrued expenses payable	15,000
Income taxes payable	3,000
Total current liabilities	$187,000

Determine (a) the working capital, (b) the current ratio, and (c) the quick ratio.

Solution 7.23

(a)

$$\text{Working capital} = \text{Current assets} - \text{Current liabilities}$$
$$\$197,000 - \$187,000 = \$10,000$$

(b)

$$\text{Current ratio} = \frac{\text{Current assets}}{\text{Current liabilities}} = \frac{\$197,000}{\$187,000} = 1.05$$

(c)

Quick ratio equals:

$$\frac{\text{Cash} + \text{Marketable securities} + \text{Accounts receivable}}{\text{Current liabilities}}$$

$$\frac{\$5,000 + \$10,000 + \$80,000}{\$187,000} = 0.51$$

Solved Problem 7.24. Liquidity Analysis

Based upon the answer to Solved Problem 7.23, does the Nelson Safe Company have good or poor liquidity if the industry averages are a current ratio of 2.3 and a quick ratio of 1.2?

Solution 7.24

Nelson Safe Company's ratios are significantly below the industry norms. As a result, the company's liquidity is quite poor. Nelson will have difficulty meeting its current debt out of highly liquid assets.

Solved Problem 7.25. Accounts-Receivable Ratios

The Williams Wire Company reports the following accounts-receivable information:

	1992	1991
Average accounts receivable	$ 200,000	$ 216,000
Net credit sales	2,500,000	3,000,000

The terms of sale are net 15 days, meaning that the company expects payment from customers in 15 days.

(a) Compute the accounts-receivable turnover and the collection period. (b) Appraise the results.

Solution 7.25

(a)

$$\text{Accounts-receivable turnover} = \frac{\text{Net credit sales}}{\text{Average accounts receivable}}$$

$$1992: \frac{\$2,500,000}{\$200,000} = 12.50 \quad 1991: \frac{\$3,000,000}{\$216,000} = 13.89$$

$$\text{Collection period} = \frac{365 \text{ days}}{\text{Accounts-receivable turnover}}$$

1992: 365 ÷ 12.50 = 29.20 days
1991: 365 ÷ 13.89 = 26.28 days

(b) The company's management of accounts receivable is deficient. In both years, the collection period exceeded the terms of net 15 days. The situation is deteriorating, as is indicated by the increase in the collection period in 1992 compared to that of 1991. The company has significant funds tied up in accounts receivable that could be invested for a return. A careful evaluation of the credit policy is needed. Perhaps sales are being made to marginal customers.

Solved Problem 7.26. Total Sales

The Johnson Lumber Company's net accounts receivable were $275,000 at December 31, 1991, and $350,000 at December 31, 1992. Net cash sales for 1992 were $450,000. The accounts-receivable turnover for 1992 was 6. What was the company's total sales for 1992?

Solution 7.26

Average accounts receivable equals:

$$\frac{\text{Beginning accounts receivable} + \text{Ending accounts receivable}}{2}$$

$$\frac{\$275,000 + \$350,000}{2} = \$312,500$$

$$\text{Accounts-receivable turnover} = \frac{\text{Net credit sales}}{\text{Average accounts receivable}}$$

$$6 = \frac{\text{Net credit sales}}{\$312,500}$$

Net credit sales = 6 × $312,500 = $1,875,000

Since the cash sales were $450,000, the total net sales must be $2,325,000 ($1,875,000 + $450,000).

Solved Problem 7.27. Determining the Inventory Turnover

On January 1, 1992, the Harris Television Corporation's beginning inventory was $300,000. During 1992 the company purchased $1,500,000 worth of inventory. Harris had ending inventory of $600,000.

What is the inventory turnover for 1992?

Solution 7.27

Cost of goods sold:

Beginning inventory	$ 300,000
Purchases	1,500,000
Cost of goods available	$1,800,000
Less: Ending inventory	600,000
Cost of goods sold	$1,200,000

$$\text{Average inventory} = \frac{\text{Beginning inventory} + \text{Ending inventory}}{2}$$

$$\text{Inventory turnover} = \frac{\text{Cost of goods sold}}{\text{Average inventory}} = \frac{\$1,200,000}{\$450,000} = 2.67$$

Solved Problem 7.28. Financial Ratios

The Radon Watch Corporation reports the following balance-sheet information:

Current liabilities	$270,000
Bonds payable, 12%	100,000
Preferred stock, 15%, $100 par value	200,000
Common stock, $10 par value, 40,000 shares	400,000
Premium on common stock	250,000
Retained earnings	175,000

Income before taxes is $150,000. The tax rate is 34%. Common stockholders' equity in the prior year was $700,000. The market price per share of common stock is $30. Calculate (a) the net income, (b) the preferred dividends, (c) the return on common stock, (d) the interest coverage, (e) the earnings per share, and (f) the price-earnings ratio.

Solution 7.28

(a)

Income before taxes	$150,000
Taxes (34% rate)	51,000
Net income	$ 99,000

(b)

Preferred dividends = 15% × $200,000 = $30,000

(c)

Common stock	$400,000
Premium on common stock	250,000
Retained earnings	175,000
Common stockholders' equity	$825,000

Return on common stock equals:

$$\frac{\text{Net income} - \text{Preferred dividend}}{\text{Average common stockholders' equity}}$$

$$\frac{\$99,000 - \$30,000}{(\$825,000 + \$700,000) \div 2} = \frac{\$69,000}{\$762,500} = 0.09$$

(d)

Income before taxes	$150,000
Interest expense (12% × $100,000)	12,000
Income before interest and taxes	$162,000

$$\text{Interest coverage} = \frac{\text{Income before interest and taxes}}{\text{Interest expense}}$$

$$\frac{\$162,000}{\$12,000} = 13.50 \text{ times}$$

(e)

$$\text{Earnings per share} = \frac{\text{Net income} - \text{preferred dividends}}{\text{Common stock outstanding}}$$

$$= \frac{\$99,000 - \$30,000}{40,000 \text{ shares}} = \frac{\$69,000}{\$40,000} = \$1.73$$

(f)

$$\text{Price-earnings ratio} = \frac{\text{Market price per share}}{\text{Earnings per share}}$$

$$= \frac{\$30.00}{\$1.73} = 17.34 \text{ times}$$

Solved Problem 7.29. Dividend Ratios

The Waylon Chemical and Dye Company's common-stock account for 1993 and 1992 showed $40,000 of common stock at $10 par value. Additional information is as follows:

	1993	**1992**
Dividends	$2,500	$4,000

(a) Calculate the dividends per share. (b) Appraise the results.

Solution 7.29

(a)

$$\text{Dividends per share} = \frac{\text{Dividends}}{\text{Outstanding shares}}$$

$$1993: \frac{\$2,500}{4,000 \text{ shares}} = \$0.63 \quad 1992: \frac{\$4,000}{4,000 \text{ shares}} = \$1.00$$

(b) The decline in dividends per share between 1992 and 1993 will cause concern among stockholders, because declining dividends may mean that the company is not doing well. In addition, many stockholders rely on receiving dividends.

Solved Problem 7.30. Determining How a Transaction Affects Various Ratios

Column 1 lists a series of transactions. Column 2 lists various ratios. State the effect that the transaction in Column 1 has on the ratio in Column 2. Indicate your answer using only the words "increase," "decrease," or "none." Assume that the current ratio prior to the transaction was 2 to 1 and that the acid-test ratio was 1.5 to 1.

Column 1 Transaction	Column 2 Ratio
1. Payment of a short-term note payable.	Current ratio Quick ratio Working capital
2. Collection of an account receivable.	Current ratio Quick ratio Working capital
3. Sale of long-term bonds.	Current ratio Quick ratio
4. Declaration of a stock dividend.	Current ratio Quick ratio
5. Declaration of a cash dividend.	Current ratio Quick ratio Working capital

6. Sale of plant assets for cash.

Current ratio
Quick ratio
Working capital

7. Purchase of plant assets for cash.

Current ratio
Quick ratio
Working capital

8. Borrowed money from a bank with a 90-day note.

Current ratio
Quick ratio
Working capital

9. Charge an account receivable to the allowance for doubtful accounts.

Current ratio
Quick ratio
Working capital

10. Sold inventory for cash.

Current ratio
Quick ratio
Working capital

Solution 7.30

1. Current ratio:	Increase		6. Current ratio:	Increase	
Quick ratio:	Increase		Quick ratio:	Increase	
Working capital:	None		Working capital:	Increase	
2. Current ratio:	None		7. Current ratio:	Decrease	
Quick ratio:	None		Quick ratio:	Decrease	
Working capital:	None		Working capital:	Decrease	
3. Current ratio:	Increase		8. Current ratio:	Decrease	
Quick ratio:	Increase		Quick ratio:	Decrease	
Working capital:	Increase		Working capital:	None	
4. Current ratio:	None		9. Current ratio:	None	
Quick ratio:	None		Quick ratio:	None	
5. Current ratio:	Decrease		Working capital:	None	
Quick ratio:	Decrease		10. Current ratio:	None	
Working capital:	Decrease		Quick ratio:	Increase	
			Working capital:	None	

*F*inancial statement analysis is an attempt to work with reported financial figures in order to determine a company's financial strengths and weaknesses. Most analysts favor certain ratios and ignore others. Each ratio should be compared to industry norms and analyzed in light of past trends. Financial analysis also calls for an awareness of the impact of inflation and deflation on reported income. Management must also recognize that alternate methods of financial reporting may allow firms with equal performance to report different results.

Part 4

Managerial Accounting

8

Managerial Accounting

Management accounting as defined by the National Association of Accountants (NAA) is the process of identification, measurement, accumulation, analysis, preparation, interpretation, and communication of financial information, which is used by management to plan, evaluate, control, and make decisions within an organization. It ensures the appropriate use of and accountability for an organization's resources.

FINANCIAL ACCOUNTING VS. MANAGEMENT ACCOUNTING

Financial accounting is mainly concerned with the historical aspects of external reporting; that is, providing financial information to outside parties such as investors, creditors, and governments. To protect those outside parties from being misled, financial accounting is governed by what are called *generally accepted accounting principles* (GAAP).

Management accounting, on the other hand, is concerned primarily with providing information to internal managers who are charged with planning and controlling the operations of the firm and making a variety of management decisions. Due to its internal use within a company, management accounting is not subject to GAAP. More specifically, the differences between financial and management accounting are summarized below:

Financial Accounting	Management Accounting
(1) Provides data for external users	(1) Provides data for internal users
(2) Is required by FASB	(2) Is not required by FASB
(3) Is subject to GAAP	(3) Is not subject to GAAP
(4) Must generate accurate and timely data	(4) Emphasizes relevance and flexibility of data
(5) Emphasizes the past	(5) Has more emphasis on the future
(6) Looks at the business as a whole	(6) Focuses on parts as well as on the whole of a business
(7) Primarily stands by itself	(7) Draws heavily from other disciplines such as finance
(8) Is an end in itself	(8) Is a means to an end

Solved Problem 8.1. Managerial vs. Financial Accounting

For each of the following, indicate whether it is primarily identified with management accounting (MA) or financial accounting (FA):

(1) Draws heavily from other disciplines such as economics and statistics
(2) Prepares financial statements
(3) Provides financial information to internal managers
(4) Emphasizes the past rather than the future
(5) Focuses on relevant and flexible data
(6) Is not mandatory
(7) Focuses on relevant and flexible data
(8) Is not subject to generally accepted accounting principles
(9) Is built around the fundamental accounting equation of debits equal credits
(10) Draws heavily from other business disciplines

Solution 8.1

(1) MA; (2) FA; (3) MA; (4) FA; (5) MA; (6) MA; (7) MA; (8) MA; (9) FA; (10) MA

THE WORK OF MANAGEMENT

In general, the work that management performs can be classified as (a) planning, (b) coordinating, (c) controlling, and (d) decision making.

Planning: The planning function of management involves selecting long- and short-term objectives and drawing up strategic plans to achieve those objectives.

Coordinating: In performing the coordination function, management must decide how best to put together the firm's resources in order to carry out established plans.

Controlling: Controlling entails implementing a decision method and using feedback so that the firm's goals and specific strategic plans are optimally obtained.

Decision making: Decision making is the purposeful selection from a set of alternatives in light of a given objective.

Management-accounting information is important in performing all of these functions.

Controllership

The chief management accountant or the chief accounting executive of an organization is called the controller (often called comptroller, especially in the government sector). The controller is in charge of the accounting department. The controller's authority is basically of a staff nature in that the controller's office gives advice and service to other departments. At the same time, the controller has line authority over members of his or her department, such as internal auditors, bookkeepers, and budget analysts. (See Figure 8.1 for the organization chart of a typical controller's department).

The controller is basically concerned with *internal* matters; namely, financial and cost accounting, taxes, budgeting, and control functions.

Figure 8.1. Controller's Activity

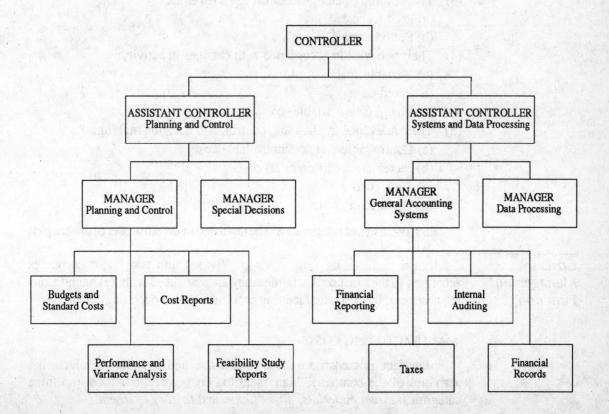

COST CONCEPTS AND TERMINOLOGY

In financial accounting, the term cost is defined as a measurement, in monetary terms, of the amount of resources used for some purpose. In managerial accounting, the term cost is used in many different ways. That is, there are different types of costs used for different purposes. Some costs are useful and required for inventory valuation and income determination. Some costs are useful for planning, budgeting, and cost control. Still others are useful for making short-term and long-term decisions.

Cost Classifications

Costs can be classified into various categories, according to:

(1) Their management function:
   (a) Manufacturing costs
   (b) Nonmanufacturing (operating) costs
(2) Their ease of traceability:
   (a) Direct costs
   (b) Indirect costs
(3) Their timing of charges against sales revenue:
   (a) Product costs
   (b) Period costs
(4) Their behavior in accordance with changes in activity:
   (a) Variable costs
   (b) Fixed costs
   (c) Mixed (semivariable) costs
(5) Their relevance to planning, control, and decision making:
   (a) Controllable and noncontrollable costs
   (b) Incremental (differential) costs
   (c) Sunk costs
   (d) Opportunity costs

Each of these cost categories will be discussed in the remainder of this chapter.

Costs by Management Function

In a manufacturing firm, costs are divided into two major categories according to the functional activities they are associated with: (a) manufacturing costs, and (b) nonmanufacturing costs, also called operating expenses.

MANUFACTURING COSTS

Manufacturing costs are those costs associated with the manufacturing activities of the company. Manufacturing costs are subdivided into three categories: *direct materials*, *direct labor*, and *factory overhead*.

DIRECT MATERIALS

Direct materials are all materials that become an integral part of the finished product. Examples are the steel used to make an automobile and the wood to make furniture. Glues, nails, and other minor items are called indirect materials (or supplies) and are classified as part of factory overhead, which is explained below.

DIRECT LABOR

Direct labor is the labor directly involved in making the product. Examples of direct-labor costs are the wages of assembly workers and the wages of machine-tool operators. Indirect labor, such as wages of supervisory personnel and janitors, is classified as part of factory overhead.

FACTORY OVERHEAD

Factory overhead can be defined as including all costs of manufacturing except direct materials and direct labor. Some of the many examples include depreciation, rent, taxes, insurance, fringe benefits, payroll taxes, and cost of idle time. Factory overhead is also called manufacturing overhead, indirect manufacturing expenses, and factory burden. Many costs overlap within their categories. For example, direct materials and direct labor when combined are called prime costs. Direct labor and factory overhead when combined are termed conversion costs (or processing costs).

NONMANUFACTURING COSTS

Nonmanufacturing costs (or operating expenses) are subdivided into selling expenses and general and administrative expenses. Selling expenses are those associated with obtaining sales and the delivery of the product. Examples are advertising and sales commissions. General and administrative expenses (G & A) include those incurred to perform general and administrative activities. Examples are executives' salaries and legal expenses. Many other examples of costs by management function and their relationships are found in Figure 8.2.

Solved Problem 8.2. Cost Classification

Classify the following costs as either manufacturing (M), selling (S), or administrative (A) in terms of their functions.

(1)	Factory supplies	(10)	Freight-in
(2)	Advertising	(11)	Employer's payroll taxes—factory
(3)	Auditing expenses	(12)	Employer's payroll taxes—sales office
(4)	Rent on general office building	(13)	President's salary
(5)	Legal expenses	(14)	Samples
(6)	Cost of idle time	(15)	Small tools
(7)	Entertainment and travel	(16)	Sanding materials used in furniture making
(8)	Freight-out	(17)	Cost of machine breakdown
(9)	Bad debts		

Solution 8.2

(1) M; (2) S; (3) A; (4) A; (5) A; (6) M; (7) S or A; (8) S; (9) A; (10) M; (11) M; (12) S; (13) A; (14) S; (15) M; (16) M; (17) M.

Figure 8.2. Costs by Management Function

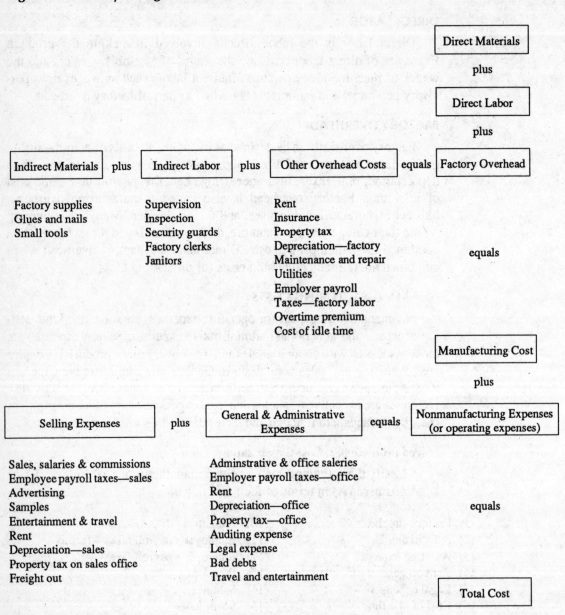

Direct Materials

plus

Direct Labor

plus

| Indirect Materials | plus | Indirect Labor | plus | Other Overhead Costs | equals | Factory Overhead |

Factory supplies
Glues and nails
Small tools

Supervision
Inspection
Security guards
Factory clerks
Janitors

Rent
Insurance
Property tax
Depreciation—factory
Maintenance and repair
Utilities
Employer payroll
Taxes—factory labor
Overtime premium
Cost of idle time

equals

Manufacturing Cost

plus

| Selling Expenses | plus | General & Administrative Expenses | equals | Nonmanufacturing Expenses (or operating expenses) |

Sales, salaries & commissions
Employee payroll taxes—sales
Advertising
Samples
Entertainment & travel
Rent
Depreciation—sales
Property tax on sales office
Freight out

Adminstrative & office saleries
Employer payroll taxes—office
Rent
Depreciation—office
Property tax—office
Auditing expense
Legal expense
Bad debts
Travel and entertainment

equals

Total Cost

Direct Costs and Indirect Costs

Costs may be viewed as either direct or indirect, depending on whether or not they are traceable to a particular object of costing. The object of costing may be a product line, a job, a department, or a sales territory.

DIRECT COSTS

Direct costs can be directly traceable to the costing object. For example, if the object of costing under consideration is a product line, then the materials and labor involved in the manufacture of the line would both be direct costs.

INDIRECT COSTS

Factory overhead items are all indirect costs since they are not directly traceable to any particular product line. Costs shared by different departments, products, or jobs, called common costs or joint costs, are also indirect costs. National advertising that benefits more than one product and sales territory is an example of an indirect cost.

Solved Problem 8.3. Cost Classification

Classify the following costs as direct (D) or indirect (ID) costs.

(1) The foreman's salary
(2) Supplies
(3) Depreciation of factory equipment
(4) Leather used in the manufacture of shoes
(5) Lubricants for machines
(6) Fringe benefits
(7) Wood in making furniture
(8) Glue in tube making
(9) FICA tax
(10) Janitorial supplies

Solution 8.3

(1) ID; (2) ID; (3) ID; (4) D; (5) ID; (6) ID; (7) D; (8) ID; (9) ID; (10) ID.

Product Costs and Period Costs

Depending upon when they are charged against revenue and whether they may be inventoried, costs are classified as: (a) *product costs* and (b) *period costs*.

PRODUCT COSTS

Product costs are inventoriable costs, identified as part of inventory on hand. They are treated as an asset until the goods they are assigned to are sold. At that time they become an expense, cost of goods sold. All manufacturing costs are product costs.

Product costs $\longrightarrow$ Asset (inventory) $\longrightarrow$ Expense (cost of goods sold)

PERIOD COSTS

Period costs are expired costs that are not necessary for production and hence are charged against sales revenues in the period in which the revenue is earned. Selling and general and administrative expenses are period costs.

Product costs $\longrightarrow$ Expense

Figure 8.3 shows the relationship of product and period costs and other cost classifications presented thus far.

Figure 8.3. Various Classifications of Costs

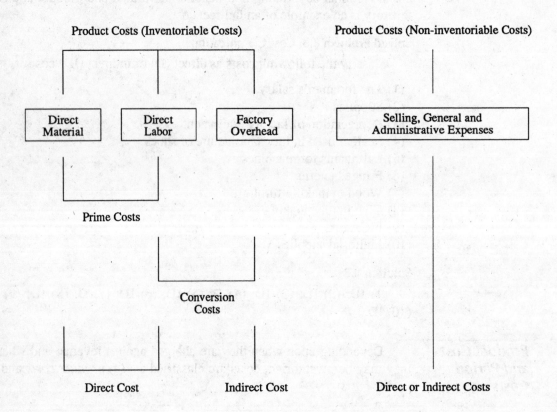

Solved Problem 8.4. Cost Classification

Classify the following costs as product costs (PC) or period expenses (PE).

(1) Pears in a fruit cocktail
(2) Overtime premium
(3) Legal fees
(4) Insurance on office equipment
(5) Advertising expenses
(6) Fringe benefits for the general office
(7) Workers' compensation
(8) Social Security taxes on direct labor
(9) Travel expenses
(10) Rework on defective products

Solution 8.4

(1) PC; (2) PC; (3) PE; (4) PE; (5) PE; (6) PE; (7) PC; (8) PC; (9) PE; (10) PC.

Variable Costs, Fixed Costs, and Mixed Costs

From a planning and control standpoint, perhaps the most important way to classify costs is by how they behave in accordance with changes in volume or some measure of activity. By behavior, costs can be classified into the following three basic categories: variable, fixed, and mixed.

Variable costs are costs that vary in total in direct proportion to changes in activity. Examples are direct materials and gasoline expenses based on mileage driven. Fixed costs are costs that remain constant in total dollar amount as the level of activity changes. Examples are rent, insurance, and taxes. Mixed (or semivariable) costs are costs that vary with changes in volume but, unlike variable costs, do not vary in direct proportion. In other words, these costs contain both variable and fixed components. Examples are the rental of a delivery truck, where a fixed rental fee plus a variable charge based on mileage is made; and power costs, where the expense consists of a fixed amount plus a variable charge based on consumption. Costs by behavior will be examined further in Chapter 11. The breakdown of costs into variable and fixed components is important in many areas of management accounting, such as break-even analysis and short-term decision making.

Solved Problem 8.5. Cost Classification

Classify the following costs as variable (V), fixed (F), or mixed (semivariable) (S) in terms of their behavior with respect to volume or level of activity:

(1) Property taxes
(2) Maintenance and repair
(3) Utilities
(4) Sales agent's salary
(5) Direct materials
(6) Insurance
(7) Depreciation by the straight-line method
(8) Sales agent's commission
(9) Depreciation by mileage—automobile
(10) Rent

Solution 8.5

(1) F; (2) S; (3) S; (4) F; (5) V; (6) F; (7) F; (8) V; (9) V; (10) F.

Costs for Planning, Control, and Decision Making

CONTROLLABLE AND NONCONTROLLABLE COSTS

A cost is said to be controllable when the amount of the cost is assigned to the head of a department and the level of the cost is significantly under the manager's influence. Noncontrollable costs are those costs not subject to influence at a given level of managerial supervision.

All variable costs such as direct materials, direct labor, and variable overhead are usually considered controllable by the department head. On the other hand, fixed costs such as depreciation of factory equipment would not be controllable by the department head, since he or she would have no power to authorize the purchase of the equipment.

Solved Problem 8.6. Cost Controllability

Which of the following costs are likely to be *fully* controllable, *partially* controllable, or *not* controllable by the chief of the production department? Enter fully (F), partially (P), or not (N).

(1) Wages paid to direct labor
(2) Rent on factory building
(3) Chief's salary
(4) Utilities
(5) Direct materials used
(6) Supplies
(7) Insurance on factory equipment
(8) Advertising
(9) Price paid for materials and supplies
(10) Idle time due to machine breakdown

Solution 8.6

(1) F; (2) N; (3) N; (4) P; (5) F; (6) P; (7) N; (8) N; (9) N; (10) P.

INCREMENTAL (OR DIFFERENTIAL) COSTS

The incremental cost is the increase or decrease in costs that is expected from a particular course of action as compared with an alternative course of action.

Solved Problem 8.7. Incremental Costs

A contractor must decide on whether to purchase a machine part from an outside supplier or to make it. The cost of buying the part is $50 per unit and the cost of producing the part is $38. What is the incremental cost?

Solution 8.7

The incremental cost is simply the cost difference between the two alternatives, or $12 ($50 − $38 = $12).

Incremental costs are relevant to future decisions, which will be taken up in detail in Chapter 14.

SUNK COSTS

Sunk costs are the costs of resources that have already been incurred whose total will not be affected by any decision made now or in the future. Sunk costs are considered irrelevant to future decisions, since they are past or historical costs.

As an example, suppose you acquired an asset for $50,000 three years ago, which is now listed at a book value of $20,000. The $20,000 book value is a sunk cost, which does not affect a future decision.

OPPORTUNITY COSTS

An opportunity cost is the net benefit foregone by selecting one alternative over the other. Suppose a company has a choice of using its capacity to produce an extra 10,000 units for a revenue of $15,000 or renting it out for $20,000. The opportunity cost of using the capacity is $20,000. Hence the company might consider renting it out to maximize its profit and minimize the opportunity cost.

Solved Problem 8.8. Incremental, Sunk, and Opportunity Costs

The Elvis Machine Tool Company is considering production for a special order for 10,000 pieces at $0.65 each, which is below the regular price. The current operational level, which is below the full capacity of 70,000 pieces, shows the operating results as contained in the following report:

Sales 50,000 @ $1		$50,000
Direct materials	$20,000	
Direct labor	10,000	
Factory overhead:		
Supervision	$3,500	
Depreciation	1,500	
Insurance	100	
Rental	400	5,500	35,500
Gross margin		$14,500

Factory overhead costs will continue regardless of the decision.

(a) What are the incremental costs, if any, in this decision problem? Prepare a schedule showing the incremental cost.

(b) Which costs, if any, represent sunk costs?

(c) What is the opportunity cost, if any, associated with giving up the special order?

Solution 8.8

(a)

	Per Unit	A Without Special Order (50,000 pieces)	B With Special Order (60,000 pieces)	Incremental Costs (B – A)
Revenue	$1.00	$50,000	$56,500	$6,500
Direct Materials	0.40	20,000	24,000	4,000
Direct Labor	0.20	10,000	12,000	2,000
Factory Overhead:				
Supervision	0.07	3,500	3,500	—
Depreciation	0.03	1,500	1,500	—
Insurance	0.002	100	100	—
Rental	0.008	400	400	—
Total Costs		$35,500	$41,500	$6,000
Income		$14,500	$15,000	$ 500

Direct materials and direct labor are incremental costs.

(b) The depreciation expense ($1,500) is a sunk cost.

(c) The opportunity cost is $500, since by rejecting the special order the company would give up the opportunity of making $500 more with this special order.

INCOME STATEMENTS AND BALANCE SHEETS OF A MANUFACTURER

Figure 8.4 illustrates the income statement of a manufacturer. An important characteristic of the income statement is that it is supported by a schedule of cost of goods manufactured (see Figure 8.5).

This schedule shows the specific costs (i.e., direct materials, direct labor, and factory overhead) that have gone into the goods completed during the period. Since the manufacturer carries three types of inventory (raw materials, work-in-process, and finished goods), all three items must be incorporated into the computation of the cost of goods sold. These inventory accounts also appear on the balance sheet for a manufacturer, as shown in Figure 8.6.

Figure 8.4

Manufacturer's Income Statement
for the Year Ended December 31, 1992

Sales		$320,000
Less: Cost of goods sold		
Finished goods, Dec. 31, 1991	$ 18,000	
Cost of goods manufactured		
(see Schedule, Figure 8.5)	121,000	
Cost of goods available for sale	$139,000	
Finished goods, Dec. 31, 1992	21,000	
Cost of goods sold		$118,000
Gross margin		$202,000
Less: Selling and administrative expenses		60,000
Net income		$142,000

Figure 8.5

Manufacturer's Schedule
of Cost of Goods Manufactured

Direct materials		
Inventory, Dec. 31, 1991	$23,000	
Purchases	64,000	
Cost of direct materials		
available for use	$87,000	
Inventory, Dec. 31, 1992	7,800	
Direct materials used		$ 79,200
Direct labor		25,000
Factory overhead:		
Indirect labor	$ 3,000	
Indirect material	2,000	
Factory utilities	500	
Factory depreciation	800	
Factory rent	2,000	
Miscellaneous	1,500	9,800
Total manufacturing costs incurred during 1992		$114,000
Add: Work-in-process inventory, Dec. 31, 1991		9,000
Manufacturing costs to account for		$123,000
Less: Work-in-process inventory, Dec. 31, 1992		2,000
Cost of goods manufactured (to income statement, Figure 8.4)		$121,000

Figure 8.6

Manufacturer's
Current Asset Section of Balance Sheet
December 31, 1992

Current assets:		
Cash		$ 25,000
Accounts receivable		78,000
Inventories:		
Raw materials	$ 7,800	
Work-in-process	2,000	
Finished goods	21,000	30,800
Total		$133,800

Solved Problem 8.9. Income Statement

Heavens Consumer Products, Inc., has the following sales and cost data for 1992.

Selling and administrative expenses	$ 25,000
Direct materials purchase	12,000
Direct labor	18,000
Sales	160,000
Direct materials inventory, beginning	3,000
Direct materials inventory, ending	2,000
Work-in-process, beginning	14,000
Work-in-process, ending	13,500
Factory depreciation	27,000
Indirect materials	4,000
Factory utilities	2,000
Indirect labor	5,500
Maintenance	2,000
Insurance	1,000
Finished goods inventory, beginning	6,000
Finished goods inventory, ending	4,000

(a) Prepare a schedule of costs of goods manufactured for 1992.

(b) Prepare an income statement for 1992.

Solution 8.9

(a)

Heaven Consumer Products, Inc.
Schedule of Cost of Goods Manufactured
for the Year Ended December 31, 1992

Direct materials:		
Beginning materials inventory	$ 3,000	
Add: Purchases	12,000	
Cost of materials available for use	$15,000	
Less: Ending materials inventory	2,000	
Direct materials used		$ 13,000
Direct labor		18,000
Factory overhead:		
Factory depreciation	$27,000	
Indirect materials	4,000	
Factory utilities	2,000	
Indirect labor	5,500	
Maintenance	2,000	
Insurance	1,000	
		41,500
Total manufacturing costs		$72,500
Add: Beginning work-in-process		14,000
		$86,500
Less: Ending work-in-process		13,500
Cost of goods manufactured		$73,000

(b)

Heaven Consumer Products, Inc.
Income Statement
for the Year Ended December 31, 1992

Sales		$160,000
Less: Cost of goods sold		
Beginning finished goods inventory	$ 6,000	
Add: Cost of goods manufactured	73,000	
Cost of goods available for sale	$79,000	
Less: Ending finished goods inventory	4,000	
Cost of goods sold		75,000
Gross profit		$ 85,000
Less: Selling and administrative expenses		25,000
Net income		$ 60,000

Solved Problem 8.10. Missing Numbers

For each of the following cases, determine the missing data. Each case is independent of the others.

	Case 1	Case 2	Case 3
Beginning direct materials	$ 5,000	$ 3,000	$ 3,000
Purchases of direct materials	17,000	45,000	10,000
Ending direct materials	(a)	7,000	(m)
Direct materials used	(b)	(f)	6,000
Direct labor	16,000	(g)	4,000
Factory overhead	3,000	20,000	6,000
Total manufacturing costs	(c)	85,000	(n)
Beginning work-in-process	6,000	6,000	5,000
Ending work-in-process	6,000	4,000	(o)
Cost of goods manufactured	23,000	(h)	10,000
Sales	52,000	125,000	23,000
Beginning finished goods	8,000	7,000	7,000
Costs of goods manufactured	23,000	(i)	10,000
Ending finished goods	(d)	(j)	6,000
Cost of goods sold	27,000	(k)	(p)
Gross profit	(e)	60,000	(q)
Selling and adm. expenses	5,000	8,500	4,000
Net income	20,000	(l)	8,000

Solution 8.10

(a) $18,000; (b) 4,000; (c) $23,000; (d) $4,000; (e) $25,000 (f) $41,000; (g) $24,000; (h) $87,000; (i) $87,000; (j) $29,000; (k) $65,000; (l) $51,500; (m) $7,000; (n) $16,000; (o) $11,000; (p) $11,000; (q) $12,000

The answers above are computed as follows:

Case 1

Cost of goods manufactured	$23,000
– Beginning work-in-process	6,000
+ Ending work-in-process	6,000
Total manufacturing costs	$23,000 (c)

Total manufacturing costs	$23,000
– Direct labor	16,000
– Factory overhead	3,000
Direct materials used	$ 4,000 (b)

Beginning direct materials	$ 5,000
+ Purchase of direct materials	17,000
– Direct materials used	4,000
Ending direct materials	$18,000 (a)

Beginning finished goods	$ 8,000
+ Cost of goods manufactured	23,000
– Cost of goods sold	27,000
Ending finished goods	$ 4,000 (d)

Sales	$ 52,000
– Cost of goods sold	27,000
Gross profit	$ 25,000 (e)

Case 2

Beginning direct materials	$ 3,000
+ Purchase of direct materials	45,000
– Ending direct materials	7,000
Direct materials used	$ 41,000 (f)

Total manufacturing costs	$ 85,000
– Direct materials used	41,000
– Factory overhead	20,000
Direct labor	$ 24,000 (g)

Total manufacturing costs	$ 85,000
+ Beginning work-in-process	6,000
– Ending work-in-process	4,000
Cost of goods manufactured	$ 87,000 (h)

Sales	$125,000
– Gross profit	60,000
Cost of goods sold	$ 65,000 (k)

Beginning finished goods	$ 7,000
+ Cost of goods manufactured	87,000
– Cost of goods gold	65,000
Ending finished goods	$ 29,000 (j)

Gross profit	$ 60,000
– Selling and administrative expenses	8,500
Net income	$ 51,500 (l)

Case 3

Beginning direct materials	$ 3,000
+ Purchases of direct materials	10,000
– Direct materials used	6,000
Ending direct materials	$ 7,000 (m)

Direct materials used	$ 6,000
+ Direct labor	4,000
+ Factory overhead	6,000
Total manufacturing costs	$ 16,000 (n)

Total manufacturing costs	$ 16,000
+ Beginning work-in-progress	5,000
– Cost of goods manufactured	10,000
Ending work-in-process	$ 11,000 (o)

Beginning finished goods	$ 7,000
+ Cost of goods manufactured	10,000
– Ending finished goods	6,000
Cost of goods sold	$11,000 (p)

Sales	$23,000
– Cost of goods sold	11,000
Gross profit	$12,000 (q)

*M*anagerial accounting is the accumulation and analysis of cost data to provide information for external reporting, for internal planning and control of an organization's operations, and for short-term and long-term decisions. It is important to realize that there are different costs used for different purposes. The management/cost accountant must determine how to use cost data in order to supply the most appropriate cost information. The next two chapters present the cost-accounting systems.

9

Job-Order Costing

A cost-accumulation system is a product-costing system. This process accumulates manufacturing costs such as materials, labor, and factory overhead and assigns them to cost objectives, such as finished goods and work-in-process. Product costing is necessary not only for inventory valuation and income determination but also for establishing the unit sales price. We will discuss the essentials of the cost-accumulation system that is used to measure the manufacturing costs of products. This is essentially a two-step process; involving (1) the measurement of costs that are applicable to manufacturing operations during a given accounting period and (2) the assignment of these costs to products.

There are two basic approaches to cost accounting and accumulation: (1) job-order costing and (2) process costing (which will be discussed in the next chapter).

JOB-ORDER COSTING AND PROCESS COSTING COMPARED

The distinction between job-order costing and process costing centers largely around how product costing is accomplished. With job-order costing, the focus is to apply costs to specific jobs or batches, which may consist of either a single physical unit or a few like units.

Under process costing, accounting data are accumulated by the production department (or cost center) and averaged over all of the production that occurred in the department. Here there is mass production of like units that are manufactured on a continuous basis through a series of uniform production steps known as processes. Figure 9.1 summarizes the basic differences between these two methods.

Figure 9.1

Differences between Job-Order Costing and Process Costing

	Job-order costing	Process costing
1. Cost unit	Job, order, or contract	Physical unit
2. Costs are accumulated	By jobs	By departments
3. Subsidiary record	Job-cost sheet	Cost of production report
4. Used by	Custom manufacturers	Processing industries
5. Permits computation of (a)	a unit cost for inventory costing purposes and	A unit cost to be used to compute the costs of
(b)	a profit or loss on each job	goods completed and work in process

JOB-ORDER COSTING

Job-order cost accounting is the cost-accumulation system under which costs are accumulated by jobs, contracts, or orders. This costing method is appropriate when the products are manufactured in identifiable lots or batches or when the products are manufactured to customer specifications. Job-order costing is widely used by custom manufacturers such as printing, aircraft, and construction companies. It may also be used by service businesses such as auto-repair shops and professional services. Job-order costing keeps track of costs as follows: Direct material and direct labor are traced to a particular job. Costs not directly traceable—factory overhead, for example—are applied to individual jobs using a predetermined overhead (application) rate.

Job-Cost Records

A job-cost sheet is used to record various production costs for work-in-process inventory. A separate cost sheet is kept for each identifiable job, accumulating the direct materials, direct labor, and factory overhead assigned to that job as it moves through production.

The form varies according to the needs of the company. Figure 9.2 presents the basic records or source documents used for job costing. These include:

(1) The job-cost sheet is the key document in the system. It summarizes all of the manufacturing costs—direct materials, direct labor, and applied factory overhead (to be discussed in detail later)—of producing a given job or batch of products. One sheet is maintained for each job, and the file of job-cost sheets for unfinished jobs is the subsidiary ledger for the work-in-process inventory account. When the jobs are completed and transferred, the job-order sheets are transferred to a completed jobs file and the number of units and their unit costs are recorded on inventory cards supporting the finished goods inventory account.

Figure 9.2. Basic Records in a Job-Cost System

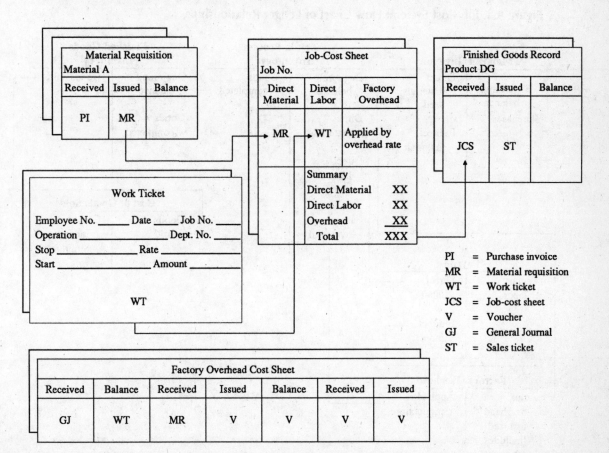

(2)   The materials requisition form shows the type, quantity and price of each type of material issued for production.

(3)   The work ticket shows who worked on what job for how many hours and at what wage rate. This is also called a time ticket and is illustrated in Figure 9.2.

(4)   The factory overhead cost sheet summarizes the various factory overhead costs incurred.

(5)   The memo for applied factory overhead shows how the factory overhead applied rate has been developed.

(6)   The finished goods record is maintained for each type of product manufactured and sold. Each record contains a running record of units and costs of products received, sold, and on hand.

The general flow of costs through a job-cost system is shown in Figure 9.3.

Figure 9.3. Job-Cost System: Flow Chart of Ledger Relationships

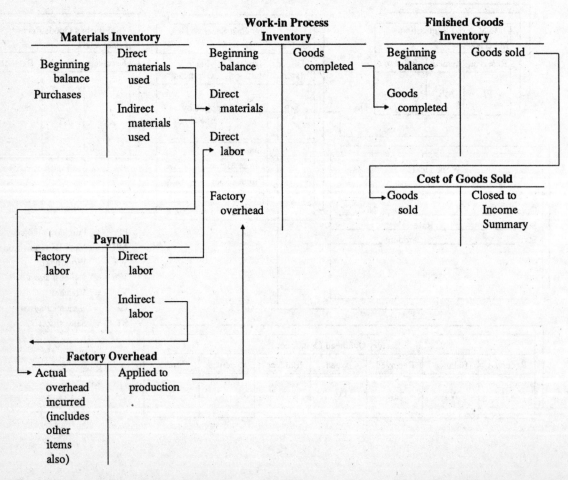

Job-Order Costing: Illustration

To illustrate a job-order cost system, especially the relationship between the general ledger accounts and the subsidiary records, examine the information presented below.

This illustration covers the month of June, for which the beginning inventories were as follows:

Materials inventory (Material A, $10,000; Material B, $6,000; indirect materials $4,000)	$20,000
Work-in-process inventory (Job No. 310: direct materials, $4,200; direct labor, $5,000; and overhead, $4,000)	13,200
Finished goods inventory (500 units of Product X at a cost of $11 per unit)	5,500

Assume that Job No. 310 was completed in June and that, of the two jobs started in June (Nos. 320 and 510), only Job No. 510 is incomplete at the end of the month. The transactions, and the journal entries to record them, are given below:

1. Purchased $10,000 of Material A and $15,000 of Material B on account.

Materials Inventory	25,000	
Accounts Payable		25,000

To record purchase of direct materials.

2. Issued direct materials: Material A to Job No. 310, $1,000; to Job No. 320, $8,000; and to Job No. 510, $2,000; Material B to Job No. 310, $2,000; to Job No. 320, $6,000; and to Job No. 510, $4,000. Indirect materials issued to all jobs, $1,000.

Work-In-Process Inventory	23,000	
Factory Overhead	1,000	
Material Inventory		24,000

To record direct and indirect materials issued.

3. Factory payroll for the month, $25,000; social security and income taxes withheld, $4,000.

Payroll Summary	25,000	
Various Liability Accounts for Taxes Withheld		4,000
Accrued Wages Payable		21,000

To record factory payroll for June.

4. Factory payroll paid, $19,000.

Accrued Wages Payable	19,000	
Cash		19,000

To record cash paid to factory employees in June.

5. Payroll costs distributed: direct labor, $20,000 (Job No. 310, $5,000; Job No. 320, $12,000; and Job No. 510, $3,000); and indirect labor, $5,000.

Work-In-Process Inventory	20,000	
Factory Overhead	5,000	
Payroll Summary		25,000
To distribute factory labor costs incurred.		

6. Other factory overhead costs incurred:

Payroll Taxes Accrued	$ 3,000
Repairs (on account)	1,000
Property Taxes Accrued	4,000
Heat, Light, and Power (on account)	2,000
Depreciation	5,000
	$15,000

Factory Overhead	15,000	
Accounts Payable		3,000
Accrued Payroll Taxes		3,000
Accrued Property Taxes Payable		4,000
Accumulated Depreciation		5,000
To record factory overhead costs incurred.		

7. Factory overhead applied to production (at rate of 80 % of direct labor cost):

Job No. 310, Product Y (0.80 × $5,000)	$ 4,000
Job No. 320, Product Z (0.80 × $12,000)	9,600
Job No. 510, Product W (0.80 × $3,000)	2,400
	$16,000

Work-In-Process Inventory	16,000	
Factory Overhead		16,000
To record application of overhead to production.		

It is important to note that as factory overhead costs are incurred, they are recorded in a subsidiary ledger and debited to the factory overhead account, as shown in journal entries 2, 5, and 7. The factory overhead costs applied to production are periodically credited to the factory overhead account and debited to the work-in-process account (as illustrated in journal entry 7). The issue of factory overhead application will be discussed in detail later in the chapter.

8. Jobs completed and transferred to finished goods inventory (see Figure 9.4 for details):

Job No. 310 (4,000 units of Product Y @ $6.30)	$25,200
Job No. 320 (10,000 units of Product Z @ $3.56)	35,600
	$60,800

| Finished Good Inventory | 60,800 | |
| Work-In-Process Inventory | | 60,800 |

To record completed production for June.

9. Sales on account for the month: 500 units of Product X for $8,000, cost, $5,500; and 10,000 units of Product Z for $62,000, cost, $35,600 (Job No. 320).

| Accounts Receivable | 70,000 | |
| Sales | | 70,000 |

To record sales on account ($8,000 + $62,000) for June.

| Cost of Goods Sold | 41,100 | |
| Finished Goods Inventory | | 41,100 |

To record cost of goods sold ($5,500 + $35,600) for June.

After the above entries have been posted to the accounts of the company, the work-in-process inventory and finished goods inventory accounts would appear (in T-account form) as follows:

Work-in-Process Inventory

June 1 balance	13,200	Completed	60,800
Direct materials used	23,000		
Direct labor cost incurred	20,000		
Overhead applied	16,000		

Finished Goods Inventory

| June 1 balance | 5,500 | Sold | 41,100 |
| Completed | 60,800 | | |

The work-in-process inventory account has a balance at June 28 of $11,400, which agrees with the total costs charged thus far to Job No. 510, as is shown in Figure 9.4. These costs consist of direct materials, $6,000; direct labor, $3,000, and factory overhead, $2,400. The finished goods inventory account has a balance at June 28 of $25,200. The finished goods inventory card for Product Y supports this amount (see Figure 9.4), showing that there are indeed units of Product Y on hand having a total cost of $25,200.

Note that the entries in the ledger accounts given above are often made from summaries of costs and are thus entered only at the end of the month. On the other hand, in order to keep management informed as to costs incurred, the details of the various costs incurred may be recorded more frequently, often daily.

Figure 9.4. Job-Cost Sheets and Supporting Inventory Cards

Material Requisition Material A		
Received	Issued	Balance
		$10,000
$10,000		20,000
	$1,000	19,000
	8,000	11,000
	2,000	9,000

Material Requisition Material B		
Received	Issued	Balance
		$ 6,000
$15,000		21,000
	$2,000	19,000
	6,000	13,000
	4,000	9,000

Job Cost Sheet (Product Y)   Job No. 310

Date	Direct Materials	Direct Labor	Factory Overhead Applied
June	$4,200	$ 5,000	$4,000
	A 1,000	5,000	4,000
	B 2,000	$10,000	$8,000
	$7,200		

Job completed (4,000 units of Product Y @ $6.30). Total cost, $25,200.

Job Cost Sheet (Product Z)   Job No. 320

Date	Direct Materials	Direct Labor	Factory Overhead Applied
June	A 8,000	$12,000	$9,600
	B 6,000		
	$14,000		

Job completed (10,000 units of Product Z @ $3.56). Total cost, $35,600.

Job Cost Sheet (Product W)   Job No. 510

Date	Direct Materials	Direct Labor	Factory Overhead Applied
June	A 2,000	$3,000	$2,400
	B 4,000		

Job completed (4,000 units of Product W). Cost to date, $11,400.

Finished Goods Record Product X		
Received	Issued	Balance
		$5,500
	$5,500	– 0 –

Finished Goods Record Product Y		
Received	Issued	Balance
$25,200		$25,200

Finished Goods Record Product Z		
Received	Issued	Balance
$35,600		$35,600
	$35,600	– 0 –

The above example should be studied until the real advantages of using overhead rates (including predetermined rates) are clear. Three jobs were worked on during the month. Job No. 310 was started last month and completed in June. Job No. 320 was started and completed in June. And Job No. 510 was started but not finished in June. Each required different amounts of direct materials and direct labor (and, perhaps, different types of direct labor). Under these conditions, there is simply no way to apply overhead to products without the use of a rate based on some level of activity. Note also that the use of a predetermined overhead rate permits the computation of unit costs of Job Nos. 310 and 320 at the time of their completion rather than waiting until the end of the month. But this advantage is secured only at the cost of keeping more detailed records of the costs incurred. As we shall see below, the other major cost system—process costing—requires far less recordkeeping, but the computation of unit costs is more complex.

Solved Problem 9.1. Costing of a Job

Holden Works collects its cost data by the job-order cost system. For Job 123, the following data is available:

Direct Materials		Direct Labor	
7/14 Issued	$1,200	Week of July 20	180 hrs. @$6.50
7/20 Issued	650	Week of July 26	140 hrs. @ 7.25
7/25 Issued	350		
	$2,200		

Factory overhead is applied at the rate of $4.50 per direct labor hour.

(a) What is the cost of Job 123?
(b) What is the sales price of the job, assuming that it was contracted with a markup of 40% of cost?

Solution 9.1

(a) The cost of the job is:

Direct material		$2,200
Direct labor:		
180 hrs. × $6.50	$1,170	
140 hrs. × $7.25	1,015	2,185
Factory overhead applied:		
320 hrs. × $4.50		1,440
Cost of Job 123		$5,825

(b) The sales price of the job is:
$5,825 + 40%($5,825) = $5,825 + $2,330 = $8,155

Solved Problem 9.2. Accounting for a Job

The following account appears in the ledger after only part of the postings have been completed for June:

Work-in-Process

Balance, June	$132,200
Direct materials	134,500
Direct labor	112,000
Factory overhead	220,000
	$598,700

Jobs finished during June are summarized as follows:

Job 101	$ 56,700
Job 107	230,200
Job 111	127,500
	$414,400

(a) Prepare the journal entry to record the jobs completed and (b) determine the cost of the unfinished jobs at June 30.

Solution 9.2

(a) The journal entry is:

Finished Goods	414,400	
Work-In-Process		414,400

(b) The cost of unfinished jobs is:
$598,700 – $414,400 = $184,300

Factory Overhead Application

Many items of factory overhead cost are incurred for the entire factory and for the entire accounting period and cannot be specifically identified with particular jobs. Furthermore, the amount of actual factory overhead costs incurred is not usually available until the end of the accounting period. But it is often critical to make cost data available for pricing purposes as each job is completed. Therefore, in order for job costs to be available on a timely basis, it is customary to apply factory overhead by using a predetermined factory overhead rate.

PREDETERMINED FACTORY OVERHEAD RATE

Regardless of the cost-accumulation system used (i.e., job-order or process), factory overhead is applied to a job or process. The predetermined overhead rate is determined as follows:

$$\text{Predetermined overhead rate} = \frac{\text{Budgeted annual overhead}}{\substack{\text{Budgeted annual activity units} \\ \text{(direct labor hours, machine hours, etc.)}}}$$

Budgeted activity units used in the denominator of the formula, more often called the denominator activity level, are measured in direct labor hours, machine hours, direct labor costs, production units, or any other representative surrogate of production activity.

DISPOSITION OF UNDER- AND OVERAPPLIED OVERHEAD

Inevitably, actual overhead cost incurred and during a period and factory overhead costs applied will differ. Conventionally, at the end of the year, the difference between actual overhead and applied overhead is closed to cost of goods sold if it is immaterial. On the other hand, if a material difference exists, work-in-process, finished goods, and cost of goods sold are adjusted on a proportionate basis based on units or dollars at year-end for the deviation between actual and applied overhead. Underapplied overhead and overapplied overhead results are as follows:

Underapplied overhead = applied overhead < actual overhead

Overapplied overhead = applied overhead > actual overhead

Solved Problem 9.3. Applied Overhead

Two companies have prepared the following budgeted data for the year 1992:

	Company X	Company Y
Predetermined rate based on	Machine hours	Direct labor cost
Budgeted overhead	$200,000 (1)	$240,000 (1)
Budgeted machine hours	100,000 (2)	
Budgeted direct labor cost		160,000 (2)
Predetermined overhead rate (1)/(2)	$2 per machine hour	150% of direct labor cost

Now assume that actual overhead costs and the actual level of activity for 1992 for each firm are shown as follows:

	Company X	Company Y
Actual overhead costs	$198,000	$256,000
Actual machine hours	96,000	
Actual direct labor cost		176,000

Note that for each company, the actual cost and activity data differ from the budgeted figures used in calculating the predetermined overhead rate. The computation of the resulting underapplied and overapplied overhead for each company is provided below:

Solution 9.3

	Company X	Company Y
Actual overhead costs	$198,000	$256,000
Factory overhead applied to work-in-process during 1992:		
96,000 actual machine hours × $2	192,000	
$176,000 actual direct labor cost × 150%		264,000
Underapplied (overapplied) factory overhead	$ 6,000	($ 8,000)

Solved Problem 9.4. Cost of a Job

A company uses a budgeted overhead rate in applying overhead to production orders on a labor-cost basis for Department A and on a machine-hour basis for Department B. At the beginning of the year, the company made the following predictions:

	Department A	Department B
Factory overhead	$72,000	$75,000
Direct labor cost	64,000	17,500
Machine hours	500	10,000

The predetermined overhead rates for each department are:

Department A: $72,000 ÷ $64,000 = $1.125 per labor dollar, or 112.5%
Department B: $75,000 ÷ 10,000 = $7.50 per machine hour

During the month of January, the cost record for a job order, No. 105, that was processed through both departments shows the following:

	Department A	Department B
Materials issued	$30	$45
Direct labor cost	36	25
Machine hours	6	15

The total applied overhead for job order No. 105 follows:

Department A: $36 × 1.125	$ 40.50
Department B: 15 × $7.50	112.50
	$153.00

Assuming that job order No. 105 consisted of 30 units of product, what is the total cost and unit cost of the job?

Solution 9.4

	Department A	Department B
Direct material	$ 30.00	$ 45.00
Direct labor	36.00	25.00
Applied overhead	40.50	112.50
Total	$106.50	$182.50

Hence the total cost of the job is $106.50 + $182.50 = $289; the unit cost is $9.63 ($289 ÷ 30 units).

Solved Problem 9.5. Applied Overhead

Refer to Solved Problem 9.4 and assume, at the end of the year, that actual factory overhead amounted to $80,000 in Department A and $69,000 in Department B. Assume further that the actual direct labor cost was $74,000 in Department A and the actual machine hours were 9,000 in Department B. Compute the overapplied or underapplied overhead for each department.

Solution 9.5

Department A: Applied overhead (1.125 × $74,000)	$83,250
Actual overhead	80,000
Overapplied overhead	$ 3,250
Department B: Applied overhead ($7.50 × 9,000)	$67,500
Actual overhead	69,000
Underapplied overhead	$ (1,500)

*U*nit costs are necessary for inventory valuation, income determination, and pricing. Two basic cost-accumulation systems are: (1) job-order costing and (2) process costing.

Job-order costing attaches costs to specific jobs by means of cost sheets established for each job. Direct material and direct labor costs are traced to specific jobs; factory overhead costs are applied by jobs, using a predetermined overhead rate. This chapter also discussed ways in which to develop the overhead application rate. In the next chapter, we discuss process-cost accounting.

10

Process Costing

Process costing is a cost-accumulation system that aggregates manufacturing costs by departments or by production processes. Total manufacturing costs are accumulated by two major categories, direct materials and conversion costs (the sum of direct labor and factory overhead applied). Unit cost is determined by dividing the total costs charged to a cost center by the output of that cost center. In that sense, the unit costs are averages.

Process costing is appropriate for companies that produce a continuous mass of like units through a series of operations or processes. Process costing is generally used in such industries as petroleum, chemicals, oil refinery, textiles, and food processing.

STEPS IN PROCESS-COSTING CALCULATIONS

There are basically five steps to be followed in accounting for process costs. They are summarized below.

(1) Summarize the flow of physical units.

The first step of the accounting provides a summary of all units on which some work was done in the department during the period. *Input must equal output.* This step helps to detect lost units during the process. The basic relationship may be expressed in the following equation:

$$\begin{pmatrix} \text{Beginning Inventory} \\ + \\ \text{Units for the Period} \end{pmatrix} = \begin{pmatrix} \text{Units Completed and Transferred Out} \\ + \\ \text{Ending Inventory} \end{pmatrix}$$

(2) Compute output in terms of equivalent units.

In order to determine the unit costs of the product in a processing environment, it is important to measure the total amount of work done during an accounting period. A special problem arises in processing industries in connection with how to deal with work still in process, that is, the work partially completed at the end of the period. The partially completed units are measured on an equivalent whole-unit basis for process-costing purposes.

Equivalent units are a measure of how many whole units of production are represented by the units completed plus the units partially completed. For example, 100 units that are 60% completed are the equivalent of 60 completed units in terms of conversion costs.

(3) Summarize the total costs to be accounted for by cost categories.

This step summarizes the total costs assigned to the department during the period.

(4) Compute the unit costs per equivalent unit.

The unit costs per equivalent is computed as follows:

$$\text{Unit Cost} = \frac{\text{Total Costs Incurred During the Period}}{\text{Equivalent Units of Production During the Period}}$$

(5) Apply total costs to units completed and transferred out and to units in ending work-in-process.

Cost-of-Production Report

The process-costing method uses what is called the cost-of-production report. It summarizes both total and unit costs charged to a department and indicates the allocation of total costs between work-in-process inventory and the units completed and transferred out to the next department or the finished goods inventory.

The cost-of-production report covers all five steps described above. It is also the source for monthly journal entries as well as a convenient compilation from which cost data may be presented to management.

Ledger Accounts Used in a Process System

In order to assign costs to processing departments and to compute unit costs of output, it is desirable to have at least one work-in-process inventory account for each production center, such as:

Work-in-process inventory: Department A
Work-in-process inventory: Department B

It may be useful to have subdivisions of each of these departmental accounts for every input factor for which unit costs are to be computed and reported. The following are examples (see Figure 10.1):

Work-in-process, Department A: Materials
Work-in-process, Department B: Conversion costs

PROCESS-COST COMPUTATION: NO BEGINNING INVENTORY

The first illustration of unit-cost computations under a process system assumes for simplicity that there is no beginning work-in-process inventory. A company produces and sells a chemical product that is processed in two departments. In Department A the basic materials are crushed, powdered, and mixed. In Department B the product is tested, packaged, and labeled, before being transferred to the finished-goods inventory.

Figure 10.1. Process-Cost System: Flow Chart of Ledger Relationships.

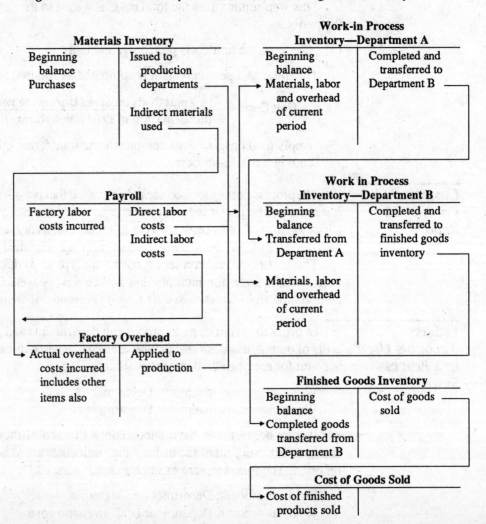

Assume the following for Production Department A for May. Materials are added when production is begun; therefore, all finished units and all units in the ending work-in-process inventory will have received a full complement of materials.

Actual production costs:
  Direct materials used, 18,000 gallons costing $27,000.
  Direct labor and factory overhead, $25,000.
Actual production:
  Completed and transferred to Production Department B, 8,000 gallons.
  Ending work-in-process, 10,000 gallons, 20% complete as to conversion.

(1) Summarize the flow of physical units.

To be accounted for:
  Added this period   18,000 gallons

Accounted for as follows:
  Completed this period   8,000 gallons
  In process, end of period   10,000
    Total   18,000 gallons

(2) Compute output in terms of equivalent units

	Materials (gallon)	Conversion Cost
Units completed	8,000	8,000
Ending work-in-process (10,000 gallons)		
100% of materials	10,000	
20% of conversion cost		2,000
Equivalent units produced	18,000	10,000

Steps (3) through (5)

	Cost of Production		
	Total Cost	Equivalent Production (gallon)	Unit Cost
Materials	$27,000	18,000	$1.50
Conversion cost	25,000	10,000	2.50
To be accounted for	$52,000		$4.00
Ending work-in-process:			
Materials	$15,000	10,000	$1.50
Conversion cost	5,000	2,000	2.50
Total work-in-process	$20,000		
Completed and transferred	32,000	8,000	4.00
Total accounted for	$52,000		

Journal Entries	Work-In-Process, Department A: Materials	27,000	
	Materials Inventory		27,000
	To record cost of materials issued during May.		

	Work-in-Process, Department A: Conversion Cost	25,000	
	Accrued Payroll and Various Other Accounts		25,000
	To record cost of direct labor and factory overhead during May.		

	Work-in-Process, Department B: Cost transferred in	32,000	
	Work-in-Process, Department A: Materials (8,000 gallons × $1.50)		12,000
	Work-in-Process, Department A: Conversion Cost (8,000 gallons × $2.50)		20,000

After the preceding entries have been posted, the balances of the work-in-process accounts of Department A will be as follows:

| Work-in-Process, Department A: Materials | $15,000 |
| Work-in-Process, Department A: Conversion Costs | 5,000 |

These balances agree with the results computed in the cost-of-production report.

Weighted Average vs. First-In, First-Out (FIFO)

When there is a beginning inventory of work-in-process, the production completed during the period comes from different batches, some from work partially completed in a prior period, and some from new units started in the current period. Since costs tend to vary from period to period, each batch may carry a different unit cost. There are two ways to treat the costs of the beginning inventory. One is weighted-average costing and the other is first-in, first-out (FIFO) costing.

WEIGHTED-AVERAGE COSTING

Under the weighted-average method of costing, both units of work-in-process at the beginning of the period and their costs are combined with current production units started in the current period and their costs, and an average cost is computed. In determining equivalent production units, no distinction is made between work partially completed in the prior period and the units started and completed in the current period. In other words, all units in the beginning inventory are treated as if they were produced in the current period. Thus there is only one average cost for goods completed.

Equivalent units under weighted-average costing may be computed as follows:

Units Completed + [Ending Work-in-Process × Degree of Completion (%)].

FIRST-IN, FIRST-OUT

Under FIFO, on the other hand, beginning work-in-process inventory costs are separated from added costs applied in the current period. Thus there are two unit costs for the period: (1) beginning work-in-process units completed and (2) units started and completed in the same period. Under FIFO, the beginning work-in-process is assumed to be completed and transferred first. Equivalent units under FIFO costing may be computed as follows:

Units Completed + [Ending Work-in-Process × Degree of Completion (%)]
– [Beginning Work-in-Process × Degree of Completion (%)]

Solved Problem 10.1. Equivalent Production

The quantity schedule for Department 2 at the Lyon Transport Company for the month of June 1992 is shown below.

Quantities	
Units-in-process at beginning (all materials; 50% conversion	8,000
Units started	76,000
Available	84,000
Units transferred to next department	78,000
Units still in-process (all materials; 66.67% conversion)	6,000
Accounted for	84,000

Compute the equivalent production units for materials and conversion costs for the month, under (a) weighted-average cost and (b) FIFO cost.

Solution 10.1

(a) Weighted-average cost

	Materials	**Conversion**
Units completed and transferred out	78,000	78,000
Add: Ending work-in-process amount completed (all materials; 66.67% conversion costs)	6,000	4,000
Equivalent production units	84,000	82,000*

(b) FIFO

	Materials	Conversion
Units completed and transferred out	78,000	78,000
Add: Ending work-in-process amount completed (all materials; 66.67% conversion costs	6,000	4,000
Equivalent production units	84,000	82,000
Less: Beginning work-in-process (all materials; 50% conversion costs)	8,000	4,000
	76,000	78,000*

* Note that 82,000 units under the weighted-average method include units fully or partially completed last month and on hand in Department 2's beginning inventory, while 78,000 units under FIFO represent only work completed during the current period.

Let us look at another comprehensive illustration. The following data relates to the activities of Department A during the month of January:

	Units
Beginning work-in-process (all materials; 66.67% complete as to conversion)	1,500
Started this period	5,000
Available	6,500
Completed and transferred	5,500
Ending work-in-process (all materials; 60% complete as to conversion)	1,000
Accounted for	6,500

Equivalent production in Department A for the month is computed, using weighted-average costing, as follows:

	Materials	Conversion Costs
Units completed and transferred	5,500	5,500
Ending work-in-process		
Materials (100%)	1,000	
Conversion costs (60%)		600
Equivalent production	6,500	6,100

Equivalent production in Department A for the month is computed, using FIFO costing, as follows:

	Materials	Conversion Costs
Units completed and transferred	5,500	5,500
Ending work-in-process		
Materials (100%)	1,000	
Conversion costs (60%)		600
Equivalent production for weighted average	6,500	6,100
Minus: Beginning work-in-process		
Materials (100%)	1,500	
Conversion costs (66.67%)		1,000
Equivalent production for FIFO	5,000	5,100

In the next illustration we will discuss, step by step, the weighted-average and FIFO methods.

The Portland Cement Manufacturing Company, Inc., manufactures cement. Its processing operations involve quarrying, grinding, blending, packing, and sacking. For cost-accounting and control purposes, there are four processing centers: Raw Materials No. 1, Raw Materials No. 2, Clinker, and Cement. Separate cost-of-production reports are prepared in detail with respect to these cost centers. The following information pertains to the operation of Raw Materials No. 2 Department for July 1991:

	Materials	Conversion
Units in process July 1		
800 bags	complete	60% complete
Costs	$12,000	$56,000
Units transferred out		
40,000 bags		
Current costs	$41,500	$521,500
Units in process July 31		
5,000 bags	complete	30% complete

Using weighted-average costing and FIFO costing, we will compute the following:

(a) Equivalent production units and unit costs by elements.
(b) Cost of work-in-process for July.
(c) Cost of units completed and transferred.

(a)

Computation of Output in Equivalent Units

	Physical Flow	Materials	Conversion
Work-in-process, beginning	800(60%)		
Units transferred in	44,200*		
Units to account for	45,000		
Units completed and transferred out	40,000	40,000	40,000
Work-in-process, ending	5,000(30%)	5,000	1,500
Units accounted for	45,000		
Equivalent units used for weighted-average costing		45,000	41,500
Less: Old equivalent units for work done on beginning inventory in prior period		800	480
Equivalent units used for FIFO		44,200	41,020

*(40,000 + 5,000) − 800 = 45,000 − 800 = 44,200

Cost of Production Report, Weighted Average
Raw Materials No. 2 Department
for the Month Ended July 31, 1991

	Work-in-Process Beginning	Current Costs	Total Costs	Equivalent Units	Average Unit Cost
Materials	$12,000	$ 41,500	$ 53,500	45,000	$ 1.1889
Conversion costs	56,000	521,500	577,500	41,500	13.9157
	$68,000	$563,000	$631,000		$15.1046

Cost of goods completed $604,184
  40,000 × $15.1046

Work-in-process, ending:
  Materials, 5,000 × $1.1889 $ 5,944.50
  Conversion costs, 1,500 × 13.9156   20,873.40 $ 26,817.90
                 $631,000 (rounded)

Cost of Production Report, FIFO
Raw Materials No. 2 Department
for the Month Ended July 31, 1991

	Total Costs	Equivalent Units	Unit Cost
Work-in-process, beginning	$ 68,000		
Current costs:			
Materials	41,500	44,200	$ 0.9389
Conversion costs	521,500	41,020	12.7133
Total costs to account for	$631,000		$13.6522

Cost of goods completed in units:		40,000	
• Work-in-process, beginning to be transferred out first	$ 68,000		
• Additional costs to complete $800 \times (1-.6)^* \times \$12.7133$	4,068.26		
• Cost of goods started and completed this month $39,200 \times \$13.6522$	535,166.24	$607,234.50	
Work-in-process, end:			
Materials			
$5,000 \times \$.9389$	$ 4,694.50		
Conversion			
$1,500 \times \$12.7133$	19,069.95	$ 23,764.45	
Total costs accounted for		$631,000 (rounded)	

* $(1 - 0.6) = .4$ means that it takes an additional 40% work to complete 800 work-in-process units.

A summary follows:

	Weighted Average		FIFO	
	Materials	**Conversion**	**Materials**	**Conversion**
(a) Equivalent units	45,000	41,500	44,200	41,020
Unit costs	$1.1889	$13.9157	$.9389	$12.7133
(b) Cost of work-in-process	$26,818.05		$23,764.45	
(c) Cost of units completed and transferred	$604,184		$607,234.50	

Note the difference in unit costs between the weighted-average and FIFO methods. From the perspective of cost control, FIFO costing is superior to the weighted-average method because of its focus on current period costs.

Solved Problem 10.2. Cost-of-Production Report

Texas Texturizing is a texturizer of polyester yarn. On June 1, 1991, the company had an inventory of 10,000 pounds that was complete as to materials but only three-quarters complete as to conversion. The beginning work-in-process cost was $15,000 ($10,000 for material and $5,000 for conversion). During the period, 160,000 pounds were completed. The material and conversion costs for the period were $140,000 and $76,600, respectively. The inventory at the end of the period consisted of 40,000 pounds that were complete as to materials but only one-quarter complete as to conversion. Prepare a cost-of-production report using the weighted-average costing method.

Solution 10.2

Texas Texturizing
Cost-of-Production Report
for the Month of June
(weighted average)

Physical flow

Work-in-process, beginning	10,000 (75%)
Started	190,000
In-process	200,000
Completed	160,000
Work-in-process, ending	40,000 (25%)
Accounted for	200,000

Equivalent units in process:

	Materials	Conversion
Units completed	160,000	160,000
Equivalent units, ending work-in-process	40,000	10,000
Equivalent units in-process	200,000	170,000

Total costs to be accounted for:
Cost per equivalent unit:

	Materials	Conversion	Total
Work-in-process, beginning	$ 10,000	$ 5,000	$ 15,000
Current costs	140,000	76,600	216,600
Total costs in-process	$150,000	$ 81,600	$231,600
Equivalent units in-process	$200,000	$170,000	
Cost per equivalent unit	$0.75	$0.48	$1.23

Accounting for total costs:

Completed and transferred out (160,000 × $1.23)			$196,800
Work-in-process, ending			
Materials (40,000 × $0.75)		$30,000	
Conversion (10,000 × $0.48)		4,800	34,800
Total costs accounted for			$231,600

Solved Problem 10.3. Cost-of-Production Report

Using data from Solved Problem 10.2, prepare a cost-of-production report using the FIFO method.

Solution 10.3

Texas Texturizing
Cost-of-Production Report
for the Month of June
(FIFO)

Physical flow

Work-in-process, beginning	10,000 (75%)
Started	190,000
In-process	200,000
Completed	160,000
Work-in-process, ending	40,000 (25%)
	200,000

Equivalent units manufactured:

	Materials	Conversion
Units completed	160,000	160,000
Equivalent units, ending work-in-process	40,000	10,000
Equivalent units in process	200,000	170,000
Less: Equivalent units, beginning work-in-process	10,000	7,500
Equivalent units manufactured	190,000	162,500

Total costs to be accounted for:
Cost per equivalent unit manufactured:

	Materials	Conversion	Total
Work-in-process, beginning			$ 15,000
Current costs	140,000	76,600	216,600
Total costs in process	$140,000	$76,600	$231,600
Equivalent units manufactured	190,000	162,500	
Cost per equivalent unit	$ 0.7368	$ 0.4714	$ 1.2082

Accounting for total costs:

Completed and transferred out:
  First batch:
    Beginning inventory $15,000.00
    Costs to complete:
      Materials $ 0.00
      Conversion $(1 - 0.75)$
        $\times$ 10,000 $\times$ $0.4714 $1,178.50   1,178.50 $ 16,178.50

  Second batch:
    (160,000 − 10,000) $\times$
      $1.2082   181,230.00
                                                                        $197,408.50

Work-in-process, ending
  Materials (40,000 $\times$ $0.7368) $29,472.00
  Conversion (10,000 $\times$ $0.4714)   4,714.00   34,186.00
  Total costs accounted for $231,594.50*

*$5.50 rounding error.

JOINT PRODUCT AND BYPRODUCT COSTS

When two or more types of products result from a single production process, the outputs are referred to as either joint products or byproducts, depending on their relative importance. Joint products are those that have a relatively significant sales value, while byproducts are those whose sales value is relatively minor in comparison with the value of the main, or joint, products.

Joint costs are the cost of inputs that are required for the joint products as a group. They cannot be identified directly with any of the joint products that emerge from the process. An example of a joint cost is the price paid for a steer by a packing house. Various joint products such as different cuts of meat, hides, glue, and fertilizer emerge. (The last two might be classified as byproducts if their value is relatively small.) It is impossible to tell how much of the cost of each steer pertains to T-bone steaks, hamburger, hides, and so forth. Any assignment of the joint cost to the joint products is arbitrary. The point in the production process at which joint products are separated is the split-off point. After that point each type of product can be separately identified and is independent of the others. Separate decisions can be made as to whether to sell the joint products as they are or to process them further before sale.

Accounting for Joint Products

Three different bases of allocating joint costs to products have sometimes been advocated:

(1) The physical unit basis.
(2) The sales value basis.
(3) The net realizable value basis.

We will discuss only the physical unit basis. The physical unit basis of allocating joint cost to the resulting joint products assigns an equal share of the joint cost to the outputs on the basis of some physical measure, such as gallons or pounds, contained in each output.

Assume that two chemical products result from a single production process. During a given period, the total input costs of the joint process amounted to $400,000. The output consisted of 200,000 gallons of Product A and 300,000 gallons of Product B.

The total cost allocated to each type of product can be computed as follows:

$$\frac{\text{Quantity of each product}}{\text{Total output quantity}} \times \text{Joint cost} = \text{Total cost allocated each joint product}$$

Thus:

$$\text{Product A, total cost} = \frac{200,000 \text{ gallons}}{500,000 \text{ gallons}} \times \$400,000 = \$160,000$$

$$\text{Product B, total cost} = \frac{300,000 \text{ gallons}}{500,000 \text{ gallons}} \times \$400,000 = \$240,000$$

Methods of Accounting for Byproduct Costs

Byproducts were already defined as products resulting from a single production process but whose sales value is relatively minor in comparison with the value of the main, or joint, products.

Because the relative value of the byproducts is not very important, it is usually considered undesirable to use a refined accounting method in dealing with byproduct costs. Thus the methods used to allocate joint costs to joint products (physical unit basis, sales value basis, and net realizable value basis) are not used in accounting for byproducts because the value of the resulting information would not be worth the cost of obtaining it.

Several different methods of accounting for byproducts are in use. Their main difference lies in whether or not they assign an inventoriable cost to byproducts in the period in which they are produced.

There are two methods that do not assign a cost to byproduct inventory in the period of production:

(1) Revenue from byproduct sales is treated as sales revenue, or miscellaneous revenue, in the period in which the byproduct is sold.
(2) Revenue from byproduct sales is treated as a deduction from cost of goods sold in the period in which the byproduct is sold.

*P*rocess costing makes no attempt to cost any specific lot in process. All costs, direct and indirect, are accumulated by departments for periods of time and an average cost for the period is computed. The choice of the system, job-order or process, depends on the nature of the manufacturing operation and the desired information.

Process costing is used by manufacturers whose products are produced on a continuous basis, with units receiving equal attention in each processing center. The five steps in process costing determination are: the check of a physical flow, computation of equivalent units, summary of costs, calculation of the unit costs, and calculation of the cost of goods completed and the ending work-in-process. Methods of accounting for joint and byproduct costs were also illustrated. The next chapter looks at cost behavior and the break-even point.

11

Cost Behavior and Cost-Volume-Profit Analysis

Not all costs behave in the same way. There are certain costs that vary in proportion to changes in volume or activity, such as labor hours and machine hours. There are other costs that do not change even though volume changes. An understanding of cost behavior is important:

(1) For break-even and cost-volume-profit analysis.
(2) To appraise divisional performance.
(3) For flexible budgeting.
(4) To make short-term choice decisions

Cost-volume-profit analysis is the systematic investigation of the interrelationships between sales prices, sales volume, mix of products sold, variable and fixed costs, and profits.

A FURTHER LOOK AT COSTS BY BEHAVIOR

As was discussed in Chapter 8, depending on how a cost will react or respond to changes in the level of activity, costs may be viewed as variable, fixed, or mixed (semivariable). This classification is made within a specified range of activity, called the *relevant range*. The relevant range is the volume zone within which the behavior of variable costs, fixed costs, and selling prices can be predicted with reasonable accuracy.

Variable Costs

As previously discussed, variable costs vary in total with changes in volume or level of activity. Examples of variable costs include the costs of direct materials, direct labor, and sales commissions.

Fixed Costs

Fixed costs remain constant in total dollar amounts as the volume or level of activity changes. Examples include advertising expense, salaries, and depreciation.

Mixed (Semivariable) Costs

Mixed costs contain both a fixed element and a variable one. Salespersons' compensation, including salary and commission, is an example. Note that factory overhead, taken as a whole, is a perfect example of mixed costs. Figure 11.1 displays how each of these three types of costs varies with changes in volume.

ANALYSIS OF MIXED (SEMIVARIABLE) COSTS

For planning, control, and decision-making purposes, mixed costs must be separated into their variable and fixed components.

There are several methods available for this purpose, including the high-low method, the scattergraph method, and the least-squares method. Only the high-low method will be discussed here. (The other methods are discussed in cost and managerial accounting textbooks such as Horngren and Foster's *Cost Accounting* and Garrison's *Managerial Accounting*.)

Figure 11.1. Cost-Behavior Patterns.

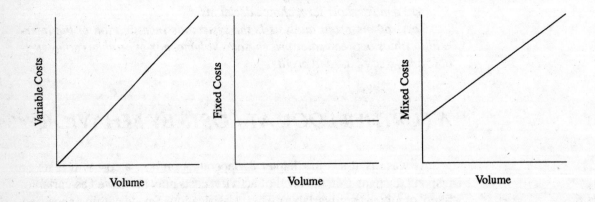

The High-Low Method

The high-low method, as the name indicates, uses two extreme data points to determine the values of the fixed-cost portion and the variable cost per unit of activity. The extreme data points are the highest and lowest total costs revealed by past cost patterns.

The high-low method is explained, step by step, as follows:

Step 1: Select the highest cost-volume pair and the lowest pair.

Step 2: Compute the variable cost per unit of activity, using the formula:

$$\text{Variable Cost per Unit} = \frac{\text{Difference in Total Cost}}{\text{Difference in Activity}}$$

Step 3: Compute the fixed cost portion as:

$$\text{Fixed-cost portion} = \text{Total mixed cost} - \text{Variable cost}$$

Assume for illustration purposes that Alvin Manufacturing Company decides to relate total factory overhead costs to direct labor hours (DLH) to develop a cost-volume formula. Twelve monthly observations are collected. They are given in Table 11.1 and plotted as shown in Figure 11.2.

Table 11.1

Month	Direct Labor Hours (x) (Thousands)	Factory Overhead (y) (Thousands)
January	9 hours	$ 15
February	19	20
March	11	14
April	14	16
May	23	25
June	12	20
July	12	20
August	22	23
September	7	14
October	13	22
November	15	18
December	17	18
Total	174 hours	$225

The high-low points selected from the monthly observations are thus

	DLH	Factory Overhead
High	23 hours	$25 (May pair)
Low	7	14 (September pair)
Difference	16 hours	$11

Variable cost per unit, therefore, is

$$\frac{\text{Difference in cost}}{\text{Difference in activity}} = \frac{\$11}{16 \text{ hours}} = \$0.6875 \text{ per DLH}$$

Figure 11.2. Scatter Diagram.

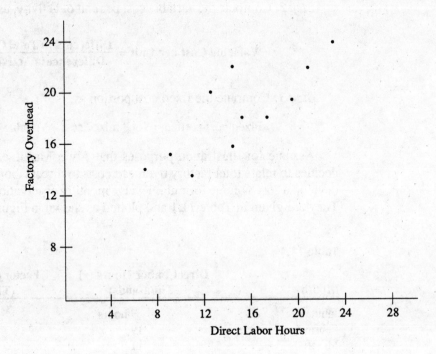

The fixed-cost portion is computed as follows

	High	**Low**
Factory overhead	$25.0000	$14.0000
Less: Variable expense ($0.6875 per DLH)	(15.8125)	(4.8125)
Fixed cost	$ 9.1875	$ 9.1875

Therefore the cost-volume formula for factory overhead is:

$9,187.50 fixed plus $0.6875 per DLH

Solved Problem 11.1. High-Low Method

Following are the highest and lowest levels of direct labor hours and the repair costs of Jason Manufacturing Corporation:

	Direct Labor Hours (DHL)	Repair Costs
Highest level	25,000 hours	$99,000
Lowest level	10,000	64,500

Determine (a) the variable cost per unit and (b) the fixed-cost component of the repair cost by using the high-low method.

Solution 11.1

	DHL	Overhead Costs
Highest level	25,000 hours	$99,000
Lowest level	10,000	64,500
Difference	15,000 hours	$34,500

(a) Variable cost per DLH = $34,500/15,000 hours = $2.30 per DLH.
(b) The fixed component is

Total overhead costs at 25,000 DLH	$99,000
Less: Variable costs (25,000 @ $2.30)	57,500
Fixed	$41,500

Total repair costs, therefore, are $41,500 fixed + $2.30 DLH.

COST-VOLUME-PROFIT (CVP) ANALYSIS

Cost-volume-profit (CVP) analysis, together with cost-behavior information, helps managerial accountants perform many useful analyses. CVP analysis deals with how profit and costs change with a change in volume. More specifically, it looks at the effects on profits of changes in such factors as variable costs, fixed costs, selling prices, volume, and mix of products sold. By studying the relationships of costs, sales, and net income, management is better able to cope with many planning decisions.

Questions Answered by CVP Analysis

CVP analysis tries to answer the following questions:

(1) What sales volume is required to break even?
(2) What sales volume is necessary to earn a desired profit?
(3) What profit can be expected on a given sales volume?
(4) How would changes in selling price, variable costs, fixed costs, and output affect profits?
(5) How would a change in sales mix affect the break-even volume and profit potential?

Concepts of Contribution Margin (CM)

In order to compute the break-even point and perform various CVP analyses, note the following important concepts.

CONTRIBUTION MARGIN

The contribution margin (CM) is the excess of sales (S) over the variable costs (VC) of the product or service. It is the amount of money available to cover fixed costs (FC) and to generate profit. As an equation, $CM = S - VC$.

UNIT-CONTRIBUTION MARGIN

The unit CM is the excess of the unit selling price (p) over the unit variable cost (v). Symbolically, unit $CM = p - v$.

CONTRIBUTION-MARGIN RATIO

The CM ratio is the contribution margin as a percentage of sales:

$$\text{CM Ratio} = \frac{CM}{S} = \frac{S-VC}{S} = 1 - \frac{VC}{S}$$

Here VC/S is the variable cost ratio, and the CM ratio is 1 minus the variable cost ratio. For example, if variable costs are 40% of sales, then the variable cost ratio is 40% and the CM ratio is 60%.

To illustrate the various concepts of CM, consider the following data for Avon Toy Store:

	Total	Per Unit	Percent
Sales (1,500 units)	$37,500	$25	100
Less: Variable costs	15,000	10	40
Contribution margin	$22,500	$15	60
Less: Fixed costs	15,000		
Net income	$ 7,500		

From the data listed above, CM, unit CM, and the CM ratio are computed as follows:

$$CM = S - VC = \$37,500 - \$15,000 = \$22,500$$

$$\text{Unit CM} = p - v = \$25 - \$10 = \$15$$

$$\text{CM Ratio} = \frac{CM}{S} = \frac{\$22,500}{\$37,500} = 1 - \frac{\$15,000}{\$37,500} = 1 - 0.4 = 0.6 = 60\%$$

Solved Problem 11.2. Missing Amounts

In each of the following cases, find the missing amounts:

	Sales in Units	Sales in Dollars	Variable Expenses
Case 1	5,000	$90,000	$40,000
Case 2	3,000	(c)	4,000
Case 3	10,000	50,000	(e)

	Contribution Margin per Unit	Fixed Costs	Net Income
Case 1	$(a)	$15,000	$ (b)
Case 2	3	(d)	2,000
Case 3	(f)	20,000	5,000

Solution 11.2

(a) Unit CM = ($90,000 − $40,000) ÷ 5,000 units = $10 per unit

(b) Net income = $90,000 − $40,000 − $15,000 = $35,000

(c) CM = 3,000 units × $3 = $9,000

$$\text{Sales} - \$4,000 = \$9,000$$

$$\text{Sales} = \$13,000$$

(d) $13,000 − $4,000 − Fixed costs = $2,000

$$\text{Fixed costs} = \$7,000$$

(e) $50,000 − Variable expenses − $20,000 = $5,000

$$\text{Variable expenses} = \$25,000$$

(f) Unit CM = ($50,000 − $25,000) ÷ 10,000 units = $2.50

Solved Problem 11.3. Missing Amounts

In each of the following cases, find the missing amounts:

	Sales in Dollars	Variable Expenses	Contribution Margin Ratio	Fixed Costs	Net Income
Case 1	$100,000	$50,000	(a)%	$30,000	$ (b)
Case 2	200,000	(c)	30	(d)	5,000
Case 3	(e)	(f)	40	25,000	25,000

Solution 11.3

(a) CM ratio = ($100,000 – $50,000) ÷ $100,000 = 50%

(b) Net income = $100,000 – $50,000 – $30,000 = $20,000

(c) $$\frac{\$200,000 - \text{Variable expenses}}{\$200,000} = 30\%$$

   Variable expenses = $140,000

(d) $200,000 – $140,000 – Fixed costs = $5,000
   Fixed costs = $55,000

(e) CM – Fixed costs = Net income
   CM – $25,000 = $25,000
   CM = $50,000

   By definition, the CM ratio = CM ÷ Sales.
   40% = $50,000 ÷ Sales
   Therefore, Sales = $125,000.

(f) CM = Sales – Variable expenses
   $50,000 = $125,000 – Variable expenses
   Variable expenses = $75,000

Break-Even Analysis

The break-even point represents the level of sales revenue that equals the total of the variable and fixed costs for a given volume of output at a particular capacity use rate. It can be computed using the following formulas:

$$\text{Break-Even Point in Units} = \frac{\text{Fixed Costs}}{\text{Unit CM}}$$

$$\text{Break-Even Point in Dollars} = \frac{\text{Fixed Costs}}{\text{CM Ratio}}$$

Or, in a single product case,

Break-Even Point in Dollars = Break-Even Point in Units × Unit Sales Price

Solved Problem 11.4. Break-Even Point

Assume fixed costs equal $15,000, selling price is $25, and variable cost per unit is $10. Therefore, unit CM = $25 – $10 = $15, and the CM ratio = 60%. Compute the break-even point in units and dollars.

Solution 11.4

Break-even point in units = $15,000 ÷ $15 = 1,000 units
Break-even point in dollars = $15,000 ÷ 0.6 = $25,000

Or, alternatively,

$$1,000 \text{ units} \times \$25 = \$25,000$$

Solved Problem 11.5. Break-Even Sales

Fixed costs are estimated at $90,000 and variable costs are expected to be 70% of sales. What is the break-even sales?

Solution 11.5

Since the variable cost ratio is 70%, the CM ratio is 30%.

$$\text{Break-even point in dollars} = \$90,000 \div 0.3 = \$300,000$$

GRAPHICAL APPROACH

The graphical approach to obtaining the break-even point is based on the so-called *break-even (B-E) chart,* as shown in Figure 11.3. Sales revenue, variable costs, and fixed costs are plotted on the vertical axis, while units of output are plotted on the horizontal axis. The break-even point is the point at which the total sales revenue line intersects the total cost line. The chart can also effectively report profit potentials over a wide range of activity and therefore be used as a tool for discussion and presentation.

The *profit-volume (P-V) chart,* as shown in Figure 11.4, focuses directly on how profits vary with changes in volume. Profits are plotted on the vertical axis, while units of output are shown on the horizontal axis. The P-V chart provides a quick, condensed comparison of how alternatives on pricing, variable costs, or fixed costs may affect net income as volume changes. The P-V chart can be easily constructed from the B-E chart.

DETERMINATION OF TARGET INCOME VOLUME

Besides determining the break-even point, CVP analysis determines the sales required to attain a particular income level or target net income. The formula is

$$\text{Target Income Sales Volume} = \frac{\text{Fixed Costs} + \text{Target Income}}{\text{Unit CM}}$$

Solved Problem 11.6. Target Income Volume

Assume fixed costs equal $15,000, selling price per unit is $25, and variable cost per unit is $10. Assume further that the company wishes to attain a target income of $15,000 before taxes. Compute the target income volume required.

Figure 11.3. Break-Even Chart.

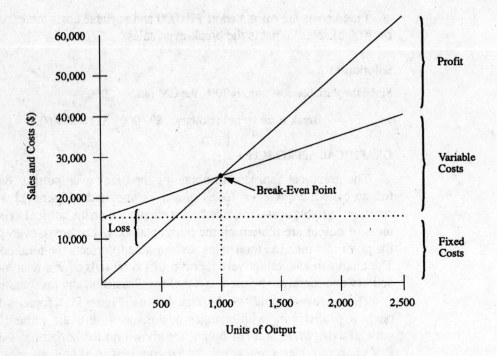

Figure 11.4. Profit-Volume (P-V) Chart.

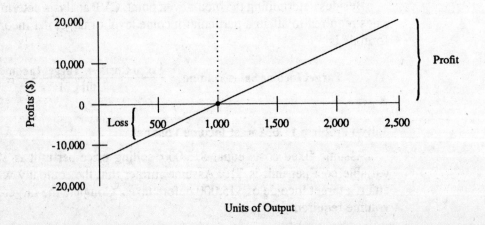

Solution 11.6

$$\text{Target income sales volume} = \frac{\text{Fixed costs} + \text{Target income}}{\text{Unit CM}}$$

$$\frac{\$15,000 + \$15,000}{\$25 - \$10} = \frac{\$30,000}{\$15} = 2,000 \text{ units}$$

Solved Problem 11.7. Contribution Margin and Break-Even

The following information is given for Angeles Stores:

Selling price per unit	$ 10
Variable cost per unit	6
Total fixed costs	50,000

Determine the following:

(a) Contribution margin per unit
(b) Contribution-margin ratio
(c) Break-even sales in units
(d) Break-even sales in dollars
(e) Sales in units required to achieve a net income of $4,000

Solution 11.7

(a) Contribution margin per unit = $10 – $6 = $4
(b) Contribution-margin ratio = $4 ÷ $10 = 40%
(c) Break-even sales in units = $50,000 ÷ $4 = 12,500 units
(d) Break-even sales in dollars = $50,000 ÷ 0.4 = $125,000
    or, alternatively, 12,500 units × $10 = $125,000
(e) Target income sales in units = ($50,000 + $4,000) ÷ $4 = 13,500 units

MARGIN OF SAFETY

The margin of safety is a measure of the difference between actual sales and break-even sales, sales being in dollars or in units. The amount by which sales revenue may drop before losses begin, it is expressed as a percentage of expected sales:

$$\text{Margin of Safety} = \frac{\text{Expected Sales} - \text{Break-Even Sales}}{\text{Expected Sales}}$$

The margin of safety is often used as a measure of operating risk. The larger the ratio the safer the situation, since there is less risk of reaching the break-even point.

Solved Problem 11.8. Margin of Safety

Assume that Avon Toy Store projects sales of $35,000, with a break-even sales level at $25,000. What is the projected margin of safety?

Solution 11.8

$$\frac{\$35,000 - \$25,000}{\$35,000} = 28.57\%$$

Solved Problem 11.9. Break-Even Computations

The following information is given for the Foster Tool Company:

Fixed costs	$30,000 per period
Variable cost per unit	$5
Selling price per unit	$8

(a) Compute the break-even sales in units and in dollars.
(b) Calculate the margin of safety at the 12,000-unit level.
(c) Find the net income when sales are $120,000.
(d) Compute the sales in units required to produce a net income of $10,000.
(e) Find the break-even point in units if variable costs are increased by $1 per unit and if total fixed costs are decreased by $5,000.

Solution 11.9

(a) Break-even point in units = $30,000 ÷ ($8 – $5) = 10,000 units

Break-even point in dollars = $30,000 ÷ [($8 – $5) ÷ $8] =

$30,000 ÷ 0.375 = $80,000 or 10,000 units × $8 = $80,000

(b)

$$\text{Margin of safety} = \frac{12,000 \text{ units} - 10,000 \text{ units}}{12,000 \text{ units}} = 16.7\%$$

(c)

Sales	$120,000	
Variable costs	75,000	(15,000 units* @ $5)
CM	$ 45,000	
Fixed costs	30,000	
Net income	$ 15,000	

* 15,000 units = $120,000 ÷ $8

(d) Target income volume = ($30,000 + $10,000) ÷ ($8 – $5) = 13,333 units (rounded)

(e) Break-even point in units = $25,000 ÷ ($8 – $6) = 12,500 units

...e concepts of contribution margin have many applications in profit
...ng and short-term decision making. Many what-if scenarios can be
...ed using them as planning tools. Some applications are illustrated

...roblem 11.10. Impact on Income

...me that Avon Toy Store has a CM of 60% and fixed costs of
...per period. Assume that the company expects sales to go up by
...or the next period. How much will income increase?

...1.10

...the CM concepts, we can quickly compute the impact of a change
...profits. The formula for computing the impact is:

...ange in Net Income = Dollar Change in Sales × CM Ratio

...Increase in Net Income = $10,000 × 60% = $6,000

...e the income will go up by $6,000, assuming there is no change

...iven a change in unit sales instead of dollars, then the formula

...ge in Net Income = Change in Unit Sales × Unit CM

...11.11. Impact On Income

...t the store expects sales to go up by 400 units. How much
...ease, assuming a selling price of $25, variable cost per unit
...ange in fixed costs?

...'s unit CM is $15. The income will increase by

400 units × $15 = $6,000

...12. Expected Net Income

...von Toy Store has a CM of 60% and fixed costs of
...,uuu per period. What net income is expected on sales of $47,500?

Solution 11.12

The answer is the difference between the CM and the fixed costs:

CM: $47,500 × 60%	$28,500
Less: Fixed costs	15,000
Net income	$13,500

Solved Problem 11.13. Advertising Budget

Avon Toy Store is considering increasing its advertising budget by $5,000, which, in turn would increase sales revenue by $8,000. Should the advertising budget be increased?

Solution 11.13

The answer is no, since the increase in the CM is less than the increased cost:

Increase in CM: $8,000 × 60%	$4,800
Increase in advertising	5,000
Decrease in net income	$ (200)

Sales Mix Analysis

Break-even and cost-volume-profit analysis requires some additional computations and assumptions when a company produces and sells more than one product. In multiproduct firms, sales mix is an important factor in calculating an overall company break-even point.

Different selling prices and different variable costs result in different unit CM and CM ratios. As a result, the break-even points and cost-volume-profit relationships vary with the relative proportions of the products sold, called the sales mix.

In break-even and CVP analysis, it is necessary to predetermine the sales mix and then compute a weighted-average unit CM. The weighted-average unit CM is an average of unit CMs of products involved, the weights being sales-mix ratios. It is also necessary to assume that the sales mix does not change for a specified period. The break-even formula for the company as a whole is:

$$\text{Break–Even Sales in Units (or in Dollars)} = \frac{\text{Fixed Costs}}{\substack{\text{Weighted-Average Unit CM} \\ \text{(or CM Ratio)}}}$$

Solved Problem 11.14. Break-Even Point

Assume that Knibex, Inc. produces cutlery sets of high-quality wood and steel. The company makes a deluxe cutlery set and a standard set that have the following unit CM data:

	Deluxe	Standard
Selling price	$20	$10
Variable cost per unit	12	5
Unit CM	$ 8	$ 5
Sales mix	60%	40%
Fixed costs	$136,000	$136,000

What is the break-even point in units for each product?

Solution 11.14

The weighted-average unit CM = ($8)(0.6) + ($5)(0.4) = $6.80. Therefore the company's break-even point in units is

$$\$136,000 \div \$6.80 = 20,000 \text{ units}$$

which is divided as follows:

Deluxe: 20,000 units × 60% =		12,000 units
Standard: 20,000 units × 40% =		8,000
		20,000 units

Solved Problem 11.15. Break-Even Point

The Tape Red Company has three major products, whose contribution margins are shown below:

	Product		
	A	B	C
Sales price	$15	$10	$8
Variable cost	10	6	5
CM/unit	5	4	3

Total fixed costs are $100,000.

Compute the break-even point in units in total and for each product if the three products are sold in the proportion of 30, 50, and 20%, respectively.

Solution 11.15

Average contribution margin per unit = $5(30%) + $4(50%) + $3(20%) = $4.10 per unit

$$\text{Company's break-even point} = \frac{\$100,000}{\$4.10} = 24,390 \text{ units (rounded)}$$

which will be broken up, per product, as:

A	30% × 24,390 units =	7,317 units
B	50% × 24,390 units =	12,195 units
C	20% × 24,390 units =	4,878 units

Assumptions Underlying Break-Even and CVP Analysis

The basic break-even and CVP models are subject to a number of limiting assumptions:

(a) The selling price per unit is constant throughout the entire relevant range of activity.

(b) All costs are classified as fixed or variable.

(c)   The variable cost per unit is constant.

(d)   There is only one product or a constant sales mix.

(e)   Inventories do not change significantly from period to period.

(f)   Volume is the only factor affecting variable costs.

ABSORPTION VS. DIRECT COSTING

Currently, the most commonly accepted theory of product costing holds that the cost of producing a product includes direct materials, direct labor, and an apportioned share of the many factory overhead costs. This method of assigning costs to products, called absorption (full) costing, is the method generally required for tax purposes.

Because all costs, including fixed overhead, are applied to production under absorption costing, variations in unit-product cost may result solely from variations in production volume. If fixed costs are $200,000 and 20,000 units are produced, unit fixed cost is $10; if volume is 40,000, unit fixed cost is $5. Because these variations are not controllable at the production manager level and may obscure other significant variations in cost, they can be excluded from product cost through use of a costing technique referred to as direct (variable or marginal) costing.

Under direct costing, all variable manufacturing costs are charged to the product, and all fixed costs (including fixed manufacturing costs) are charged to expense. Thus all manufacturing costs must first be classified as fixed or variable. Direct materials and direct labor costs are usually completely variable. But factory overhead costs must be separated into variable and fixed portions. All variable costs (direct materials, direct labor, and variable overhead) are assigned to production and become part of the unit costs of the products produced. All fixed costs are assumed to be costs of the period and are charged to expenses.

In summary, the only difference between absorption costing and direct costing is in the treatment of fixed manufacturing costs. Under absorption costing they are treated as product costs, and under direct costing they are treated as period costs.

Absorption and Direct Costing Compared

The differences between (a) direct and (b) absorption costing can be seen from an illustration comparing the income statements that would result from applying each technique to the same data. Assume the following information:

Beginning inventory	– 0 –	Variable costs (per unit)	
Production (units)	10,000	Direct materials	$2.00
Sales (units)	9,000	Direct labor	1.00
		Factory overhead	0.30
		Total	$3.30
Fixed factory overhead	$ 6,000		
Selling expenses	15,000	Variable selling expenses	
Administrative expenses	12,000	(per unit)	$0.20
Total	$33,000	Selling price (per unit)	$8.00

INCOME STATEMENT UNDER DIRECT COSTING

Under direct costing, the year's income statement would be as shown in Figure 11.5.

Figure 11.5. Income Statement Under Direct Costing.

Sales (9,000 units at $8)		$72,000
Cost of goods sold:		
Variable production costs incurred		
(10,000 units at $3.30)	$33,000	
Less: Inventory (1,000 units at $3.30)	3,300	29,700
Manufacturing margin		$42,300
Variable selling expenses (9,000 units at $0.20)		1,800
Marginal income		$40,500
Period costs:		
Factory overhead	$ 6,000	
Selling expenses	15,000	
Administrative expenses	12,000	33,000
Net income		$ 7,500

Note that all of the fixed manufacturing costs are considered costs of the period and are not included in inventories. The fixed factory overhead is treated as a period cost and is deducted, along with the selling and administrative expenses in the period incurred. That is,

Direct materials	$XX
Direct labor	XX
Variable factory overhead	XX
Product cost	$XX

INCOME STATEMENT UNDER ABSORPTION COSTING

Figure 11.6 contains the income statement that would be prepared under absorption costing.

Figure 11.6. Income Statement Under Absorption Costing.

Sales (9,000 units at $8)		$72,000
Cost of goods sold:		
Variable costs of production (10,000 units at $3.30)	$33,000	
Fixed overhead costs	6,000	
Total costs of producing 10,000 units	$39,000	
Less: Inventory (1,000 units at $3.90*)	3,900	35,100
Gross margin on sales		$36,900
Operating expenses:		
Selling ($15,000 fixed plus 9,000 at $0.20 each)	$16,800	
Administrative	12,000	28,800
Net income		$ 8,100

*$3.90 = $3.30 + $0.60 ($6,000 ÷ 10,000 units)

Note that the fixed manufacturing costs are included as part of the product cost and that some of these costs are included in the ending inventory. Under absorption costing, the cost to be inventoried includes all manufacturing costs, both variable and fixed. Nonmanufacturing (operating) expenses, i.e., selling and administrative expenses, are treated as period expenses and thus are charged against the current revenue:

Direct materials	$XX
Direct labor	XX
Variable factory overhead	XX
Fixed factory overhead	XX
Product cost	$XX

The ending inventory is priced at so-called full cost; that is, the cost of ending inventory includes fixed factory overhead.

Two important facts should be noted:

(1) Effects of the two costing methods on net income:

    (a) When production exceeds sales, a larger net income will be reported under absorption costing.

    (b) When sales exceeds production, a larger net income will be reported under direct costing.

    (c) When sales and production are equal, net income will be the same under both methods.

(2) Reconciliation of the direct and absorption costing net income figures:

    (a) The difference in net income can be reconciled as follows:

$$\begin{pmatrix} \text{Difference in} \\ \text{Net Income} \end{pmatrix} = \begin{pmatrix} \text{Change in} \\ \text{Inventory} \end{pmatrix} \times \begin{pmatrix} \text{Fixed Factory} \\ \text{Overhead Rate} \end{pmatrix}$$

(b) The above formula applies only if the fixed overhead rate per unit does not change between the periods.

We can prove:

(1) Since the difference in net income is $8,100 – $7,500 = $600, the absorption costing shows a larger net income.
(2) Reconciliation of difference in net income:

Change in inventory	Fixed factory overhead rate	Difference in net income
1,000	× $0.60 ($6,000 ÷ 10,000 units) =	$600

MANAGERIAL USE OF DIRECT COSTING

It is important to realize that direct costing is used for internal management only. It highlights the concept of contribution margin and focuses on the costs by behavior rather than by function. Its managerial uses include: (1) relevant cost analysis; (2) break-even and cost-volume-profit (CVP) analyses; and (3) short-term decision making.

Direct costing is, however, not acceptable for external reporting or income-tax reporting. Companies that use direct costing for internal reporting must convert to absorption costing for external reporting.

Solved Problem 11.16. Income Statement Preparation

Assume the following data concerning operation of the Ames Manufacturing Company for the month of September:

Number of units sold	100 units
Selling price per unit	$ 20
Variable manufacturing cost/unit	5
Fixed manufacturing costs	300
Variable selling and administrative cost/unit	4
Fixed selling and administrative costs	110

Prepare an income statement for the month of September, using the absorption-costing (traditional) and direct-costing (contribution) formats.

Solution 11.16

Ames Manufacturing Company
Income Statement
for the Month Ended September 30

Absorption Costing			Direct Costing			
Sales		$2,000	Sales			$2,000
Less: Cost of goods sold		800*	Less: Variable costs			
Gross margin		$1,200	Manufacturing		500	
			Selling/Adm.		400	900
			Contribution margin			$1,100
Less: Operating expenses			Less: Fixed costs			
Selling/ Adm.		510**	Manufacturing		$300	
			Selling/Adm.		110	410
Net income		$ 690	Net income			$ 690

* $800 = (100 units × $5) + $300
**$510 = $110 + (100 units × $4)

*A*n understanding of cost behavior is extremely useful for managerial planning and decision-making purposes. It allows managerial accountants to perform short-term planning analysis, such as break-even analysis. Cost-volume-profit analysis is useful as a frame of reference, as a vehicle for expressing overall managerial performance, and as a planning device via break-even techniques and what-if scenarios. Breaking down the costs by behavior, which is reflected in a contribution (direct-costing) income statement, facilitates the use of various short-term profit-planning tools on the part of managerial accountants. Budgets and standards will be discussed in the next chapter.

12

Budgeting and Standard Cost Systems

A comprehensive (master) budget is a formal statement of management's expectations regarding sales, expenses, volume, and other financial transactions of an organization for the coming period. Simply stated, a budget is a set of pro forma (projected, planned, or budgeted) financial statements. It consists basically of a pro forma income statement, pro forma balance sheet, and cash budget.

A budget is a tool for both planning and control. At the beginning of the period, the budget is a plan or standard; at the end of the period it serves as a control device to help management measure company performance against the plan so that future performance may be improved.

One of the most important phases of responsibility accounting (to be discussed in more detail in the following chapter) is establishing standard costs and evaluating performance by comparing actual costs with the standard costs. The difference between the actual costs and the standard costs is called the variance and is calculated for individual cost centers. Variance analysis is a key tool for measuring performance of a cost center.

TYPES OF BUDGETS

A budget is typically either an operating budget, which reflects the results of operating decisions, or a financial budget, reflecting the financial decisions of the firm.

The operating budget consists of:

- Sales budget
- Production budget
- Direct materials budget
- Direct labor budget
- Factory overhead budget
- Ending-inventory budget
- Selling and administrative expense budget
- Pro forma income statement

The financial budget consists of:

- Cash budget
- Pro forma balance sheet

The major steps in preparing the budget are as follows:

(1) Prepare a sales forecast.
(2) Determine expected production volume.
(3) Estimate manufacturing costs and operating expenses.
(4) Determine cash flow and other financial effects.
(5) Formulate projected financial statements.

To illustrate how all these budgets are put together, we will focus on a manufacturer company called the Darcel Company, which produces and markets a single product. We will assume that the company develops the master budget for 1992 on a quarterly basis. We will use the *direct costing (contribution)* method throughout the illustration.

Operating Budget

THE SALES BUDGET

The sales budget is the starting point in preparing the master budget, since estimated sales volume influences nearly all other items appearing throughout the master budget. The sales budget ordinarily indicates how many units of each product is expected to be sold. After sales volume has been estimated, the sales budget is constructed by multiplying the expected sales in units by the expected unit sales price. The sales budget generally includes a computation of expected cash collections from credit sales, which will be used later for cash budgeting.

The Darcel Company
Sales Budget
for the Year Ending December 31, 1992

	1 Qtr.	2 Qtr.	3 Qtr.	4 Qtr.	Total
Expected sales in units	800	700	900	800	3,200
Unit sales price	× $ 80	× $ 80	× $ 80	× $ 80	× $ 80
Total sales	$64,000	$56,000	$72,000	$64,000	$256,000

Schedule of Expected Cash Collections

	1 Qtr.	2 Qtr.	3 Qtr.	4 Qtr.	Total
Accounts receivable, 12/31/1991	$ 9,500[*]				$ 9,500
1st quarter sales ($64,000)	44,800[†]	$17,920[‡]			62,720
2d quarter sales ($56,000)		39,200	$15,680		54,880
3d quarter sales ($72,000)			50,400	$20,160	70,560
4th quarter sales ($64,000)				44,800	44,800
Total cash collections	$54,300	$57,120	$66,080	$64,960	$242,460

---

[*] The entire accounts receivable balance of $9,500 is assumed to be collectible in the first quarter.

[†] 70% of a quarter's sales are collected in the quarter of sale.

[‡] 28% of a quarter's sales are collected in the quarter following, and the remaining 2% are uncollectible.

THE PRODUCTION BUDGET

After sales are budgeted, the production budget can be determined. The number of units expected to be manufactured to meet budgeted sales and inventory requirements is set forth in the production budget. The expected volume of production is determined by subtracting the estimated inventory at the beginning of the period from the sum of the units expected to be sold and the desired inventory at the end of the period. The production budget is illustrated as follows:

The Darcel Company
Production Budget
for the Year Ending December 31, 1992

	1 Qtr.	2 Qtr.	3 Qtr.	4 Qtr.	Total
Planned sales*	800	700	900	800	3,200
Desired ending inventory†	70	90	80	100‡	100
Total needs	870	790	980	900	3,300
Less: Beginning inventory§	80	70	90	80	80
Units to be produced	790	720	890	820	3,220

*   Taken from the sales budget illustrated above.
†   10% of the next quarter's sales
‡   Estimated
§   The same as the previous quarter's ending inventory

Solved Problem 12.1. Sales and Production Budgets

The Barker Company manufactures two models of adding machines, A and B. The production and sales data for the month of June 1992 are given as follows:

	A	B
Inventory (units) June 1	4,500	2,250
Desired inventory (units) June 30	4,000	2,500
Expected sales volume (units)	7,500	5,000
Unit sales price	$75	$120

Prepare a sales budget and a production budget.

Solution 12.1

Barker Company
Sales Budget

Product	Sales Volume	Unit Selling Price	Total Sales
A	7,500	$ 75	$ 562,500
B	5,000	120	600,000
			$1,162,500

Barker Company
Production Budget

	Product A	Product B
Expected sales in units	7,500	5,000
Ending inventory, desired	4,000	2,500
Total needs	11,500	7,500
Less: Beginning inventory	4,500	2,250
Total production (in units)	7,000	5,250

THE DIRECT MATERIAL BUDGET

When the level of production has been computed, a direct material budget should be constructed to show how much material will be required for production and how much material must be purchased to meet this production requirement.

The purchase will depend on both expected usage of materials and inventory levels. The formula for computation of the purchase is:

Purchase in units = Usage + Desired ending material inventory units
– Beginning inventory units

The direct material budget is usually accompanied by a computation of expected cash payments for materials.

The Darcel Company
Direct Material Budget
for the Year Ending December 31, 1992

	1 Qtr.	2 Qtr.	3 Qtr.	4 Qtr.	Total
Units to be produced	790	720	890	820	3,220
Material needs per unit (lbs)	× 3	× 3	× 3	× 3	× 3
Material needs for production	2,370	2,160	2,670	2,460	9,660
Desired ending inventory of materials*	216	267	246	250[†]	250
Total needs	2,586	2,427	2,916	2,710	9,910
Less: Beginning inventory of materials[‡]	237	216	267	246	237
Materials to be purchased	2,349	2,211	2,649	2,464	9,673
Unit price	× $2	× $2	× $2	× $2	× $2
Purchase cost	$4,698	$4,422	$5,298	$4,928	$19,346

Schedule of Expected Cash Disbursements

Accounts payable, 12/31/1991	$2,200				$ 2,200
1st quarter purchases ($4,698)	2,349	2,349§			4,698
2nd quarter purchases ($4,422)		2,211	2,211		4,422
3rd quarter purchases ($5,298)			2,649	2,649	5,298
4th quarter purchases ($4,928)				2,464	2,464
Total disbursements	$4,549	$4,560	$4,860	$5,113	$19,082

---

*   10 percent of the next quarter's units needed for production
†   Estimated
‡   The same as the prior quarter's ending inventory
§   50% of a quarter's purchases are paid for in the quarter of purchase; the remainder are paid for in the following quarter.

THE DIRECT LABOR BUDGET

The production requirements set forth in the production budget also provide the starting point for the preparation of the direct labor budget. To compute direct labor requirements, expected production volume for each period is multiplied by the number of direct labor hours required to produce a single unit. The direct labor hours to meet production requirements is then multiplied by the direct labor cost per hour to obtain budgeted total direct labor costs.

The Darcel Company
Direct Labor Budget
for the Year Ending December 31, 1992

	1 Qtr.	2 Qtr.	3 Qtr.	4 Qtr.	Total
Units to be produced	790	720	890	820	3,220
Direct labor hours per unit	× 5	× 5	× 5	× 5	× 5
Total hours	3,950	3,600	4,450	4,100	16,100
Direct labor cost per hour	× $5	× $5	× $5	× $5	× $5
Total direct labor cost	$19,750	$18,000	$22,250	$20,500	$80,500

THE FACTORY OVERHEAD BUDGET

The factory overhead budget should provide a schedule of all manufacturing costs other than direct materials and direct labor. Using the contribution approach to budgeting requires the development of a predetermined overhead rate for the variable portion of the factory overhead. In developing the cash budget, remember that depreciation does not entail a cash outlay. It must therefore be deducted from the total factory overhead when computing cash disbursement for factory overhead.

To illustrate the factory overhead budget, assume that total factory overhead is budgeted at $6,000 fixed (per quarter), plus $2 per hour of direct labor; depreciation expenses are $3,250 each quarter; and all overhead costs involving cash outlays are paid for in the quarter incurred.

The Darcel Company
Factory Overhead Budget
for the Year Ending December 31, 1992

	1 Qtr.	2 Qtr.	3 Qtr.	4 Qtr.	Total
Budgeted direct labor hours	3,950	3,600	4,450	4,100	16,100
Variable overhead rate	× $2	× $2	× $2	× $2	× $2
Variable overhead budgeted	$ 7,900	$ 7,200	$ 8,900	$ 8,200	$32,200
Fixed overhead budgeted	6,000	6,000	6,000	6,000	24,000
Total budgeted overhead	13,900	13,200	14,900	14,200	56,200
Less: Depreciation	3,250	3,250	3,250	3,250	13,000
Cash disbursement for overhead	$10,650	$ 9,950	$11,650	$10,950	$43,200

THE ENDING-INVENTORY BUDGET

The desired ending-inventory budget provides the information required for the construction of budgeted financial statements. Specifically, it will help compute the cost of goods sold on the budgeted income statement. It also will provide the dollar value of the ending materials and finished goods inventory that appear on the budgeted balance sheet.

The Darcel Company
Ending-Inventory Budget
for the Year Ending December 31, 1992

	Ending Inventory Units	Unit Cost	Total
Direct materials	250 pounds	$ 2	$ 500
Finished goods	100 units	$41*	$4,100

* The unit variable cost of $41 is computed as follows:

	Unit Cost	Unit	Total
Direct materials	$2	3 pounds	$ 6
Direct labor	5	5 hours	25
Variable overhead	2	5 hours	10
Total variable manufacturing cost			$41

THE SELLING AND ADMINISTRATIVE EXPENSE BUDGET

The selling and administrative expense budget lists the operating expenses involved in selling the products and in managing the business. In order to complete the budgeted income statement in contribution format, variable selling and administrative expense per unit must be computed.

The Darcel Company
Selling and Administrative Expense Budget
for the Year Ending December 31, 1992

	1 Qtr.	2 Qtr.	3 Qtr.	4 Qtr.	Total
Expected sales in units	800	700	900	800	3,200
Variable selling and admin. exp. per unit[*]	× $4	× $4	× $4	× $4	× $4
Budgeted variable expense	$ 3,200	$ 2,800	$3,600	$ 3,200	$12,800
Fixed selling and administrative expenses:					
Advertising	1,100	1,100	1,100	1,100	4,400
Insurance	2,800				2,800
Office salaries	8,500	8,500	8,500	8,500	34,000
Rent	350	350	350	350	1,400
Taxes			1,200		1,200
Total budgeted selling and administrative expenses[†]	$15,950	$12,750	$14,750	$13,150	$56,600

[*] Includes sales agents' commissions, shipping, and supplies
[†] Paid for in the quarter incurred

Financial Budget

THE CASH BUDGET

The cash budget is prepared for the purpose of cash planning and control. It presents the expected cash inflow and outflow for a designated time period. The cash budget helps management keep cash balances in reasonable relationship to the company's operating requirements. The objective of the budget is to avoid unnecessary idle cash and possible cash shortages.

The cash budget consists typically of four major sections:

(1) The receipts section, which is the beginning cash balance, cash collections from customers, and other receipts;

(2) The disbursements section, which comprises all cash payments made by purpose;

(3) The cash surplus or deficit section, which simply shows the difference between the cash-receipts section and the cash-disbursements section; and

(4) The financing section, which provides a detailed account of the borrowings and repayments expected during the budgeting period.

For illustrative purposes, the following assumptions will be made:

(1) The company desires to maintain a $5,000 minimum cash balance at the end of each quarter.
(2) All borrowing and repayment must be in multiples of $500 at an interest rate of 10% per annum.
(3) Interest is computed and paid as the principal is repaid.
(4) Borrowing takes place at the beginning of each quarter, and repayment is made at the end of each quarter.

The Darcel Company
Cash Budget
for the Year Ending December 31, 1992

	1 Qtr.	2 Qtr.	3 Qtr.	4 Qtr.	Total
Cash balance, beginning	10,000	9,401	5,461	9,106	10,000
Add: Receipts:					
Collection from customers	54,300	57,120	66,080	64,960	242,460
Total cash available	64,300	66,521	71,541	74,066	252,460
Less: Disbursements:					
Direct materials	4,549	4,560	4,860	5,113	19,082
Direct labor	19,750	18,000	22,250	20,500	80,500
Factory overhead	10,650	9,950	11,650	10,950	43,200
Selling and admin.	15,950	12,750	14,750	13,150	56,600
Machinery purchase	—	24,300	—	—	24,300
Income tax	4,000	—	—	—	4,000
Total disbursements	54,899	69,560	53,510	49,713	227,682
Cash surplus (deficit)	9,401	(3,039)	18,031	24,353	24,778
Financing:					
Borrowing	—	8,500	—	—	8,500
Repayment	—	—	(8,500)	—	(8,500)
Interest	—	—	(425)		(425)
Total financing	—	8,500	(8,925)	—	(425)
Cash balance, ending	9,401	5,461	9,106	24,353	24,353

Solved Problem 12.2. Cash Receipts

The following data is given for Erich Food Stores:

	September	October	November	December
Cash sales	$ 7,000	$ 6,000	$ 8,000	$ 6,000
Credit sales	50,000	48,000	62,000	80,000
Total sales	$57,000	$54,000	$70,000	$86,000

Past experience indicates that:

(1) No collections are made in the month of sale.
(2) 80% of the sales of any month are collected in the following month.
(3) 19% of sales are collected in the second following month.
(4) 1% of sales are uncollectible.

Calculate the total cash receipts for November and December.

Solution 12.2

	November	December
Cash receipts:		
Cash sales	$ 8,000	$ 6,000
Cash collections:		
September sales: $50,000 (19%)	9,500	
October sales: $48,000 (80%)	38,400	
$48,000 (19%)		9,120
November sales: $62,000 (80%)		49,600
Total cash receipts	$55,900	$64,720

The Budgeted Income Statement

The budgeted income statement summarizes the various revenue and expenses projections for the budgeting period. For control purposes, however, the budget can be divided into quarters or even months, depending on the need.

The Darcel Company
Budgeted Income Statement
for the Year Ending December 31, 1992

Sales (3,200 units @ $80)		$256,000
Less: Variable expenses		
Variable cost of goods sold		
(3,200 units @ $41)	$131,200	
Variable selling & admin.	12,800	144,000
Contribution margin		$112,000
Less: Fixed expenses		
Factory overhead	$ 24,000	
Selling and Admin.	43,800	67,800
Net operating income		$ 44,200
Less: Interest expense		425
Net income before taxes		$ 43,775
Less: Income taxes (20%)		8,755
Net income		$ 35,020

The Budgeted Balance Sheet

The budgeted balance sheet is developed by beginning with the balance sheet for the year just ended and adjusting it, using all the activities that are expected to take place during the budgeting period. Some of the reasons why the budgeted balance sheet must be prepared are:

(1) It could disclose some unfavorable financial conditions that management might want to avoid.
(2) It serves as a final check on the mathematical accuracy of all the other schedules.
(3) It helps management perform a variety of ratio calculations.
(4) It highlights future resources and obligations.

STANDARD COSTS AND VARIANCE ANALYSIS

Standard costs are costs that are established in advance to serve as targets to be met; after the fact, management will determine how well those targets were actually met. The standard cost is based on physical and dollar measures. It is determined by multiplying the standard quantity of an input by its standard price.

Variance analysis based on standard costs and flexible budgets would be a typical tool for control of a cost center such as a production department.

General Model for Variance Analysis

Two general types of variances can be calculated for most cost items: a *price variance* and a *quantity variance*.

The price variance is calculated as follows:

$$\text{Price variance} = (\text{Actual quantity}) \times (\text{Actual price} - \text{Standard price})$$
$$= AQ\ (AP - SP)$$

The quantity variance is calculated as follows:

$$\frac{\text{Quantity}}{\text{variance}} = \left(\frac{\text{Actual}}{\text{quantity}} - \frac{\text{Standard}}{\text{quantity}}\right) \times \frac{\text{Standard}}{\text{price}}$$
$$= (AQ - SQ)\ SP$$

It is important to note the following:

(1) A price variance and a quantity variance can be calculated for all three variable cost items: direct materials, direct labor, and the variable portion of factory overhead. The variance is not called by the same name, however. For example, a price variance is called a materials-

price variance in the case of direct materials, a labor-rate variance in the case of direct labor, and a variable overhead-spending variance in the case of variable overhead.

(2) A cost variance is unfavorable (U) if the actual price (AP) or actual quantity (AQ) exceeds the standard price (SP) or standard quantity (SQ); a variance is favorable (F) if the actual price or actual quantity is less than the standard price or standard quantity.

(3) The standard quantity allowed for output is the key concept in variance analysis. This is the standard quantity that should have been used to produce actual output. It is computed by multiplying the actual output by the number of input units allowed.

MATERIALS VARIANCES

A materials-price variance is isolated at the time the materials are purchased. The purchasing department is responsible for any materials-price variance. The production department is responsible for any materials-quantity variance that occurs.

Unfavorable price variances may be caused by inaccurate standard prices, inflationary cost increases, scarcity in raw material supplies resulting in higher prices, and purchasing-department inefficiencies. Unfavorable materials-quantity variances may be explained by poorly trained workers, improperly adjusted machines, or outright waste on the production line.

Solved Problem 12.3. Materials Variances

Dallas Manufacturing Corporation uses a standard cost system. The standard variable costs for product J are as follows:

> Materials: 2 pounds at $3 per pound
> Labor: 1 hour at $5 per hour
> Factory overhead: 1 hour at $3 per hour

During March, 25,000 pounds of materials were purchased for $74,750 and used in producing 10,000 units of finished product. Direct labor costs incurred were $49,896 (10,080 direct labor hours) and variable overhead costs incurred were $34,776.

Compute the materials variances.

Solution 12.3

$$
\begin{aligned}
\text{Materials-purchase-price variance} \; &= \; \text{AQ (AP} - \text{SP)} \\
&= \; (25{,}000 \text{ pounds}) \, (\$2.99^* - \$3.00) \\
&= \; (25{,}000 \text{ pounds}) \, (-\$0.01) \\
&= \; \$250 \text{ (F)}
\end{aligned}
$$

*$2.99 = $74,750 ÷ 25,000 pounds

Materials-quantity (usage) variance $= (AQ - SQ)\,SP$
$$= (25{,}000 \text{ pounds} - 20{,}000 \text{ pounds}^*)\ (\$3.00)$$
$$= (5{,}000 \text{ pounds})\ (\$3.00)$$
$$= \$15{,}000\ (U)$$

*20,000 pounds = 10,000 units of output $\times$ 2 pounds allowed

Solved Problem 12.4. Materials Variances

The standard cost sheet for Largo Tool Corp. showed the following material cost related to one unit of product:

$$4 \text{ pieces at } \$4 \text{ per piece} = \$16 \text{ per unit}$$

During February 1992, 10,000 units were produced. The costs recorded showed the following:

$$\text{Purchase and use of material: 41,000 pieces at } \$3.80$$

Determine the materials-price variance and materials-quantity (usage) variances.

Solution 12.4

Materials-purchase-price variance $= AQ\,(AP - SP)$
$$= (41{,}000 \text{ pieces})\ (\$3.80 - \$4.00)$$
$$= \$8{,}200\ (F)$$

Materials-quantity (usage) variance $= (AQ - SQ)\,SP$
$$= (41{,}000 - 40{,}000^*)\ (\$4.00)$$
$$= \$4{,}000\ (U)$$

*40,000 units = 10,000 output units $\times$ 4 pieces allowed

LABOR VARIANCES

Labor variances are calculated when labor is used for production. They are computed in a manner similar to the materials variances, except that the terms *efficiency* and *rate* are used in place of the terms *quantity* and *price*. The production department is responsible for both the price paid for labor services and the quantity of labor services used. Therefore the production department must explain why any labor variances occur.

Unfavorable rate variances may be explained by an increase in wages or the use of labor commanding higher wage rates than contemplated. Unfavorable efficiency variances may be explained by poor supervision, poor-quality workers, poor quality of materials requiring more labor time, or machine breakdowns.

Note: The symbols AQ, SQ, AP, and SP are changed to AH, SH, AR, and SR to reflect the terms "hour" and "rate."

Solved Problem 12.5. Labor Variances

Using the same data given in Solved Problem 12.3, compute the labor variances.

Solution 12.5

Labor-rate variance $\qquad$ = AH (AR – SR)
$\qquad\qquad\qquad\qquad$ = (10,080 hours) ($4.95* – $5.00)
$\qquad\qquad\qquad\qquad$ = $48,888 – $50,400
$\qquad\qquad\qquad\qquad$ = $512 (F)

*$4.95 = $49,896 ÷ 10,080 hours

Labor-efficiency variance $\qquad$ = (AH – SH) SR
$\qquad\qquad\qquad\qquad$ = (10,080 hours – 10,000 hours) ($5.00)
$\qquad\qquad\qquad\qquad$ = $50,400 – $50,000
$\qquad\qquad\qquad\qquad$ = $400 (U)

Solved Problem 12.6. Labor Variances.

The standard cost sheet for York Steel Corp. shows the following cost for a unit of product:

Direct labor: 2¾ hours at $7 an hour

During February 1992, 10,000 units were completed. The actual cost incurred was

28,000 hours at $8 per hour = $224,000

Determine the labor-rate variance and labor-efficiency variance.

Solution 12.6

Labor-rate variance $\qquad$ = AH (AR – SR)
$\qquad\qquad\qquad\qquad$ = (28,000 hours) ($8.00 – $7.00)
$\qquad\qquad\qquad\qquad$ = $28,000 (U)

Labor-efficiency variance $\qquad$ = (AH – SH) SR
$\qquad\qquad\qquad\qquad$ = (28,000 hours – 27,500 hours*) ($7.00)
$\qquad\qquad\qquad\qquad$ = $3,500 (U)

*27,500 hours = 10,000 units × 2¾ hours allowed

VARIABLE OVERHEAD VARIANCES

The variable overhead variances are computed in a way very similar to the labor variances. The production department is usually responsible for any variable overhead variance that might occur. Unfavorable variable overhead-spending variances may be caused by a large number of factors: acquiring supplies for a price different from the standard, using more supplies than expected, waste, and theft of supplies. Unfavorable variable overhead-efficiency variances might be caused by such factors as poorly trained workers, poor-quality materials, faulty equipment, work interruptions, poor production scheduling, poor supervision, and employee unrest.

When variable overhead is applied using direct labor hours, the efficiency variance will be caused by the same factors that cause the labor-efficiency variance. However, when variable overhead is applied using machine hours, inefficiency in machinery will cause a variable overhead-efficiency variance.

Solved Problem 12.7. Variable Overhead Variances

Using the same data given in Solved Problem 12.3, compute the variable overhead variances.

Solution 12.7

$$
\begin{aligned}
\text{Variable overhead-spending variance} &= \text{AH (AR - SR)} \\
&= (10{,}080 \text{ hours}) (\$3.45^* - \$3.00) \\
&= \$34{,}776 - \$30{,}240 \\
&= \$4{,}536 \text{ (U)}
\end{aligned}
$$

*$3.45 = $34,776 ÷ 10,080 hours

$$
\begin{aligned}
\text{Variable overhead-efficiency variance} &= \text{(AH - SH) SR} \\
&= (10{,}080 \text{ hours} - 10{,}000 \text{ hours}^*) \times \$3.00 \\
&= \$30{,}240 - \$30{,}000 \\
&= \$240 \text{ (U)}
\end{aligned}
$$

*10,000 hours = 10,000 units of output × 1 hour allowed

Solved Problem 12.8. Variable Overhead Variances

Variable overhead standards per finished unit for Century Metals Company are as follows: 10 hours at $2.00 per direct labor hour. During October 5,000 units were produced. Direct labor hours used were 52,000 hours. Actual variable overhead costs were $109,200. Determine the spending and efficiency variances for variable overhead.

Solution 12.8

$$
\begin{aligned}
\text{Variable overhead-spending variance} &= \text{AH (AR - SR)} \\
&= (52{,}000 \text{ hours}) (\$2.10^* - \$2.00) \\
&= (52{,}000 \text{ hours}) (\$0.10) \\
&= \$5{,}200 \text{ (U)}
\end{aligned}
$$

*$2.10 = $109,200 ÷ 52,000 hours

$$
\begin{aligned}
\text{Variable overhead-efficiency variance} &= \text{(AH - SH) SR} \\
&= (52{,}000 \text{ hours} - 50{,}000 \text{ hours}^*) \times \$2.00 \\
&= 2{,}000 \text{ hours} \times \$2.00 \\
&= \$4{,}000 \text{ (U)}
\end{aligned}
$$

*50,000 hours = 5,000 units of output × 10 hours allowed

Flexible Budgets and Performance Reports

A flexible budget is a tool that is extremely useful in cost control.

The budget, which was discussed at the beginning of the chapter, is static and inflexible in that it is geared toward a single level of activity. In contrast, the flexible budget is characterized as follows:

(1) It is geared toward a range of activity rather than a single level of activity.

(2) It is dynamic in nature rather than static. By using the cost-volume formula (or flexible budget formula), a series of budgets can be easily developed for various levels of activity.

The static (fixed) budget is geared for only one level of activity and has problems in cost control. Flexible budgeting distinguishes between fixed and variable costs, thus allowing for a budget that can be automatically adjusted (via changes in variable cost totals) to the particular level of activity actually attained. Thus variances between actual costs and budgeted costs are adjusted for volume ups and downs before differences due to price and quantity factors are computed.

The primary use of the flexible budget is to accurately measure performance by comparing actual costs for a given output with the budgeted costs for the same level of output.

To illustrate the difference between the static budget and the flexible budget, assume that the assembly department of Kato Industries, Inc. is budgeted to produce 6,000 units during June. Assume further that the company was able to produce only 5,800 units. The budget for direct labor and variable overhead costs is as follows:

Kato Industries, Inc.
Assembly Department
The Direct Labor and Variable Overhead Budget
for the Month of June

Budgeted production	6,000 units
Direct labor	$39,000
Variable overhead costs:	
Indirect labor	6,000
Supplies	900
Repairs	300
	$46,200

If a static budget approach is used, the performance report will appear as follows:

Kato Industries, Inc.
Assembly Department
The Direct Labor and Variable Overhead Budget
For the Month of June

	Budget	Actual	Variance (U or F)
Production in units	6,000	5,800	200(U)
Direct labor	$39,000	$38,500	$500(F)
Variable overhead costs:			
Indirect labor	6,000	5,950	50(F)
Supplies	900	870	30(F)
Repairs	300	295	5(F)
	$46,200	$45,615	$585(F)

These cost variances are not helpful; the problem is that the budget costs are based on an activity level of 6,000 units, whereas the actual costs were incurred at an activity level below this (5,800 units). From a control standpoint, it makes no sense to compare costs at one activity level with costs at a different activity level. Such comparisons would make a production manager look good as long as the actual production is less than the budgeted production. Using the cost-volume formula and generating the budget based on the 5,800 actual units gives the following performance report:

Kato Industries, Inc.
Assembly Department
Performance Report
for the Month of June

Budgeted production		6,000 units
Actual production		5,800 units

	Cost-Volume Formula	Budget 5,800 units	Actual 5,800 units	Variance (U or F)
Direct labor	$6.50 per unit*	$37,700	$38,500	$800(U)
Variable overhead:				
Indirect labor	1.00	5,800	5,950	150(U)
Supplies	0.15	870	870	0
Repairs	0.05	290	295	5(U)
	$7.70	$44,660	$45,615	$955(U)

*Per unit cost = Budgeted cost ÷ budgeted production (i.e., $39,000 ÷ 6,000 units for direct labor).

Notice that all cost variances are unfavorable (U), as compared to the favorable cost variances on the performance report based on the static budget approach.

Solved Problem 12.9. Flexible Budget

The following shows factory overhead budget information for Los Alamitos, Inc. for the year 1992:

Indirect materials used	$0.50 per machine hour plus $6,000 fixed cost
Indirect labor	$92,000 fixed cost
Power	$0.95 per machine hour
Repairs and maintenance	$1.50 per machine hour plus $2,100 fixed cost
Depreciation	$9,500 fixed cost
Rent	$12,000 fixed cost

In 1992, the company operated at 11,000 machine hours and incurred the following overhead costs:

Indirect materials used	$11,700
Indirect labor	91,000
Power	10,650
Repairs and maintenance	19,200
Depreciation	9,500
Rent	12,500

Compare the flexible budget with the actual overhead, computing a variance for each item and for the total overhead. Indicate whether variances are favorable (F) or unfavorable (U).

Solution 12.9

	Budget (11,000 hours)	Actual (11,000 hours)	Variance (U or F)
Indirect materials used	$ 11,500	$ 11,700	$ 200 (U)
Indirect labor	92,000	91,000	1,000 (F)
Power	10,450	10,650	200 (U)
Repairs and maintenance	18,600	19,200	600 (U)
Depreciation	9,500	9,500	—
Rent	12,000	12,500	500 (U)
Total	$154,050	$154,550	$ 500 (U)

FIXED OVERHEAD VARIANCES

In order to calculate variances for fixed overhead, it is necessary to determine a standard fixed overhead rate. The standard rate is determined by dividing the standard (budgeted) fixed overhead costs by the standard amount of productive capacity, generally expressed in direct labor hours or machine hours.

The fixed overhead variance is divided into fixed overhead spending (flexible budget) variance and fixed overhead volume (capacity) variance.

(a) Fixed overhead spending variance is the difference between actual fixed overhead and budgeted fixed overhead. This variance is caused solely by events such as unexpected changes in prices and unforeseen repairs.

(b) Fixed overhead volume (capacity) variance. This variance results when the actual level of activity differs from the standard level of activity used in determining the standard fixed overhead rate. The fixed overhead volume variance is a measure of the cost of failure to operate at budgeted activity level, and may be caused by such factors as failure to meet sales targets, idleness due to poor scheduling, and machine breakdowns. The volume variance is calculated as follows:

Fixed overhead volume variance = (Budgeted activity – standard hours allowed for amount produced) × (standard fixed overhead rate)

When budgeted activity exceeds standard hours allowed for actual output, the volume variance is unfavorable (U), because it is an index of less-than-normal utilization of capacity. Note that there are no efficiency variances for fixed overhead. Fixed overhead does not change regardless of whether productive resources are used efficiently or not.

Solved Problem 12.10. Fixed Overhead Variances

The Quality Manufacturing Company has the following standard costs of factory overhead at a normal monthly production volume of 1,300 direct labor hours:

Fixed overhead (1 hour @ $5)

Fixed overhead budgeted is $6,500 per month. During the month of March, the following events occurred:

(1) Actual fixed overhead costs incurred were $6,750.

(2) Standard hour allowed for actual output: 1,250 hours (1 hour × 1,250 units of actual output).

Compute the fixed overhead spending and volume variances.

Solution 12.10

Fixed overhead spending variance (Actual fixed overhead – Budgeted fixed overhead)
= $6,750 – $6,500 = $250 (U).

Fixed overhead volume variance can be calculated as follows:

Fixed overhead volume variance
= (Budgeted activity – standard hours allowed for amount produced)
× (Standard fixed overhead rate) = (1,300 hours – 1,250 hours) × $5
= 50 hours × $5 = $250 (U)

A budget is a detailed quantitative plan outlining the acquisition and use of an organization's financial and material resources over a specific time period. It is a tool for planning. If properly constructed, it can be used as a control device. The process of formulating a master budget begins with the development of a sales budget and proceeds through a number of steps that ultimately lead to the cash budget, the budgeted income statement, and the budgeted balance sheet.

Variance analysis is essential for the appraisal of all aspects of a business. This chapter looked at the control of cost centers through standard costs. It discussed the basic mechanics of how the two major variances—the price variance and the quantity variance—are calculated for direct materials, direct labor, variable overhead, and fixed overhead. The flexible budget was emphasized in an attempt to correctly measure the efficiency of the cost center. Chapter 13 discusses responsibility accounting.

13

Responsibility Accounting

*R*esponsibility accounting is the system for collecting and reporting revenue and cost information by areas of responsibility. It operates on the premise that managers should be held responsible for their performance, the performance of their subordinates, and all activities within their responsibility center. Responsibility accounting, also called profitability accounting or activity accounting, has the following advantages:

(1) It facilitates delegation of decision making.

(2) It helps management promote the concept of management by objective. In management by objective, managers agree on a set of goals. The manager's performance is then evaluated based on his or her attainment of these goals.

(3) It provides a guide to the evaluation of performance and helps to establish standards of performance, which are then used for comparison purposes.

(4) It permits effective use of the concept of management by exception, which means that the manager's attention is concentrated on important deviations from standards and budgets.

RESPONSIBILITY ACCOUNTING SYSTEMS

An effective responsibility accounting system requires the following three basic conditions:

(1) The organization structure must be well defined. Management responsibility and authority must go hand in hand at all levels and must be clearly established and understood.

(2) Standards of performance in revenues, costs, and investments must be properly determined and well defined.

(3) The responsibility accounting reports (or performance reports) should include only those items that are controllable by the manager of the responsibility center. Also, they should highlight items calling for managerial attention.

Responsibility Centers

A well-designed responsibility accounting system establishes responsibility centers within the organization. A responsibility center is defined as a unit in the organization that has control over costs, revenues, and/or investment funds. Responsibility centers can be one of three types: *cost center*, *profit center*, or *investment center*.

COST CENTER

A cost center is the unit within the organization responsible only for costs. Examples include production and maintenance departments of a manufacturing company. Variance analysis based on standard costs and flexible budgets is a typical performance measure of a cost center. Variance analysis was discussed in Chapter 12.

PROFIT CENTER

A profit center is the unit held responsible for the revenues earned and costs incurred in that center. Examples include a sales office of a publishing company, the appliance department in a retail store, and an auto repair center in a department store. The contribution approach to cost allocation is widely used to measure the performance of a profit center.

INVESTMENT CENTER

An investment center is the unit within the organization responsible for the costs, revenues, and related investments made in that center. The division in a large decentralized organization such as the Cadillac Division of General Motors is an example of an investment center.

Figure 13.1 illustrates the manners in which responsibility accounting can be used within an organization and shows responsibility centers. This chapter discusses in detail how the performance of both profit and investment centers are evaluated.

Figure 13.1. Responsibility Centers Within a Company.

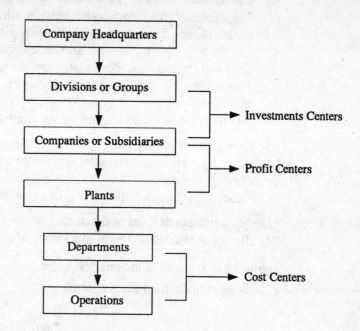

CONTROL OF PROFIT CENTERS

Segmented reporting is the process of reporting activities of profit centers such as divisions, product lines, or sales territories.

The contribution approach is widely used for segmented reporting because it emphasizes the cost behavior patterns and the controllability of costs that are generally useful for profitability analysis of various segments of an organization.

Contribution Approach for Profit Centers

The contribution approach is based on the following assumptions:

(1) Fixed costs are much less controllable than variable costs.

(2) Direct fixed costs and common fixed costs must be clearly distinguished. Direct fixed costs are those fixed costs that can be directly identified with a particular segment of an organization, whereas common fixed costs are those costs that cannot be directly identified.

(3) Common fixed costs should be clearly identified as *unallocated* in the income statement. Any attempt to allocate these types of costs, on some arbitrary basis, to the segments of the organization can destroy the value of responsibility accounting. It would lead to unfair evaluation of performance and misleading managerial decisions.

The following concepts are highlighted in the contribution approach:

(1) Contribution margin: Sales minus variable costs.
(2) Segment margin: Contribution margin minus direct (traceable) fixed costs. Direct fixed costs include discretionary fixed costs such as certain advertising, research and development (R & D), sales promotion, and engineering. They also include such traceable and committed fixed costs as depreciation, property taxes, insurance and the segment managers' salaries.
(3) Net income: Segment margin minus unallocated common fixed costs.

Segmented reporting can be made by division, product or product line, sales territory, service center, salesperson, store or branch office, or domestic or foreign operations.

Figure 13.2 illustrates two levels of segmented reporting:

(1) By segments defined as divisions.
(2) By segments defined as product lines of a division.

Figure 13.2. Segmented Income Statement.

(1) Segments Defined as Divisions

	Total Company	Segments Division 1	Segments Division 2
Sales	$150,000	$90,000	$60,000
Less: Variable costs			
Manufacturing	$ 40,000	$30,000	$10,000
Selling and administrative	20,000	14,000	6,000
Total variable costs	$ 60,000	$44,000	$16,000
Contribution margin	$ 90,000	$46,000	$44,000
Less: Direct fixed costs	70,000	43,000	27,000
Divisional segment margin	$ 20,000	$ 3,000	$17,000
Less: Unallocated common fixed costs	10,000		
Net income	$ 10,000		

(2) Segments Defined as Product Lines of Division 2

	Division 2	Segments Deluxe Model	Segments Regular Model
Sales	$60,000	$20,000	$40,000
Less: Variable costs			
Manufacturing	$10,000	$ 5,000	$ 5,000
Selling and administrative	6,000	2,000	4,000
Total variable costs	$16,000	$ 7,000	$ 9,000
Contribution margin	$44,000	$13,000	$31,000
Less: Direct fixed costs	26,500	9,500	17,000
Product line margin	$17,500	$ 3,500	$14,000
Less: Unallocated common fixed costs	500		
Divisional segment margin	$17,000		

The segment margin is the best measure of the profitability of a segment. Unallocated fixed costs are common to the segments being evaluated and should be left unallocated in order not to distort the performance results of segments.

Solved Problem 13.1. Segmented Income Statement

From the following data, prepare a segmented income statement for the Christian Company for 1991.

	Total	Divisions Alpha	Divisions Beta
Sales	$500,000	$200,000	$300,000
Direct fixed costs:	$185,000	$ 85,000	$100,000
Variable costs:			
Manufacturing	210,000	100,000	110,000
Selling and administrative	70,000	35,000	35,000
Unallocated fixed costs:			
Manufacturing	20,000	—	—
Selling and administrative	10,000	—	—

Solution 13.1

The Christian Company
Segmented Income Statement
Divisions

	Total Company	Segments Alpha	Segments Beta
Sales	$500,000	$200,000	$300,000
Less: Variable costs			
Manufacturing	$210,000	$100,000	$110,000
Selling and admin.	70,000	35,000	35,000
Total variable costs	$280,000	$135,000	$145,000
Contribution margin	$220,000	$ 65,000	$155,000
Less: Direct fixed costs	185,000	85,000	100,000
Divisional segment margin	$ 35,000	$ (20,000)	$ 55,000
Less: Unallocated common fixed costs	30,000		
Net income	$ 5,000		

CONTROL OF INVESTMENT CENTERS

The ability to measure the performance of an investment center is essential in developing management incentives, controlling an operation, and achieving organizational goals. A typical decentralized subunit is an investment center which is responsible for an organization's invested capital and the related operating income. There are two widely used measurements of performance for the investment center: the *rate of return on investment* (ROI) and *residual income* (RI).

Rate of Return on Investment (ROI)

The ROI relates operating income to invested capital. Specifically,

$$\text{ROI} = \frac{\text{Operating income}}{\text{Invested assets}}$$

Solved Problem 13.2. Return on Investment

Consider the following financial data for a division:

Operating income	$ 18,000
Invested assets	100,000

Compute the ROI.

Solution 13.2

$$ROI = \$18,000 \div \$100,000 = 18\%$$

The problem with this formula is that it only indicates how a division did and how well it fared in the company. Other than that, it has very little value from the standpoint of profit planning.

THE BREAKDOWN OF ROI—DU PONT FORMULA

In the past, managers have tended to focus only on the margin earned and have ignored the turnover of assets. However, excessive funds tied up in assets can be just as much of a drag on profitability as excessive expenses.

The Du Pont Corporation was the first major company to recognize the importance of looking at both margin and asset turnover in assessing the performance of an investment center. The ROI breakdown, known as the Du Pont formula, is expressed as a product of these two factors, as shown below:

$$ROI = \frac{\text{Operating Income}}{\text{Invested Assets}} = \frac{\text{Operating Income}}{\text{Sales}} \times \frac{\text{Sales}}{\text{Invested Assets}}$$

$$= \text{Margin} \times \text{Asset Turnover}$$

The Du Pont formula combines the income statement and balance sheet into this otherwise static measure of performance. Margin is a measure of profitability or operating efficiency. It is the percentage of profit earned on sales. This percentage shows how much profit is made on each dollar of sales. On the other hand, asset turnover measures how well a division manages its assets. It is the number of times by which the investment in assets turns over each year to generate sales.

The breakdown of ROI is based on the thesis that the profitability of a firm is directly related to management's ability to manage assets efficiently and to control expenses effectively.

Solved Problem 13.3. Return on Investment

Assume the same data as in Solved Problem 13.2. Also assume sales of $200,000. Compute the ROI.

Solution 13.3

$$ROI = \frac{\text{Operating income}}{\text{Invested assets}} = \frac{\$18,000}{\$100,000} = 18\%$$

Alternatively,

$$\text{Margin} = \frac{\text{Operating income}}{\text{Sales}} = \frac{\$18,000}{\$200,000} = 9\%$$

$$\text{Turnover} = \frac{\text{Sales}}{\text{Invested assets}} = \frac{\$200,000}{\$100,000} = 2$$

Therefore,

$$\text{ROI} = \text{Margin} \times \text{Turnover} = 9\% \times 2 = 18\%.$$

The breakdown provides division managers with insight on how to improve profitability of an investment center. Specifically, it has several advantages over the original formula for profit planning:

(1) The importance of turnover as a key to overall return on investment is emphasized in the breakdown. In fact, turnover is just as important as profit margin in enhancing overall return.

(2) The importance of sales is explicitly recognized, though not in the original formula.

(3) The breakdown stresses the possibility of trading one measure off for the other in an attempt to improve the overall performance of a company. Margin and turnover complement each other. In other words, a low turnover can be made up for by a high margin and vice versa.

The breakdown of ROI into its two components shows that a number of combinations of margin and turnover can yield the same rate of return, as shown below:

	Margin	×	Turnover	=	ROI
(1)	9%	×	2	=	18%
(2)	6	×	3	=	18
(3)	3	×	6	=	18
(4)	2	×	9	=	18

The margin–turnover relationship and its resulting ROI is illustrated in Figure 13.3.

Figure 13.3. The Margin–Turnover Relationship.

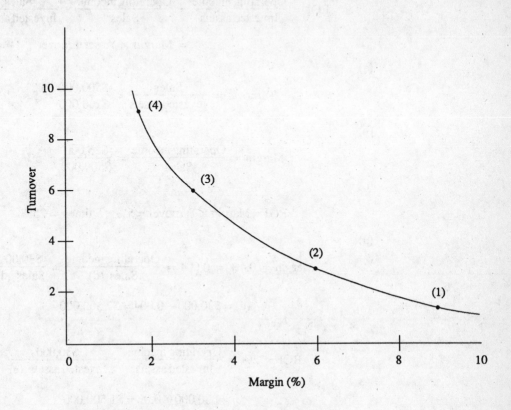

Solved Problem 13.4. Determination of Missing Items

XYZ Corporation has three divisions, whose income statements and balance sheets are summarized below:

	Division X	Division Y	Division Z
Sales	$500,000	(d)	(g)
Operating Income	$ 25,000	$30,000	(h)
Invested Assets	$100,000	(e)	$250,000
Turnover	(a)	(f)	0.4
Margin	(b)	0.4%	5%
Return on Investment (ROI)	(c)	2%	(i)

(1) Supply the missing data in the table above and summarize the results.
(2) Comment on the relative performance of each division. What questions can be raised as a result of the performance of the divisions?

Solution 13.4

(1)

$$ROI = \frac{Operating\,income}{Invested\,assets} = \frac{Operating\,income}{Sales} \times \frac{Sales}{Invested\,assets}$$

$$= Margin \times Asset\,turnover$$

(a)

$$Turnover = \frac{Sales}{Invested\,assets} = \frac{\$500,000}{\$100,000} = 5$$

(b)

$$Margin = \frac{Operating\,income}{Sales} = \frac{\$25,000}{\$500,000} = 5\%$$

(c)

$$ROI = Margin \times Turnover = 5\% \times 5\,times = 25\%$$

(d)

$$Margin = 0.4\% = 0.004 = \frac{Operating\,income}{Sales\,(d)} = \frac{\$30,000}{Sales\,(d)}$$

$$(d) = \$30,000 \div 0.004 = \$7,500,000$$

(e)

$$ROI = 2\% = \frac{Operating\,income}{Invested\,assets} = \frac{\$30,000}{Invested\,assets\,(e)}$$

$$(e) = \$30,000 \div 0.02 = \$1,500,000$$

(f)

$$Turnover = (d) \div (e) = \$7,500,000 \div \$1,500,000 = 5$$

(g)

$$Turnover = 0.4 = \frac{Sales\,(g)}{\$250,000}$$

$$(g) = 0.4 \times \$250,000 = \$100,000$$

(h)

$$Margin = 5\% = \frac{Operating\,income\,(h)}{Sales\,(g)} = \frac{(h)}{\$100,000}$$

$$(h) = 0.05 \times \$100,000 = \$5,000$$

(i)

$$ROI = 0.4 \times 5\% = 2\% \quad or \quad \$5,000 \div \$250,000 = 2\%$$

Summarizing the results gives:

	Division X	Division Y	Division Z
Turnover	5 times	5 times	0.4 times
Margin	5%	0.4%	5%
ROI	25%	2%	2%

(2) Division X enjoyed the best performance. It appears that divisions Y and Z are in trouble. Division Y turns over its assets as often as division X, but Y 's margin on sales is much lower. Thus division Y must work on improving its margin. The following questions are raised about division Y: Is the low margin due to inefficiency? Is it due to excessive overhead costs? Division Z, on the other hand, does just as well as division X in terms of profit margin: Both divisions earn 5% on sales. But division Z has a much lower turnover of capital than division X. Therefore division Z should take a close look at its investment. Is too much money tied up in receivables and inventories? Are there unused fixed assets? Is there idle cash not producing investment income?

Residual Income (RI)

Another approach to measuring performance in an investment center is residual income (RI). RI is the operating income that an investment center is able to earn above some minimum rate of return on its invested assets. RI, unlike ROI, is an absolute amount of income rather than a specific rate of return. When RI is used to evaluate divisional performance, the objective is to maximize the total amount of residual income, not to maximize the overall ROI figure.

RI = Operating income − (Minimum required rate of return × Invested assets)

Solved Problem 13.5. Residual Income

In Solved Problem 13.2, assume the minimum required rate of return is 13%. Compute the residual income of the division.

Solution 13.5

$$\$18,000 - (13\% \times \$100,000) = \$18,000 - \$13,000 = \$5,000$$

Solved Problem 13.6. Residual Income

The following data is given for the Key West division for 1991:

Return on investment (ROI)	25%
Sales	$1,200,000
Margin	10%
Minimum required rate of return	18%

(1)   Compute the division's invested assets.
(2)   Compute the division's residual income (RI).

Solution 13.6

(1)

$$\text{By definition, ROI} = \text{Margin} \times \text{Turnover.}$$
$$\text{Thus, } 25\% = 10\% \times \text{Turnover.}$$
$$\text{Turnover} = 25\% \div 10\% = 2.5$$

$$\text{Turnover} = 2.5 \text{ times} = \frac{\text{Sales}}{\text{Invested assets}} = \frac{\$1,200,000}{\text{Invested assets}}$$

Therefore invested assets = $\$1,200,000 \div 2.5 = \$480,000$

(2)

$$\text{RI} = (\text{Operating income}) - (\text{Minimum required rate of return} \times \text{Invested assets})$$

$$\text{Margin} = 10\% = 0.1 = \frac{\text{Operating income}}{\text{Sales}} = \frac{\text{Operating income}}{1,200,000}$$

Operating income = $0.1 \times \$1,200,000 = \$120,000$

RI = $\$120,000 - (18\% \times \$480,000) = \$120,000 - \$86,400 = \$33,600$

Solved Problem 13.7. ROI and Residual Income

Consider the following:

	Division A	Division B
	(Thousands of dollars)	
Invested assets	$5,000	$12,500
Operating income	$1,000	$ 2,250
ROI	20%	18%

(1)   Which division is the more successful in terms of ROI?
(2)   Using 16% as the minimum required ROI, compute the residual income for each division. Which division is more successful under this rate?

Solution 13.7

(1)   Division A is more successful, since it returns $0.20 for each dollar invested (compared to $0.18 for division B).
(2)   The residual income at 16% for each division is computed as follows:

	Division A		Division B	
	(Thousands of dollars)			
Operating income	$1,000		$2,250	
Minimum required income	800	(16% × $5,000)	2,000	(16% × $12,500)
RI	$ 200		$ 250	

Division B is more successful.

Solved Problem 13.8. Missing Information

Supply the missing data in the following table:

	Division A	Division B	Division C
Sales	$60,000	$75,000	$100,000
Operating income	(a)	$25,000	(e)
Invested assets	$30,000	(c)	$ 50,000
Return on investment (ROI)	15%	10%	20%
Minimum required rate of return	10%	(d)	(f)
Residual income (RI)	(b)	$ 5,000	0

Solution 13.8

$$ROI = \frac{Operating\ income}{Invested\ assets}$$

$$RI = (Operating\ income) - (Minimum\ required\ rate\ of\ return \times Invested\ assets)$$

(a)

$$ROI = 15\% = \frac{Operating\ income\ (a)}{\$30,000}$$

$$(a) = 15\% \times \$30,000 = \$4,500$$

(b)

$$RI = \$4,500 - (10\% \times \$30,000) = \$4,500 - \$3,000 = \$1,500$$

(c)

$$ROI = 10\% = \frac{\$25,000}{Invested\ assets\ (c)}$$

$$(c) = \$25,000 \div 10\% = \$250,000$$

(d)

$$RI = \$25,000 - [Minimum\ required\ return\ (d) \times \$250,000] = \$5,000$$

$$\$20,000 = (d) \times \$250,000$$

$$(d) = 8\%$$

(e)

$$ROI = 20\% = \frac{\text{Operating income (e)}}{\$50,000}$$

$$(e) = 20\% \times \$50,000 = \$10,000$$

(f)

$$RI = \$0 = \$10,000 - [\text{Minimum required return (f)} \times \$50,000]$$

$$(f) = 20\%$$

RI is regarded as a better measure of performance than ROI because it encourages investment in projects that would be rejected under ROI. A major disadvantage of RI, however, is that it cannot be used to compare divisions of different sizes. RI tends to favor the larger divisions due to the larger amount of dollars involved.

*T*he contribution approach attempts to measure the performance of segments *of an organization. It classifies costs as being either direct (traceable) or common to the segments. Only those costs that are directly identified with the segments are allocated; costs that are not direct to the segments are treated as common costs and are not allocated.*

Under the contribution approach we deduct variable costs from sales to arrive at the contribution margin. The direct fixed costs are then deducted from the contribution margin, yielding a segment margin. The segment margin is a performance measure for profit centers that is also useful for long-term planning and overall decision making.

A measure for investment centers is the rate of return on investment (ROI). An emphasis was placed on the breakdown of the ROI formula, commonly referred to as the Du Pont formula. The breakdown formula has several advantages over the original formula in terms of profit planning. An additional measure of investment center performance, the residual income (RI), is the operating income that an investment center is able to earn above some minimum rate of return on its invested assets.

14

Analysis of Short-Term and Capital Budgeting Decisions

*T*hroughout the manufacturing and selling functions, management needs to choose between alternative courses of action. Typical choices include: What products should the company make? How should they be produced? Where should the products be sold? What price should be charged? In the short run, management typically faces many short-term, nonroutine types of decisions. In these short-term situations, fixed costs are generally irrelevant to the decision at hand. Managerial accountants recognize as major decision tools two important concepts: relevant costs and contribution margin. (Contribution margin was discussed in Chapter 11.)

In the long run, capital budgeting is the process of making long-term planning decisions for alternative investment opportunities. Companies may make investment decisions in order to grow.

RELEVANT COSTS

For each of the above choices, management decisions ultimately rest on cost-data analysis. Cost data are the basis for profit calculations. Cost data are classified by function, behavior patterns, and other criteria, as discussed previously.

However, not all costs are of equal importance in decision making; managers must identify those costs that are relevant to a decision. Such costs are called relevant costs. The relevant costs are the expected future costs (and also revenues) that differ between the decision alternatives. Therefore, sunk costs (past and historical costs) are not considered relevant in the decision at hand. What is relevant are the incremental or differential costs.

Under the concept of relevant costs, which also may be titled the incremental, differential, or relevant cost approach, the decision involves the following steps:

(1) Gather all costs associated with each alternative.
(2) Drop the sunk costs.
(3) Drop those costs that do not differ between alternatives.
(4) Select the best alternative based on the remaining cost data.

Pricing a Special Order

A company often receives a short-term special order for its products at lower prices than usual. In normal economic times, the company may refuse such an order, since it will not yield a satisfactory profit. If times are bad, however, such an order should be accepted if the incremental revenue obtained from it exceeds the incremental costs involved. The company is better off to receive some revenue, above its incremental costs, than to receive nothing at all.

Such a price, one lower than the regular price, is called a contribution price. This approach to pricing is often called the contribution approach to pricing or the variable pricing model.

This approach is most appropriate under the following conditions:

(1) when operating in a distress situation;
(2) when there is idle capacity; and
(3) when faced with sharp competition or in a competitive bidding situation.

Solved Problem 14.1. Contribution Margin Income Statement

Assume that a company with 100,000-unit capacity is currently producing and selling only 90,000 units of product each year at a regular price of $2. If the variable cost per unit is $1 and the annual fixed cost is $45,000, prepare the contribution-income statement.

Solution 14.1

Sales (90,000 units)	$180,000	$2.00
Less: Variable cost		
(90,000 units)	90,000	1.00
Contribution margin	$ 90,000	$1.00
Less: Fixed cost	45,000	0.50
Net income	$ 45,000	$0.50

Solved Problem 14.2. Acceptance of a Special Order

The company in Solved Problem 14.1 has just received an order that calls for 10,000 units at $1.20, for a total of $12,000. The acceptance of this order will not affect regular sales. The company's president is reluctant to accept the order, however, because the $1.20 price is below the $1.50 factory unit cost (the $1.00 variable cost + $0.50 fixed cost). Should the company accept the order?

Solution 14.2

The answer is yes. The company can add to total profits by accepting this special order, even though the price offered is below the unit factory cost. At a price of $1.20, the order will contribute $0.20 per unit (CM per unit = $1.20 – $1.00 = $0.20) toward fixed cost, and profits will increase by $2,000 (10,000 units × $0.20).

Using the contribution approach to pricing, the variable cost of $1 will be a better guide than the full unit cost of $1.50. Note that the fixed costs do not change because of the presence of idle capacity.

Solved Problem 14.3. Acceptance of a Special Order

The Spartan Manufacturing Company has an annual plant capacity of 25,000 units. Predicted data on sales and costs are given below:

Sales (20,000 units @ $50)	$1,000,000
Manufacturing costs:	
Variable	
(materials, labor, and overhead)	$40 per unit
Fixed overhead	$30,000
Selling and administrative expenses;	
Variable	
(sales commission – $1 per unit)	$2 per unit
Fixed	$7,000

A special order has been received for 4,000 units at a selling price of $45 each. The order will have no effect on regular sales. The usual sales commission on this order will be reduced by half.

Should the company accept the order? Show supporting computations.

Solution 14.3

Incremental revenue (4,000 units @ $45)		$180,000
Less: Incremental costs		
Variable manufacturing		
(4,000 units @ $40)	$160,000	
Variable selling and administrative		
(4,000 @ $1.50*)	6,000	166,000
Incremental gain		$ 14,000

*$1.50 = ½ the sales commission + $1.00 = $0.50 + $1.00

The company should accept the order since it will add $14,000 to total profits.

The Make-or-Buy Decision

The decision whether to produce a component part internally or to buy it externally from an outside supplier is called a make-or-buy decision. This decision involves both quantitative and qualitative factors. The qualitative factors include concerns about product quality and the importance of long-term business relationships with a supplier. The quantitative factors deal with cost. The quantitative effects of the make-or-buy decision are best seen through the relevant cost approach.

Solved Problem 14.4. Make or Buy

Assume that a firm has prepared the following cost estimates for the manufacture of a subassembly component based on an annual production of 8,000 units:

	Per Unit	Total
Direct materials	$ 5	$ 40,000
Direct labor	4	32,000
Variable Factory Overhead Applied	4	32,000
Fixed factory overhead applied		
(150% of direct labor cost)	6	48,000
Total cost	$19	$152,000

The supplier has offered to provide the subassembly at a price of $16 each. Two-thirds of fixed factory overhead, which represents executive salaries, rent, depreciation, and taxes, continue, regardless of the decision. Should the company buy or make the product?

Solution 14.4

The key to the decision lies in the investigation of those relevant costs that change between the make-or-buy alternatives. Assuming that the productive capacity will be idle if not used to produce the subassembly, the analysis takes the following form:

	Per Unit		Total of 8,000 Units	
	Make	**Buy**	**Make**	**Buy**
Purchase price		$16		$128,000
Direct materials	$ 5		$ 40,000	
Direct labor	4		32,000	
Variable overhead	4		32,000	
Fixed overhead that can be				
avoided by not making	2		16,000	
Total relevant costs	$15	$16	$120,000	$128,000
Difference in favor of making		$ 1	$ 8,000	

Thus the company will be better off making the subassembly itself.

Solved Problem 14.5. Make or Buy

Johnson Manufacturing Corp. is using 10,000 units of part no. 300 as a component to assemble one of its products. It would cost the company $18 per unit to produce it internally, computed as follows:

Direct materials	$ 45,000
Direct labor	50,000
Variable overhead	40,000
Fixed overhead	45,000
Total cost	$180,000

Unit cost = $180,000 ÷ 10,000 units = $18

An outside vendor has just offered to supply the part for $16 per unit. If the company stops producing this part, one-third of the fixed overhead would be avoided. Should the company make or buy?

Solution 14.5

	10,000 Units	
	Make	**Buy Outside**
Purchase price		$160,000 ($16 × 10,000 units)
Direct materials	$ 45,000	
Direct labor	50,000	
Variable overhead	40,000	
Fixed overhead avoided		
by not making	15,000	
	$150,000	$160,000

The company is better off making the part itself because it will save $10,000 ($160,000 – $150,000) in costs.

The Sell-or-Process-Further Decision

When two or more products are produced simultaneously from the same input by a joint process, these products are called joint products. The term joint costs is used to describe all the manufacturing costs incurred prior to the point at which the joint products are identified as individual products, referred to as the split-off point. At the split-off point some of the joint products are in final form and saleable to the consumer, whereas others require additional processing.

In many cases, however, the company might have an option: It can sell the goods at the split-off point or process them further in the hope of obtaining additional revenue. In connection with this choice, called the sell-or-process-further decision, joint costs are considered irrelevant. The joint costs have already been incurred at the time of the decision and therefore represent sunk costs. The decision will rely exclusively on additional revenue compared to the additional costs incurred by further processing.

Solved Problem 14.6. Incremental Analysis for Further Processing

The Peters Company produces three products, A, B, and C from a joint process. Joint production costs for the year were $120,000. Product A may be sold at the split-off point or processed further. The additional processing requires no special facilities and all additional processing costs are variable. Sales values and cost needed to evaluate the company's production policy regarding product A follow:

Units Produced	Sales Value at Split-Off	Additional Cost and Sales Value after Further Processing	
		Sales	Costs
3,000	$60,000	$90,000	$25,000

Should product A be sold at the split-off point or processed further?

Solution 14.6

Incremental sales revenue ($90,000 – $60,000)	$30,000
Incremental costs, additional processing	25,000
Incremental gain	$ 5,000

In summary, product A should be processed further. The joint production cost of $120,000 is not included in the analysis; it is a sunk cost and, therefore, irrelevant to the decision.

Solved Problem 14.7. Incremental Analysis for Further Processing

Products A and B are jointly produced in department Z. Each product can be sold as is at the split-off point or processed further. During January department Z recorded a joint cost of $150,000. The following data for January is available:

Product	Quantity	Selling Prices per Unit At Split-off	Selling Prices per Unit If Processed Further	Cost after Split-off
A	10,000 units	$5.00	$5.00	$40,000
B	20,000	1.50	2.00	5,000

Analyze whether individual products should be processed beyond the split-off point.

Solution 14.7

For product A:

	(a) At Split-off	(a) At Completion	(b) Difference (Increment)
Sales	$50,000	$80,000	$ 30,000
Costs	—	40,000	40,000
Net revenue	$50,000	$40,000	$ (10,000)

Product A should be sold at the split-off point.

For product B:

	(a) At Split-off	(a) At Completion	(b) Difference (Increment)
Sales	$30,000	$40,000	$10,000
Costs	—	5,000	5,000
Net revenue	$30,000	$35,000	$ 5,000

Product B should be processed further.

Keeping or Dropping a Product Line

The decision whether to drop an old product line or add a new one must take into account both qualitative and quantitative factors. However, any final decision should be based primarily on the impact the decision will have on contribution margin or net income.

The ABC grocery store has three major product lines: produce, meats, and canned food. The store is considering the decision to drop the meat line because the income statement shows it is being sold at a loss. Figure 14.1 shows the income statement for these product lines.

Figure 14.1

	Produce	Meats	Canned Food	Total
Sales	$10,000	$15,000	$25,000	$50,000
Less: Variable costs	6,000	8,000	12,000	26,000
CM	$ 4,000	$ 7,000	$13,000	$24,000
Less: Fixed costs				
Direct	$ 2,000	$ 6,500	$ 4,000	$12,500
Allocated	1,000	1,500	2,500	5,000
Total	$ 3,000	$ 8,000	$ 6,500	$17,500
Net income	$ 1,000	$ (1,000)	$ 6,500	$ 6,500

In Figure 14.1, direct fixed costs are those costs that are identified directly with each of the product lines, whereas allocated fixed costs are the amount of common fixed costs allocated to the product lines using some base such as space occupied. The amount of common fixed costs typically continues regardless of the decision and thus cannot be saved by dropping the product line to which it is distributed.

The comparative approach showing the effects on the company as a whole with and without the meat line is shown in Figure 14.2:

Figure 14.2

	Keep Meats	Drop Meats	Difference
Sales	$50,000	$35,000	$(15,000)
Less: Variable cost	26,000	18,000	(8,000)
CM	$24,000	$17,000	$ (7,000)
Less: Fixed cost			
Direct	$12,500	$ 6,000	$ (6,500)
Allocated	5,000	5,000	—
Total	$17,500	$11,000	$ (6,500)
Net income	$ 6,500	$ 6,000	$ (500)

From Figure 14.2, we see that by dropping meats the store will lose an additional $500. Therefore the meat product line should be kept. One of the great dangers in allocating common fixed costs is that such allocations can make a product line look less profitable than it really is. Because of such an allocation, the meat line showed a loss of $1,000, but in effect it contributes $500 ($7,000 – $6,500) to the recovery of the store's common fixed costs.

Solved Problem 14.8. Income Statement by Departments

The Mead Company is considering discontinuing department B, one of the three departments it currently maintains. The following information has been gathered for the three departments:

	Dept. A	Dept. B	Dept. C
Sales	$60,000	$50,000	$80,000
Cost of goods sold:	$40,000	$42,000	$60,000
Operating expenses:			
Salaries	8,000	6,400	12,000
Rent	2,000	2,000	3,000
Utilities	1,000	2,700	2,000
Total costs	$51,000	$53,100	$77,000
Net income	$ 9,000	$ (3,100)	$ 3,000

If department B is eliminated, the space it occupies will be divided equally among departments A and C. Utilities are allocated on the basis of floor space occupied. Seventy percent of the salaries in department B would be eliminated; the other 30% would be split equally between departments A and C.

(a) Prepare a combined income statement for department A and C on the assumption that department B is dropped.
(b) Based on your analysis, should department B be eliminated?

Solution 14.8

(a)

	Dept. A	Dept. C	Total
Sales	$60,000	$80,000	$140,000
Cost of goods sold	$40,000	$60,000	$100,000
Operating expenses:			
Salaries	8,960	12,960	21,920
Rent	3,000	4,000	7,000
Utilities*	2,350	3,350	5,700
Total costs	$54,310	$80,310	$134,620
Net income	$ 5,690	$ (310)	$ 5,380

*Utilities of department B are allocated equally to departments A and C because the space occupied by department B was split equally between A and C.

(b) No, department B should not be eliminated. If eliminated, the combined net income would be $5,380; with department B the combined net income would be $8,900 ($9,000 + $3,000 – $3,100).

CAPITAL BUDGETING

Capital budgeting involves planning for the best selection among long-term investment proposals. Examples of capital budgeting applications are product-line selection, keeping or selling a business segment, leasing or buying, and which asset to invest in.

Types of Investment Projects

There are typically two types of long-term investment decisions:

(1) Selection decisions arise when the company must obtain new facilities or expand existing facilities. Examples include:

   (a) Investments in property, plant, and equipment as well as other types of assets.
   (b) Resource commitments in the form of new product development, market research, introduction of computers, refunding long-term debt, and so on.
   (c) Mergers and acquisitions in the form of buying companies or divisions to expand product lines.

(2) Replacement decisions focus on whether to replace existing facilities and equipment with new facilities and equipment. Examples include replacing an old machine with a newer, more technologically capable machine.

Features of Investment Projects

Long-term investments have three important features:

(1) They typically involve a large amount of initial cash outlays, which tend to have a long-term impact on the firm's future profitability. Therefore this initial cash outlay needs to be justified on a cost-benefit basis.
(2) There are expected recurring cash inflows (e.g., increased revenues, savings in cash operating expenses) over the life of the investment project. This frequently requires considering the time value of money.
(3) Income taxes could make a difference in the decisions to accept or reject a project. Therefore income tax factors must be taken into account in every capital budgeting decision.

Evaluation of Investment Proposals

There are several methods of evaluating investment projects:

(1) Payback period (or cash payback period)
(2) Accounting (simple or unadjusted) rate of return
(3) Net present value
(4) Internal (time-adjusted) rate of return
(5) Present value (profitability) index

The net present value (NPV) method and the internal rate of return (IRR) method are called discounted cash flow (DCF) methods. Each of these methods is discussed below.

PAYBACK PERIOD

The payback (or cash payback) period measures the length of time required to recover the amount of initial investment. It is computed by dividing the initial investment by the cash inflows generated by the project.

Solved Problem 14.9. Payback Period

Assume:

Cost of investment	$18,000
Annual after-tax cash savings	$ 3,000

Compute the payback.

Solution 14.9

$$\text{Payback period} = \frac{\text{Initial investment}}{\text{Cost savings}} = \frac{\$18,000}{\$3,000} = 6 \text{ years}$$

Decision rule: Choose the project with the shorter payback period. The rationale behind this choice is that the shorter the payback period, the less risky the project and the greater the liquidity.

The advantages of using the payback period method of evaluating an investment project are that (1) it is simple to compute and easy to understand, and (2) it handles investment risk effectively.

The shortcomings of this method are that (1) it does not recognize the time value of money, and (2) it ignores the impact of cash inflows received after the payback period. Cash flows after the payback period determine the profitability of an investment, but these are not considered.

ACCOUNTING (SIMPLE OR UNADJUSTED) RATE OF RETURN

Accounting rate of return (ARR) measures profitability by relating the required investment—or sometimes the average investment—to the future annual net income.

Solved Problem 14.10. Accounting (Simple or Unadjusted) Rate of Return

Consider the following investment:

Initial investment	$6,500
Estimated life	20 years
Cash inflows per year	$1,000
Depreciation per year	
(using straight-line method)	$325

Compute the accounting rate of return.

Solution 14.10

$$\text{ARR} = \frac{\text{Net income}}{\text{Investment}} = \frac{\$1,000 - \$325}{\$6,500} = 10.4\%$$

If average investment (usually assumed to be half the original investment) is used, then

$$\text{ARR} = \frac{\$1,000 - \$325}{\$3,250} = 20.8\%$$

This is often called the *average rate of return*.

Decision rule: Under the ARR method, choose the project with the higher rate of return.

The advantages of the ARR method are (1) that it is easily understood, (2) simple to compute, and (3) recognizes the profitability factor.

The shortcomings of this method are that (1) it fails to recognize the time value of money, and (2) it uses accounting data instead of cash flow data.

Solved Problem 14.11. Payback Period and ARR

Hanke, Inc. is a fast-food restaurant chain. Potential franchises are given the following revenue and cost information:

Building and equipment	$490,000
Annual revenue	520,000
Annual cash operating costs	380,000

The building and equipment have a useful life of 20 years. The straight-line method for depreciation is used. Ignore income taxes.

(a) What is the payback period?
(b) What is the accounting (simple) rate of return?

Solution 14.11

(a)

$$\text{The payback period} = \frac{\$490,000}{\$520,000 - \$380,000} = \frac{\$490,000}{\$140,000} = 3.5 \text{ years}$$

(b)

$$\text{Annual depreciation} = \frac{\$490,000}{20 \text{ years}} = \$24,500$$

$$\text{The accounting rate of return} = \frac{\$140,000 - \$24,500}{\$490,000} = 23.57\%$$

NET PRESENT VALUE

Net present value (NPV) is the excess of the present value (PV) of cash inflows generated by the project over the amount of the initial investment (I):

$$NPV = PV - I$$

The present value of future cash flows is computed using the so-called cost of capital (or minimum required rate of return) as the discount rate. When cash inflows are uniform, the present value would be

$$PV = A \times T_2 \ (i, n)$$

where A is the amount of the annuity, i is the discount rate, and n is the estimated life of the project. *Note:* T_2 is the present value of an annuity of $1 and is found in Table 14.2 at the end of this chapter.

Solved Problem 14.12. Net Present Value

Consider the following investment:

Initial investment	$12,950
Estimated life	10 years
Annual cash inflows	$ 3,000
Cost of capital (minimum required rate of return)	12%

Use the NPV method to determine whether the project should be accepted.

Solution 14.12

Present value of the cash inflows is:

$$PV = A \times T_2 \ (i, n)$$
$$= \$3,000 \times T_2 \ (12\%, \ 10 \ \text{years})$$

$= \$3,000 \ (5.650)$	\$16,950
Initial investment (I)	12,950
Net present value (NPV = PV − I)	\$ 4,000

Since the NPV of the investment is positive, the investment should be accepted.

Decision rule: If NPV is positive, accept the project. Otherwise, reject it.

The advantages of the NPV method are that it obviously recognizes the time value of money and it is easy to compute, whether the cash flows form an annuity or vary from period to period.

INTERNAL RATE OF RETURN

Internal rate of return (IRR), also called time-adjusted rate of return, is defined as the rate of interest that equates investment (I) with the present value (PV) of future cash inflows.

In other words,

$$\text{at IRR, } I = PV \text{ or } NPV = 0$$

Solved Problem 14.13. Internal Rate of Return

Assume the same data given in Solved Problem 14.12. Use the IRR method to determine whether the project should be accepted.

Solution 14.13

Set up the following equality (I = PV):

$$\$12,950 = \$3,000 \times T_2 \ (i, \ 10 \ \text{years})$$

$$T_2 \ (i, \ 10 \ \text{years}) = \frac{\$12,950}{\$3,000} = 4.317$$

which stands somewhere between 18% and 20% in the 10-year line of Table 14.2.

Since the IRR of the investment is greater than the cost of capital (12%), accept the project.

Decision rule: Accept the project if the IRR exceeds the cost of capital. Otherwise, reject it.

The advantage of using the IRR method is that it considers the time value of money and, therefore, is more exact and realistic than the ARR method.

The shortcomings of this method are that (1) it can be time-consuming to compute, especially when the cash inflows are not even, although most financial calculators and PCs have a key to calculate the IRR, and (2) it fails to recognize the varying sizes of investment in competing projects.

Solved Problem 14.14. Missing Numbers

Fill in the blanks for each of the following independent cases. Assume in all the cases that the investment has a useful life of 10 years.

	Annual Cash Inflow	Investment	Cost of Capital	IRR	NPV
1.	$100,000	$449,400	14%	(a)	(b)
2.	$ 70,000	(c)	14%	20%	(d)
3.	(e)	$200,000	(f)	14%	$35,624
4.	(g)	$300,000	12%	(h)	$39,000

Solution 14.14

1. (a) Set up the following equality (I = PV):

$$\$449,400 = \$100,000 \times T_2 \ (i, 10 \text{ years})$$

$$T_2 \ (i, 10 \text{ years}) = \frac{\$449,400}{\$100,000} = 4.494$$

which is very close to 18% in the 10-year line of Table 14.2.

(b) $72,200.

(PV = $100,000 × 5.216 = $521,600,
  so NPV = PV − I = $521,600 − $449,400 = $72,200)

2. (c) $293,440.

($70,000 × 4.192, the present value factor for 20% and ten years; at IRR, PV = I)

(d) $71,680.

(PV = $70,000 × 5.216 = $365,120, so NPV = PV − I = $365,120 − $293,440 = $71,680)

3. (e) $38,344.

$$(\$200,000 + 5.216 \text{ factor for } 14\% \text{ and } 10 \text{ years})$$

(f) 10%.

(NPV = PV − I; PV = NPV + I; Total PV = $35,624 + $200,000; $235,624 ÷ $38,344 = 6.145, which is the present value factor for 10% and 10 years), T_2 (10%, 10 years).

4. (g) $60,000.

(Total PV = $39,000 + $300,000 = $339,000; $339,000 ÷ 5.650 factor for 12% and 10 years = $60,000)

(h) About 15%. Set up the following equality (I = PV):

$$\$300,000 = \$60,000 \times T_2 \text{ (i, 10 years)}$$

$$T_2 \text{ (i, 10 years)} = \frac{\$300,000}{\$60,000} = 5$$

which stands halfway between 14% and 16% in the 10-year line of Table 14.2.

Solved Problem 14.15. Evaluating a Proposal

The Rango Company is considering a capital investment for which the initial outlay is $20,000. Net annual cash inflows (before taxes) are predicted to be $4,000 for 10 years. Straight-line depreciation is used. Ignoring income taxes, compute the items listed below:

(a) Payback period
(b) Accounting rate of return (ARR)
(c) Net present value (NPV), assuming a cost of capital (before tax) of 12%
(d) Internal rate of return (IRR)

Solution 14.15

(a)

$$\text{Payback period} = \frac{\text{Initial investment}}{\text{Annual cash flow}} = \frac{\$20,000}{\$4,000/\text{year}} = 5 \text{ years}$$

(b)

$$\text{Accounting rate of return (APR)} = \frac{\text{Average annual net income}}{\text{Initial investment}}$$

$$\text{Depreciation} = \frac{\$20,000}{10 \text{ years}} = \$2,000/\text{year}$$

$$\text{Accounting rate of return} = \frac{\$4,000 - \$2,000}{\$20,000} = 0.10 = 10\%$$

(c)

Net present value (NPV) = PV − I
= PV of cash inflows [discounted at the cost of capital (12%)]
− Initial investment

$$= \$4,000 \times T_2 \ (12\%, 10 \text{ years}) - \$20,000$$
$$= \$4,000 \ (5.650) - \$20,000$$
$$= \$2,600$$

(d)

Internal rate of return (IRR) = Rate that equates the amount invested (I) with the present value (PV) of cash inflows generated by the project

Therefore,

$$\$20,000 = \$4,000 \times T_2 \ (i, 10 \text{ years})$$

$$T_2 \ (i, 10 \text{ years}) = \frac{\$20,000}{\$4,000} = 5$$

which stands between 14% and 16%.

PRESENT VALUE INDEX

The present value (or profitability) index is the ratio of the total PV of future cash inflows to the initial investment, that is, PV/I. This index is used as a means of ranking projects in descending order of attractiveness.

Solved Problem 14.16. Present Value Index

Using the data in Solved Problem 14.12, compute the present value index. Should the project be accepted?

Solution 14.16.

Present value of the cash inflows is

$$PV = A \times T_2 \ (i, n)$$
$$= \$3,000 \times T_2 \ (12\%, 10 \text{ years})$$
$$= \$3,000 \ (5.650)$$
$$= \$16,950$$

Therefore the present value index is:

$$\frac{PV}{I} = \frac{\$16,950}{\$12,950} = 1.31$$

Since this project generates $1.31 for each dollar invested (i.e., its present value index is greater than 1), accept the project.

Decision rule: If the present value index is greater than 1, which means that the present value (PV) is greater than I, then accept the project.

The present value index has the advantage of putting all projects on the same relative basis regardless of size.

Solved Problem 14.17. Ranking Projects

Rand Corporation is considering five different investment opportunities. The company's cost of capital is 12%. Data on these opportunities under consideration are given below:

Project	Investment	PV at 12%	NPV	IRR	Present Value Index (rounded)
(a)	$35,000	$39,325	$4,325	16%	1.12
(b)	20,000	22,930	2,930	15	1.15
(c)	25,000	27,453	2,453	14	1.10
(d)	10,000	10,854	854	18	1.09
(e)	9,000	8,749	(251)	11	0.97

Rank these five projects in descending order of preference, according to the present value index.

Solution 14.17

	PV Index	Order of Preference
(a)	1.12	2
(b)	1.15	1
(c)	1.10	3
(d)	1.09	4
(e)	0.97	5

Effect of Income Taxes on Investment Decisions

Income taxes make a difference in many capital budgeting decisions. Sometimes projects which are attractive on a before-tax basis have to be rejected on an after-tax basis and vice versa. Income taxes typically affect both the amount and the timing of cash flows. Since net income, not cash inflows, is subject to tax, after-tax cash inflows are not usually the same as after-tax net income.

Not all costs are of equal importance in decision making. Managerial accountants must identify those costs that are relevant to a decision. The relevant costs are the expected future costs that differ between the decision alternatives. Therefore sunk costs are irrelevant since they are past and historical costs. Also, costs that continue regardless of the decision are irrelevant.

What is relevant are the incremental or differential costs. The relevant cost approach helps managerial accountants make short-term, nonroutine decisions such as whether to accept a below-normal selling price, which products to emphasize, whether to make or buy, whether to sell or process further, and how to optimize capacity.

We have examined the process of evaluating investment projects. We have also discussed five commonly used criteria for evaluating capital budgeting projects, including the net present value (NPV) and internal rate of return (IRR) methods.

Since income taxes could make a difference in the accept-or-reject decision, tax factors must be taken into account in every decision.

Table 14.1

Present Value of $1.00

$$\frac{1}{(1+i)^n} = T_1 (i, n)$$

PERIODS	4%	6%	8%	10%	12%	14%	16%	18%	20%	22%	24%	26%	28%	30%	40%
1	.962	.943	.926	.909	.893	.877	.862	.847	.833	.820	.806	.794	.781	.769	.714
2	.925	.890	.857	.826	.797	.769	.743	.718	.694	.672	.650	.630	.610	.592	.510
3	.889	.840	.794	.751	.712	.675	.641	.609	.579	.551	.524	.500	.477	.455	.364
4	.855	.792	.735	.683	.636	.592	.552	.516	.482	.451	.423	.397	.373	.350	.260
5	.822	.474	.681	.621	.567	.519	.476	.437	.402	.370	.341	.315	.291	.269	.186
6	.790	.705	.630	.564	.507	.456	.410	.370	.335	.303	.275	.250	.227	.207	.133
7	.760	.665	.583	.513	.452	.400	.354	.314	.279	.249	.222	.198	.178	.159	.095
8	.731	.627	.540	.467	.404	.351	.305	.266	.233	.204	.179	.157	.139	.123	.068
9	.703	.592	.500	.424	.361	.308	.263	.225	.194	.167	.144	.125	.108	.094	.048
10	.676	.558	.463	.386	.322	.270	.227	.191	.162	.137	.116	.099	.085	.073	.035
11	.650	.527	.429	.350	.287	.237	.195	.162	.135	.112	.094	.079	.066	.056	.025
12	.625	.497	.397	.319	.257	.208	.168	.137	.112	.092	.076	.062	.052	.043	.018
13	.601	.469	.368	.290	.229	.182	.145	.116	.093	.075	.061	.050	.040	.033	.013
14	.577	.442	.340	.263	.205	.160	.125	.099	.078	.062	.049	.039	.032	.025	.009
15	.555	.417	.315	.239	.183	.140	.108	.084	.065	.051	.040	.031	.025	.020	.006
16	.534	.394	.292	.218	.163	.123	.093	.071	.054	.042	.032	.025	.019	.015	.005
17	.513	.371	.270	.198	.146	.108	.080	.060	.045	.034	.026	.020	.015	.012	.003
18	.494	.350	.250	.180	.130	.095	.069	.051	.038	.028	.021	.016	.012	.009	.002
19	.475	.331	.232	.164	.116	.083	.060	.043	.031	.023	.017	.012	.009	.007	.002
20	.456	.312	.215	.149	.104	.073	.051	.037	.026	.019	.014	.010	.007	.005	.001
21	.439	.294	.199	.135	.093	.064	.044	.031	.022	.015	.011	.008	.006	.004	.001
22	.422	.278	.184	.123	.083	.056	.038	.026	.018	.013	.009	.006	.004	.003	.001
23	.406	.262	.170	.112	.074	.049	.033	.022	.015	.010	.007	.005	.003	.002	
24	.390	.247	.158	.102	.066	.043	.028	.019	.013	.008	.006	.004	.003	.002	
25	.375	.233	.146	.092	.059	.038	.024	.016	.010	.007	.005	.003	.002	.001	
26	.361	.220	.135	.084	.053	.033	.021	.014	.009	.006	.004	.002	.002	.001	
27	.347	.209	.125	.076	.047	.029	.018	.011	.007	.005	.003	.002	.001	.001	
28	.333	.196	.116	.069	.042	.026	.016	.010	.006	.004	.002	.002	.001	.001	
29	.321	.185	.107	.063	.037	.022	.014	.008	.005	.003	.002	.001	.001	.001	
30	.308	.174	.099	.057	.033	.020	.012	.007	.004	.003	.002	.001	.001		
40	.208	.097	.046	.022	.011	.005	.003	.001	.001						

Table 14.2

Present Value of an Annuity of $1.00*

$$\frac{1}{i}\left[1 - \frac{1}{(1+i)^n}\right] = T_2\,(i, n)$$

PERIODS	4%	6%	8%	10%	12%	14%	16%	18%	20%	22%	24%	25%	26%	28%	30%	40%
1	0.962	0.943	0.926	0.909	0.893	0.877	0.862	0.847	0.833	0.820	0.806	0.800	0.794	0.781	0.769	0.714
2	1.886	1.833	1.783	1.736	1.690	1.647	1.605	1.566	1.528	1.492	1.457	1.440	1.424	1.392	1.361	1.224
3	2.775	2.673	2.577	2.487	2.402	2.322	2.246	2.174	2.106	2.042	1.981	1.952	1.923	1.868	1.816	1.589
4	3.630	3.465	3.312	3.170	3.037	2.914	2.798	2.690	2.589	2.494	2.404	2.362	2.320	2.241	2.166	1.849
5	4.452	4.212	3.993	3.791	3.605	3.433	3.274	3.127	2.991	2.864	2.745	2.689	2.635	2.532	2.436	2.035
6	5.242	4.917	4.623	4.355	4.111	3.889	3.685	3.498	3.326	3.167	3.020	2.951	2.885	2.759	2.643	2.168
7	6.002	5.582	5.206	4.868	4.564	4.288	4.039	3.812	3.605	3.416	3.242	3.161	3.083	2.937	2.802	2.263
8	6.733	6.210	5.747	5.335	4.968	4.639	4.344	4.078	3.837	3.619	3.421	3.329	3.241	3.076	2.925	2.331
9	7.435	6.802	6.247	5.759	5.328	4.946	4.607	4.303	4.031	3.786	3.566	3.463	3.366	3.184	3.019	2.379
10	8.111	7.360	6.710	6.145	5.650	5.216	4.833	4.494	4.192	3.923	3.682	3.571	3.465	3.269	3.092	2.414
11	8.760	7.887	7.139	6.495	5.938	5.453	5.029	4.656	4.327	4.035	3.776	3.656	3.544	3.335	3.147	2.438
12	9.385	8.384	7.536	6.814	6.194	5.660	5.197	4.793	4.439	4.127	3.851	3.725	3.606	3.387	3.190	2.456
13	9.986	8.853	7.904	7.103	6.424	5.842	5.342	4.910	4.533	4.203	3.912	3.780	3.656	3.427	3.223	2.468
14	10.563	9.295	8.244	7.367	6.628	6.002	5.468	5.008	4.611	4.265	3.962	3.824	3.695	3.459	3.249	2.477
15	11.118	9.712	8.559	7.606	6.811	6.142	5.575	5.092	4.675	4.315	4.001	3.859	3.726	3.483	3.268	2.484
16	11.652	10.106	8.851	7.824	6.974	6.265	5.669	5.162	4.730	4.357	4.033	3.887	3.751	3.503	2.283	2.489
17	12.166	10.477	9.122	8.022	7.120	6.373	5.749	5.222	4.775	4.391	4.059	3.910	3.771	3.518	3.295	2.492
18	12.659	10.828	9.372	8.201	7.250	6.467	5.818	5.273	4.812	4.419	4.080	3.928	3.786	3.529	3.304	2.494
19	13.134	11.158	9.604	8.365	7.366	6.550	5.877	5.316	4.844	4.442	4.097	3.942	3.799	3.539	3.311	2.496
20	13.590	11.470	9.818	8.514	7.469	6.623	5.929	5.353	4.870	4.460	4.110	3.954	3.808	3.546	3.316	2.497
21	14.029	11.764	10.017	8.649	7.562	6.687	5.973	5.384	4.891	4.476	4.121	3.963	3.816	3.551	3.320	2.498
22	14.451	12.042	10.201	8.772	7.645	6.743	6.011	5.410	4.909	4.488	4.130	3.970	3.822	3.556	3.323	2.498
23	14.857	12.303	10.371	8.883	7.718	6.792	6.044	5.432	4.925	4.499	4.137	3.976	3.827	3.559	3.325	2.499
24	15.247	12.550	10.529	8.985	7.784	6.835	6.073	5.451	4.937	4.507	4.143	3.981	3.831	3.562	3.327	2.499
25	15.622	12.783	10.675	9.077	7.843	6.873	6.097	5.467	4.948	4.514	4.147	3.985	3.834	3.564	3.329	2.499
26	15.983	13.003	10.810	9.161	7.896	6.906	6.118	5.480	4.956	4.520	4.151	3.988	3.837	3.566	3.330	2.500
27	16.330	13.211	10.935	9.237	7.943	6.935	6.136	5.942	4.964	4.524	4.154	3.990	3.839	3.567	3.331	2.500
28	16.663	13.406	11.051	9.307	7.984	6.961	6.152	5.502	4.970	4.528	4.157	3.992	3.840	3.568	3.331	2.500
29	16.984	13.591	11.158	9.370	8.022	6.983	6.166	5.510	4.975	4.531	4.159	3.994	3.841	3.569	3.332	2.500
30	17.292	13.765	11.258	9.427	8.055	7.003	6.177	5.517	4.979	4.534	4.160	3.995	3.842	3.569	3.332	2.500
40	19.793	15.046	11.925	9.779	8.244	7.105	6.234	5.548	4.997	4.544	4.166	3.999	3.846	3.571	3.333	2.500

* Payments (or receipts) at the *end* of each period.

15

Taxation of Individuals

The federal income tax is imposed annually, at graduated rates, on a figure known as taxable income. Taxable income is gross income less certain authorized deductions and exemptions. Gross income is the starting point in the computation of tax liability.

The basic legal concept of taxable income can be outlined as follows:

All Income
– Exclusions
= Adjusted gross income (AGI)
– Regular (or standard deduction) and personal exemptions
= <u>Taxable income</u>

BASIC FILING INFORMATION FOR 1992

Forms To Use   A taxpayer is permitted to use one of three forms to file his or her personal tax return: Form 1040EZ, Form 1040A, or Form 1040.

FORM 1040EZ

The simpler Form 1040EZ may be used by taxpayers (1) whose filing status is single; (2) who are not 65 years of age or blind; (3) whose taxable income is less than $50,000; (4) whose income consists only of wages, salaries, and/or tips, dividends, and interest of $400 or less; and (5) who does not itemize deductions. No deductions, other than a standard deduction and personal exemption, can be taken on the return. If taxpayers do not meet all of these requirements, they cannot use Form 1040EZ. They must use Form 1040A or Form 1040.

FORM 1040A

If a taxpayer does not qualify to use Form 1040EZ, he or she may be able to use Form 1040A. Form 1040A may be used by an individual who does not itemize personal deductions and whose gross income consists only of wages, salary, tips, annuities and pensions, taxable social security, unemployment compensation, dividends, and interest. Taxpayers may deduct individual retirement account (IRA) contributions. Taxpayers may also claim credits for withholding, child care, and earned income.

If a taxpayer does not meet all of the above requirements, he or she cannot use Form 1040A. For example, a taxpayer may want to claim itemized deductions which cannot be claimed on Form 1040A.

FORM 1040

A taxpayer may pay less tax by filing Form 1040 because he or she is entitled to take itemized deductions, have certain adjustments to income, and have credits that cannot be taken on Form 1040A or Form 1040EZ.

Types of Taxpayers

Individuals may not be subject to tax at the same rates. First, tax rates are generally higher for higher levels of income. Second, even at the same level of income, tax rates vary depending on an individual's filing status. Specifically, there are six different categories of filing status under 1992 law, each of them requiring application of a given tax rate schedule. The six categories of individual filing status are as follows:

Schedule X: Single
Schedule Y: Married filing separately
Schedule Y: Married filing jointly
           Surviving spouse
Schedule Z: Head of household
           Certain married individuals living apart

For 1992, the basic tax rate structure for individuals applies rates of 15, 28, and 31% to taxable income.

DETERMINING TAXABLE INCOME

Gross Income Defined

Gross income, for tax purposes, includes the following items:

(1) Compensation for services, including fees, commissions, fringe benefits, and similar items;

(2) Gross income derived from a business;

(3) Gains derived from the sale of stock and other property.

(4) Interest;

(5) Rents;

(6) Royalties;

(7) Dividends;

(8) Alimony;

(9) Annuities;

(10) Pensions;

(11) Income from discharge of indebtedness;

(12) Distributive share of partnership gross income;

(13) Distributive share of income from an S corporation; and

(14) Income from an interest in an estate or trust.

Solved Problem 15.1. Computation of Gross Income

For the tax year 1992, Harold Baer had the following items of income:

Salary	$80,000
Cash dividends	2,000
Interest income	3,000
Sale of stock for $12,500 that he had purchased for $10,000	2,500

What is the total income subject to tax?

Solution 15.1

Salary	$80,000
Cash dividends	2,000
Interest income	3,000
Sale of stock for $12,500 that he had purchased for $10,000	2,500
Total income subject to tax	$87,500

Exclusions from Income

The Internal Revenue Code excludes the following types of income: (1) the first $5,000 of company-paid death benefits; (2) gifts and inheritances; (3) municipal bond interest; (4) compensation for injuries or sickness; (5) amounts received from accident and health plans; (6) accident and health premiums paid by an employer for an employee; (7) combat pay for members of the armed forces; (8) a portion of social security benefits; (9) meals and lodging furnished to the employee for the convenience of the employer; (10) up to $125,000 of the gain from the sale of a principal residence by an individual who is 55 or over; and (11) certain employee fringe benefits.

Solved Problem 15.2. Exclusions from Gross Income

For the tax year 1992, Walter Weldon had the following items of income:

Municipal bond interest	$ 40,000
Gift from father	10,000
Inheritance received from Aunt Maude	35,000
Employee death benefit received from death of his mother	25,000
	$110,000

What is Weldon's 1992 adjusted gross income?

Solution 15.2

The computation of AGI would be as follows:

	Nontaxable	Taxable
Municipal bond interest	$40,000	
Gift from his father	10,000	
Inheritance received from Aunt Maude	35,000	
Employee death benefit received from death of his mother	5,000	$20,000
Total nontaxable income	$90,000	
AGI		$20,000

The Determination of Adjusted Gross Income (AGI)

The determination of adjusted gross income (AGI) is applicable only to individuals. Generally, it represents gross income less business expenses, expenses attributable to the production of rents and royalties, the capital loss deduction, and certain expenses such as the payment of alimony. These deductions are said to be *for* AGI.

Items deductible for adjusted gross income include individual retirement account (IRA) payments, deductions for self-employment tax, payments made to a Keogh retirement plan, the penalty for early withdrawal of savings, and alimony paid. IRAs are savings programs that let an individual set aside money for retirement. Some individuals' contributions are deductible if they are not covered by another pension plan. If an employer does not provide a retirement plan, the IRA deduction is the smaller of either (1) compensation or (2) the actual contribution to the IRA up to $2,000.

Solved Problem 15.3. Computation of Adjusted Gross Income If Taxpayer Is Eligible to Deduct an IRA Payment

For the tax year 1992, Pierre Goode earned a salary of $100,000. Since he was not covered by an employer retirement plan, he opened up an IRA and made the maximum allowable payment for the year. What is his 1992 AGI?

Solution 15.3

Salary	$100,000
Less: Maximum allowable payment to IRA for 1991	2,000
AGI	$ 98,000

Solved Problem 15.4. Computation of Adjusted Gross Income If Taxpayer Is Not Eligible to Deduct Cost of IRA Makes Payment to Plan

For the tax year 1992, Pamela Drake had a salary of $90,000. She was covered by her employer's retirement plan. If she makes a $2,000 payment to an IRA, what is her 1992 AGI?

Solution 15.4

Pamela's 1992 AGI is $90,000. Since she is covered by her employer's pension plan, she cannot deduct her IRA payment for tax purposes.

Capital Gains and Losses

A capital asset is any asset held for investment purposes, such as stocks and bonds. The Internal Revenue Code gives special tax treatment to long-term capital gains. Effective January 1, 1991, capital gains were taxed at a rate not to exceed 28%. This rate is below the maximum tax rate of 31%, which will apply to net ordinary income. Property must be held more than one year to qualify for long-term capital gain or loss treatment. The first step in computing net capital gain or loss is to combine long-term capital gains and losses. Then combine all short-term capital gains and losses. The final step is to combine the total of the net long-term gains or losses with the short-term capital gains or losses. The result is either a net long-term capital gain (NLTCG) or loss (NLTCL) or a net short-term capital gain (NSTCG) or loss (NSTCL).

Solved Problem 15.5. Netting Capital Gains and Losses

Give the result of netting capital gains and losses and the description indicating whether it is a long-term or short-term capital gain or loss.

Stock	Short-Term Capital Gain (STCG)	Short-Term Capital Loss (STCL)	Long-Term Capital Gain (LTCG)	Long-Term Capital Loss (LTCG)	Result and Description of Netting
V	$9,000	($6,000)			
W	4,000	(8,000)			
X			$8,000	($2,000)	
Y			7,500	(8,500)	
Z	5,000	(1,000)		(9,000)	

Solution 15.5

Stock	Short-Term Capital Gain (STCG)	Short-Term Capital Loss (STCL)	Long-Term Capital Gain (LTCG)	Long-Term Capital Loss (LTCG)	Result and Description of Netting	
V	$9,000	($6,000)			$ 3,000	Net short-term capital gain
W	4,000	(8,000)			($4,000)	Net short-term capital loss
X			$8,000	($2,000)	$6,000	Net long-term capital gain
Y			7,500	(8,500)	($1,000)	Net long-term capital loss
Z	5,000	(1,000)		(9,000)	($5,000)	Net long-term capital loss

Capital gains can always be used to offset capital losses. If there are excess capital losses, up to $3,000 of excess long-term and short-term capital losses can be used to offset ordinary income for a tax year. Any excess nondeductible losses above $3,000 can be carried over and used in future tax years.

Solved Problem 15.6. Computation of Adjusted Gross Income Utilizing Capital Gains and Losses

For 1992, Doris Cooper had a salary of $40,000. From stock sales, she had a long-term capital gain of $1,000 and a short-term capital loss of $5,000. Compute her 1992 AGI.

Solution 15.6

Salary		$40,000
Long-term capital gain	$ 1,000	
Short-term capital loss	(5,000)	
Losses exceeding gains	(4,000)	
Excess losses up to limit		(3,000)
AGI		$37,000

Disallowed excess capital losses for the year of $1,000 ($4,000 – $3,000) can be carried over and used as a capital loss in the following tax year. For example, if Cooper earned a salary of $45,000 in 1993, she could offset the $1,000 capital loss carryover from 1992 against her salary to arrive at an AGI of $44,000.

Social Security Benefits

Under the Internal Revenue Code, a portion of social security benefits is taxable if adjusted gross income exceeds certain base amounts. The taxable portion of social security benefits is equal to the lesser of 50% of the benefits received or the amount determined by the following formula:

Adjusted gross income (excluding social security benefits)	$XXX
Plus: 50% of social security benefits	XXX
Subtotal	$XXX
Less: Base amount ($32,000 for married persons filing jointly, zero for married person filing separately, and $25,000 for other taxpayers	XXX
Subtotal	$XXX
× 50%	50%
Amount to be included in gross income	$XXX

Solved Problem 15.7. Computation of Taxable Social Security Benefits to Be Included in AGI

Fred Dexter is single and received $6,000 in social security benefits in 1992. If he also earned a salary of $23,000 for the year, (a) what amount of social security benefits would he be required to include in his gross income? and (b) What would be Dexter's 1992 AGI?

Solution 15.7

(a)

Social security benefits: $6,000 × 50% =	$ 3,000
Salary	23,000
Total	$26,000
Less: Base amount for single person	25,000
Excess amount	$ 1,000
× 50%	50%
Amount to be included in gross income	$ 500

(b)

Dexter's total AGI would be $23,500 ($23,000 + $500).

Deductions from AGI

Deductions from AGI (sometimes called itemized deductions), which are a subtotal, include medical expenses in excess of 7.5% of AGI, interest on a home mortgage, charitable donations, and certain other deductions. Itemized deductions reduce taxable income only if their total is larger than the standard deduction (an amount specified by statute). If their total is less than the standard deduction, itemized deductions provide no tax benefit. Other amounts deducted from AGI to determine taxable income include exemptions for certain individuals.

Solved Problem 15.8. Computation of Deductible Medical Expense

During 1992, Renata Gillespie had gross income of $25,000, paid alimony of $10,000, and incurred medical expenses of $3,125. What is Renata's 1992 medical expense deduction?

Solution 15.8

Alimony is a deduction for AGI. Renata will be permitted to deduct excess medical expenses of $2,000, computed as follows:

Total medical costs		$3,125
Gross income	$25,000	
Less: Alimony	10,000	
Adjusted gross income	$15,000	
Statutory percentage	7.5%	
Less: Medical deduction limitation		1,125
Excess medical expense deduction		$2,000

THE PHASEOUT FOR ITEMIZED DEDUCTIONS

For 1992, taxpayers whose adjusted gross income exceeds a threshold amount must reduce certain itemized deductions by 3%. The threshold amounts are $52,625 for married persons filing separately and $105,250 for all other taxpayers. These amounts will be adjusted annually for inflation. However, certain itemized deductions, designated Group I deductions, cannot be reduced more than 80%. To make the calculation, a taxpayer must divide all itemized deductions into two groups.

The first group (Group I) of deductions includes qualifying personal property taxes, interest other than investment interest, contributions, moving expenses, state and local income taxes, and miscellaneous itemized deductions. These itemized deductions cannot be reduced more than 80%. The second group (Group II) includes medical expenses, investment interest to the extent of net investment income, casualty and theft losses, and gambling losses to the extent of gambling gains.

Solved Problem 15.9. Computation of Deductible Expenses Based Upon AGI of $205,250

Barry and Tina Minton are married taxpayers filing a joint return for 1992. Since they both work, they have adjusted gross income of $205,250 and the following itemized deductions:

Group I

Contributions to recognized charities	$ 3,000
Mortgage interest	3,000
State and local income taxes	9,000
Miscellaneous deductions	1,000
Total	$16,000

Group II

Casualty loss	$ 1,500
Investment interest	500
Total	$ 2,000

Calculate the total itemized deductions for 1992.

Solution 15.9

The total itemized deductions would be $15,000, calculated as follows:

Group I Limitation

Deductions $16,000 × 80% (maximum reduction)	$ 12,800
Adjustment for 3% of the adjusted	
gross income over $105,250:	$105,250
Adjusted gross income	$205,250
Less: Threshold amount	105,250
Amount subject to 3% adjustment	$100,000
	× 3%
3% adjustment	$ 3,000

Group I deductions	$16,000
Less: 3% adjustment	3,000
Group I allowable itemized deductions	$13,000
Add: Group II deductions	2,000
Total itemized deductions	$15,000

Solved Problem 15.10. Computation of Deductible Expenses Based Upon AGI of $605,250

Paul and Bertha Trammell are wealthy married taxpayers filing a joint return for 1992. They have adjusted gross income of $605,250 and the following itemized deductions:

Group I

Contributions to recognized charities	$ 2,000
Mortgage interest	3,500
State and local income taxes	10,000
Miscellaneous deductions	500
Total	$16,000

Group II

Casualty loss	$1,500
Investment interest	500
Total	$2,000

Calculate the total itemized deductions for 1992.

Solution 15.10

Group I Limitation

Expenses $16,000 × 80% (maximum reduction)	$ 12,800
Adjustment for 3% of the adjusted gross income over $105,250:	
Adjusted gross income	$605,250
Less: Threshold amount	105,250
Amount subject to 3% adjustment	$500,000
	× 3%
3% adjustment	$ 15,000

Since the $15,000 exceeds the maximum reduction permitted of $12,800 ($16,000 × 80%), the taxpayer will reduce the Group I expenses by only $12,800.

Group I deductions	$16,000
Less: Maximum adjustment permitted	12,800
Group I allowable itemized deductions	$ 3,200
Add: Group II deductions	2,000
Total itemized deductions	$ 5,200

Solved Problem 15.11. Indicating Whether a Deduction Is Used to Reduce AGI or Deducted from AGI as an Itemized Deduction, or not Deductible

Expense item	Used to Reduce AGI	Deducted from AGI	Not Deductible
Stock losses			
Alimony			
IRA contribution where permitted			
Tax penalties			
Interest paid to IRS for late payment of tax			
Penalty for early withdrawal of savings certificate			
Federal withholding taxes			
State withholding taxes			
Tax preparation fees			
Interest on home mortgage			

Consumer interest paid on charge
   accounts.
Moving expenses required by new job
Real estate taxes paid on home
Charitable contribution
Medical expenses
Theft of computer from sole proprietorship

Solution 15.11

Expense item	Used to Reduce AGI	Deducted from AGI	Not Deductible
Stock losses	X		
Alimony	X		
IRA contribution where permitted	X		
Tax penalties			X
Interest paid to IRS for late payment of tax			X
Penalty for early withdrawal of savings certificate	X		
Federal withholding taxes			X
State withholding taxes		X	
Tax preparation fees		X	
Interest on home mortgage		X	
Consumer interest paid on charge accounts			X
Moving expenses required by new job		X	
Real estate taxes paid on home		X	
Charitable contribution		X	
Medical expenses		X	
Theft of computer from sole proprietorship	X		

STANDARD DEDUCTION AND EXEMPTIONS

The Standard Deduction

If the total of the itemized deductions, after all adjustments, is less than the standard deduction, the taxpayer or taxpayers are permitted to take a standard deduction, which is a fixed amount. The taxpayer or taxpayers compare their itemized deductions with their applicable standard deduction and reduce their adjusted gross income by the larger of the two amounts.

The standard deduction for 1992 in each category is as follows:

	1992
Married filing separately	$3,000
Single	3,600
Head of household	5,250
Married filing jointly	6,000

If a single taxpayer has attained age 65 by year-end, or is legally blind, the taxpayer may add $900 per person for 1992 to the basic standard deduction or an additional maximum amount of $1,800. For taxpayers filing a joint return, the additional amount is $700 per person for 1992 or an additional maximum amount of $1,400 per person.

Exemptions

For 1992, one personal exemption of $2,300 is allowed per taxpayer. In the case of a joint return, there are two personal exemptions. However, if a taxpayer can be claimed as a dependent on someone else's tax return, the taxpayer cannot claim a personal exemption for him or herself. In addition to the personal exemptions, a dependency exemption of $2,300 is allowed to the taxpayer for each person who is a dependent. The Code specifies five tests for dependency status. The following five tests must be passed before a dependency exemption can be claimed:

(1) *Gross income test*. The dependent's gross income must be less than the exemption amount ($2,300 in 1992) unless the dependent is a child of the taxpayer and is under age 19 or a full-time student under the age of 24.

(2) *Support test*. More than 50% of the support of the individual must be furnished by the taxpayer. In certain cases, no one provides more than half the support of a person. Instead, two or more persons collectively provide over 50% of another person's support. In this situation, the individuals providing support can agree among themselves who will take the dependency exemption provided that they meet certain other tests. This type of arrangement is known as a multiple support agreement. All others who sign the statement agree not to claim the supported person as a dependent for the year in question.

(3) *Relationship test*. To be a dependent, the individual must be either a relative of the taxpayer or a member of the taxpayer's household. Individuals who may be claimed as dependents of the taxpayer include a son or daughter of the taxpayer, stepsons or stepdaughters, brothers, sisters, a father or mother of the taxpayer, stepfather or stepmother, nephew, niece, aunt, uncle, etc.

(4) *Joint return test*. If the potential dependent is married, the dependent must not have filed a joint return with his or her spouse for the year in question.

(5) *Citizen or residency test*. To be a dependent, the individual must be either a United States citizen, resident or national or a resident of Canada or Mexico for some part of the tax year.

Solved Problem 15.12. Determining Who Is a Dependent

Joe Thomas provided $3,000 of support for his mother. Joe's sister provided $1,000. The mother spent $5,000 of her savings for her own support. Can Joe claim his mother as a dependent?

Solution 15.12

No. Since Joe's mother provided over half of her own support, she cannot be claimed as a dependent.

Solved Problem 15.13. Computation of Taxable Income

For 1992, Kent Worth, age 70 and single, had the following items of income:

Salary	$60,000
Royalty income	10,000
Income from partnership	5,000
Dividend income	4,000
Municipal bond interest income	3,000

He paid $6,000 in alimony to his ex-wife. He also has itemized deductions of $3,800. What is his 1992 taxable income?

Solution 15.13

Salary	$60,000
Royalty income	10,000
Income from partnership	5,000
Dividend income	4,000
AGI	$79,000
Less: The greater of the standard deduction ($3,600) plus the additional standard ($900) or $4,500 or itemized deductions of $3,800	4,500
	$74,500
Less: One exemption	2,300
Taxable income	$72,200

Pursuant to the Internal Revenue Code, municipal bond interest is nontaxable.

The Phaseout Rule for Exemptions

The exemption per person is $2,300 in 1992. For 1992, if a taxpayer's adjusted gross income exceeds a threshold amount, determined by filing status, the exemption is reduced by 2% for each $2,500, or fraction thereof, by which adjusted gross income exceeds the threshold amount. In the case of married persons filing separately, the $2,500 amount is reduced to $1,250. This reduction is effective for tax years beginning after 1990 and before 1996.

The threshold amounts before inflation indexing are as follows:

Single taxpayer	$105,250
Joint returns or surviving spouse	157,900
Head of household	131,550
Married persons filing separately	78,950

Thus if married taxpayers filing jointly had an AGI of $282,900, their exemptions would be completely phased out pursuant to the following computation:

AGI	$282,900
Less: Threshold amount	157,900
Balance	$125,000
Divided by	$ 2,500
Units of $2,500	$ 50
×	2
Percentage of phaseout applicable to exemptions	100%

Solved Problem 15.14. The Phaseout Rule for Exemptions

Bradley and Helen O'Hara are a married couple with two children. For 1992, their adjusted gross income is $207,900. (a) Without the phaseout of the deduction for personal exemptions, what is their total exemption deduction? (b) What will be the amount of their exemption after the phaseout?

Solution 15.14

(a) Without the phaseout of the deduction for personal exemptions, the total exemptions would be $9,200 ($2,300 × 4).

(b) The O'Haras' adjusted gross income, however, exceeds the $157,900 applicable threshold by $50,000 ($207,900 – $157,900). This $50,000 amount represents 20 full "units" of $2,500. As a result, the applicable percentage for reducing their personal exemptions is 40% (2% × 20). The taxpayers will lose $3,680 ($9,200 × 40%) of their personal exemptions, which reduces the allowable exemption amount to $5,520 ($9,200 – $3,680).

DETERMINATION OF TAX

After determining taxable income, the next step is to determine the taxpayer's tax liability based on taxable income before the reduction by any applicable tax credits.

Applicable Tax Rates and the Tax Calculation

Most taxpayers will compute their tax liability using the tax table for taxable income up to $50,000. For 1992, the basic tax structure applies rates of 15, 28, and 31%. The 28% rate starts at the following taxable amounts:

Filing Status	15% Up to	28% Rate Applies to Taxable Income Over	31% Rate Applies to Taxable Income Over
Single	$21,450	$21,450	$51,900
Head of household	28,750	28,750	74,150
Married filing joint	35,800	35,800	86,550
Married filing separately	17,900	17,900	43,250

Solved Problem 15.15. Calculating the Personal Tax Liability

Frank and Barbara Flood, who are married, had taxable income of $90,000 for 1992. Based upon the above personal tax rates, what is their 1992 tax liability?

Solution 15.15

15% tax on $35,800	$ 5,370
28% tax on $50,700 ($86,500 – $35,800)	14,196
31% tax on $ 3,500 ($90,000 – $86,500)	1,085
$90,000	
Total tax	$20,651

Tax Credits

A tax credit should not be confused with an income tax deduction, which reduces taxable income. A tax credit reduces the tax liability dollar-for-dollar. Tax credits include those permitted for child care, the earned income credit, and the credit for foreign taxes paid.

Solved Problem 15.16. Calculating the Personal Tax Liability after Deducting a Tax Credit

Carlo Floyd, an individual with a gross tax liability of $6,000, earned a tax credit of $500 because he paid foreign taxes. What is his regular income tax liability?

Solution 15.16

Carlo's regular tax liability would be $5,500, computed as follows:

Gross tax liability	$6,000
Less: Tax credit	500
Regular income tax	$5,500

SELF-EMPLOYMENT INCOME

A tax is imposed on self-employment income. Self-employment income is the net earnings from self-employment such as a sole proprietorship. For 1992, the self-employment tax is 15.3% on self-employment income up to $55,500 and 2.9% on self-employment income in excess of $55,500 up to $130,200.

Solved Problem 15.17. Calculating Self-Employment Income

In 1992, Colin Atwood had $50,000 in net earnings from self-employment and received $1,000 in other wages that are subject to social security taxes. What is Colin's self-employment tax for 1992?

Solution 15.17

Colin's income subject to the self-employment tax is $50,000. Thus, his self-employed tax is $50,000 × 15.3% = $7,650.

Taxpayers are required to report all their taxable income. According to the Internal Revenue Code, taxpayers are also permitted to exclude all exempt income. They may also deduct certain expenses and exemptions in accordance with the rules and regulations of the tax law.

Businesses and individuals also require a knowledge of taxes so that informed decisions can be made regarding the consequences of alternative choices of action. The tax consequences of business decisions are vital pieces of information because they can severely impact the profitability and economic survival of an enterprise. The significant role that taxes play on other entities such as partnerships and corporations will be discussed in Chapter 16.

16

Taxation of Partnerships and Corporations

Taxes are an inherent part of all profitable businesses. While individuals are concerned with personal income tax decisions, entrepreneurs must choose whether to operate as a partnership or corporation. Businesses that operate as a sole proprietorship are taxed as part of the individual owner's personal income. The tax advantages and disadvantages of each entity are many. This chapter introduces some of the tax complexities that influence the choice of which business form to choose.

PARTNERSHIP TAXATION

Partnerships are not considered to be separate tax entities for the purpose of paying federal income taxes and are therefore not required to pay taxes. Instead, partnership members are subject to a tax on their share of partnership income, whether or not the income is actually distributed to them. An operating partnership may also be classified as a syndicate, group, pool, joint venture, or other unincorporated organization.

Solved Problem 16.1. Calculating the Effect of Partnership Net Income on Adjusted Gross Income (AGI)

The partnership of Dole, Hawser, and Hall share profits and losses equally. For the tax year 1992, the partnership earned $100,000 and recorded tax deductible expenses of $70,000. For 1992 the partnership made no cash distributions of profits to partners. Hall, one of the partners, also had dividend income of $20,000 and interest income of $30,000. (a) What is the partnership's 1992 distributable income? (b) What is Hall's 1992 AGI?

Solution 16.1

(a)

Partnership income	$100,000
Less: Partnership expenses	70,000
Partnership distributable income	$ 30,000

(b) A partner must add to taxable income his or her share of partnership income whether or not that income is actually distributed to the partner. Thus Hall's 1992 AGI would be $60,000, calculated as follows:

Partnership income ($30,000 × ⅓)	$10,000
Dividend income	20,000
Interest income	30,000
AGI	$60,000

Tax Filing Requirements for a Partnership

Partnerships are required to file an information tax return (Form 1065), which shows the total earnings of the partnership for the year, together with each partner's distributive share of income and expense. A partnership must file Form 1065 by the 15th day of the 4th month following the close of its tax year.

Solved Problem 16.2. Determining the Due Date for a Partnership Tax Return

The partnership of Reed, Davis, and Hadley had a December 31, 1992, year-end. When is the partnership tax return due?

Solution 16.2

A partnership must file Form 1065 by the 15th day of the 4th month following the close of its tax year. Thus the partnership tax return is due April 15, 1993.

Selecting the Partnership's Tax Year

The Internal Revenue Code generally requires partnerships to adopt, retain, or change to the same tax year as partners who own a majority interest (more than 50%) in the partnership's capital and profits. If partners owning a majority interest have different tax years, the partnership must adopt the same tax year as a partner having an interest of 5% or more of the partnership capital and profits. If the tax year cannot be determined under either of these rules, the partnership must adopt a calendar year.

Solved Problem 16.3. Determining the Partnership's Year-End

The Dawson Dredging Company, a newly formed partnership, consists of ten persons, each of whom own an equal interest. Eight of the partners file their tax return using a November 30 year end. What year-end must the partnership adopt?

Solution 16.3

The partnership must use a November 30 year-end since 80% of the partners use November 30. Under the Internal Revenue Code, the tax year must be the same as that of more than 50% of the partners.

Determination of the Basis of Partnership Interest

No gain or loss is recognized to the partnership in exchange for an interest in the partnership. The contributing partner's basis in the partnership interest received is the sum of the money contributed plus the original basis of any other property transferred to the partnership.

Solved Problem 16.4. Determining the Basis of a Partner's Interest in the Partnership

In return for the contribution of property with a cost basis of $100,000 and a fair market value of $200,000 and cash of $25,000 to Baxter Hardware, a partnership, Jason Leonard received a 20% capital interest worth $225,000. (a) What is Jason's nontaxable gain? (b) What is Jason's basis in the partnership?

Solution 16.4

(a) Jason's nontaxable gain is $100,000, calculated as follows:

Value of partnership interest		$225,000
Less:		
Cost basis of property contributed	$100,000	
Cash contributed	25,000	125,000
Nontaxable gain		$100,000

(b) Jason's basis in the partnership is $125,000 (cost basis of property contributed of $100,000, plus cash contributed of $25,000).

Tax Treatment of Partnership Income and Losses

Under the conduit principle, each partner must report his or her distributive share of income, losses, deductions, and credits for the partnership's taxable year that ends within the partner's taxable year. If both the partnership's and the partner's tax year ends on December 31, 1992, each partner must report his or her share of the partnership's income, deductions, etc., on a personal tax return (Form 1040) for 1992. If the individual partner is on a calendar year, while the partnership is on a fiscal year end, i.e., June 30, 1992, the partner must include his or her pro rata share of partnership net income and losses, whether actually distributed or undistributed, for the partnership year that ends within the personal tax year.

Solved Problem 16.5. Reporting Each Partner's Distributive Share of Income, Losses, and Deductions

The partnership of Boxer and Jones has a fiscal year ending June 30. The partners have always shared profits and losses in the ratio of 60% to 40%. Jones files his personal tax return on a calendar-year basis. After deducting all operating expenses, the partnership realized net income of $100,000 for the year ended June 30, 1992. What amount of partnership income must Jones report for the calendar year 1992 on his personal tax return?

Solution 16.5

Jones must report $40,000 (net income of $100,000 × 40%) on his personal tax return for the calendar year 1992.

DISTRIBUTING INCOME

It is a partner's share of partnership income that triggers taxation—not a distribution of cash. Cash receipts that exceed a partner's basis in the partnership are treated as a gain on the sale of a capital asset.

Note that partners have a right to agree to distribute profits in accordance with one predetermined ratio and losses in another. Thus partners can agree to share losses in such a way as to benefit those members whose tax status warrants that they absorb a greater share of the losses. Of course, such an arrangement would require that these partners also assume a greater share of the partnership liabilities.

LOSS LIMITATIONS

A partner may not deduct partnership losses that exceed his or her partnership basis. However, such losses may be carried forward until the partner's basis is increased enough so as to permit the carryforward loss to be deducted.

Solved Problem 16.6. Calculating the Amount of a Partner's Operating Loss to Be Deducted on His or Her Personal Tax Return

Morse and Beck are operating as the Mobec Realty Partnership and share profits and losses equally. At the beginning of 1992, Morse's partnership basis is $50,000. For 1992 the partnership sustained a $160,000 operating loss, but in 1993 it earned a $140,000 profit.

(a) How much of her share of the partnership operating loss can Morse deduct on her 1992 personal tax return? (b) How much of the nondeductible loss, if any, can Morse deduct on her 1993 personal tax return?

Solution 16.6

(a) For the year 1992, Morse can only deduct $50,000 of her $80,000 share ($160,000 × 50%) of the operating loss. This results in a capital basis of zero at the beginning of 1992, and the remaining $30,000 loss ($80,000 − $50,000) will be carried forward.

(b) Morse may deduct the remaining $30,000 carryforward loss against her $70,000 distribution of profits ($140,000 × 50%), so that in 1993 she will report net partnership income of $40,000 ($70,000 − $30,000). The basis of Morse's partnership interest at the end of 1993 is now $40,000.

Distribution of Special Partnership Items

Certain items that appear on the partnership tax return are not considered in arriving at the partnership's net income. Instead, these items must be reported individually by each partner based upon previously agreed upon allocations. These individually reported partnership items include:

(1) long-term capital gains and losses;
(2) short-term capital gains and losses;
(3) gains and losses from sales of certain business property and involuntary losses;
(4) charitable contributions;
(5) dividend income; and
(6) other items specified by the Internal Revenue Code.

Solved Problem 16.7. Calculating the Distribution of Special Partnership Items

The architectural firm partnership of Blank, Daniels, Withers, and Camp had the following items of income and expense for the tax year 1992:

Professional fees received	$9,000,000
Dividends received	500,000
Net long-term capital gains	400,000
Net short-term capital gains	220,000
Salaries paid	4,500,000
Operating costs (rents, electricity)	1,300,000
Payroll and other taxes	200,000
Charitable contributions	100,000

(a) Calculate the ordinary income of the partnership. (b) Prepare a list of items to be reported separately.

Solution 16.7

(a)

Professional fees received		$9,000,000
Salaries paid	$4,500,000	
Operating costs (rents, electricity)	1,300,000	
Payroll and other taxes	200,000	6,000,000
Partnership ordinary income		$3,000,000

(b)

Items to be reported separately:

Dividends received	$500,000
Net long-term capital gains	400,000
Net short-term capital gains	220,000
Charitable contributions	100,000

CORPORATE TAXATION

If an organization is incorporated under state law, it will usually be taxed as a corporation. An ordinary business corporation files a Form 1120 or a Short Form 1120-A. The Short Form may be used if the corporation's gross receipts and total assets are under $250,000 and other requirements are met.

Corporate Tax Rates

In 1992 corporations were subject to the following graduated rate structure:

Taxable Income	Tax Rate
Not over $50,000	15%
Over $50,000 but not over $75,000	25%
Over $75,000	34%

An additional 5% tax is imposed on a corporation's taxable income in excess of $100,000. The maximum additional tax is $11,750. This provision phases out the benefit of graduated rates for corporations with taxable income between $100,000 and $335,000; corporations with income in excess of $335,000 pay, in effect, a flat tax at a 34% rate.

Solved Problem 16.8. Calculating a Corporation's Tax Liability

For 1992 the Olympic Paint Corporation reported a gross income of $400,000 and allowable deductions of $100,000. Calculate the total tax liability for 1992.

Solution 16.8

Gross income	$400,000
Less: Deductions	100,000
Taxable income	$300,000
Tax computation:	
15% of first $50,000	$ 7,500
25% of next $25,000	6,250
34% of $225,000 ($300,000 – $75,000)	76,500
5% surcharge on $200,000 ($300,000 – $100,000)	10,000
Total corporate tax	$100,250

SPECIAL DEDUCTIONS FOR CORPORATIONS

Special tax saving advantages are available to corporations. They include (1) the dividends received deduction, (2) the net operating loss (NOL) carryback and carryforward, and (3) the amortization of organizational expenditures.

The Dividends Received Deduction

The purpose of the dividends received deduction is to prevent triple taxation. Without this deduction, the first corporation would have to pay a tax on its dividend income before making a nondeductible dividend distribution to a second shareholder corporation. Later, when this second recipient corporation, after payment of a second corporate income tax, pays a nondeductible dividend to its shareholders, such income would again be subject to a tax at the shareholder level. In order to alleviate this unfairness, the second shareholder corporation is granted a dividends received deduction on its domestic dividend income.

The amount of the dividends received deduction depends on the percentage of ownership that the recipient shareholder corporation holds in the *domestic* corporation making the dividend payment. The percentages for dividends received are as follows:

Percentage of Ownership by Corporate Shareholder	Deduction Percentage
Less than 20%	70%
20% or more (but less than 80%)	80%
80% or more	100%

Solved Problem 16.9. Using the Dividends Received Deduction to Calculate a Corporation's Taxable Income

The Rax Chemical Corporation owns 25% of the voting common stock of the Domestic Pipeline, Inc. For the year 1992, Rax receives $100,000 in business income and $80,000 in dividends from Domestic Pipeline. If its deductions for 1992 totalled $100,000, what is Rax's 1991 taxable income?

Solution 16.9.

Income	$100,000
Dividends	80,000
Total	$180,000
Less:	
Deductions:	100,000
Taxable income before the dividend received deduction	$ 80,000
Less: Dividends received deduction ($80,000 × 80%)	64,000
Taxable income	$ 16,000

Net Operating Losses (NOL)

The net operating loss of a corporation may be carried back three years and forward fifteen years to offset taxable income.

Solved Problem 16.10. Calculating a Corporation's Net Operating Loss (NOL)

In 1992 the Frontline Communications Corporation reported gross income of $300,000 and operating expenses of $500,000. Frontline also received $100,000 of dividends from a domestic corporation in which it owns less than 20%. Calculate Frontline's 1992 net operating loss (NOL).

Solution 16.10

Income		$300,000
Dividends		100,000
		$400,000
Less:		
Operating expenses	$500,000	
Dividends received deduction ($100,000 × 70%)	70,000	570,000
Taxable income (or loss)		($170,000)

Note that corporations are also permitted to forego the carryback option and elect instead to carry forward the election for 15 years.

Amortization of Organizational Expenditures

Organizational expenses include the cost of obtaining the corporate charter, accounting fees, and legal expenses. A newly formed corporation can either carry organization costs as an asset, or it can elect to amortize the expenditures over a minimum 60-month period beginning with the first month of its operations.

Solved Problem 16.11. Calculating the Deduction for Organizational Expenses

The Livestock Feed Corporation was formed on July 1, 1992. The following expenses were incurred during its first year of operation (July 1, 1992, to December 31, 1992).

Expenses of temporary directors	$700
Fee paid to secretary of state of incorporation	500
Legal services incident to incorporation	300

What would be the amortization expense deduction for the six month period ending December 31, 1992?

Solution 16.11

The monthly amortization would be $25, calculated as follows:

Expenses of temporary directors	$ 700
Fee paid to secretary of state of incorporation	500
Legal services incident to incorporation	300
	$1,500

$1,500 ÷ 60 months = $25.
$25 × 6 months = $150 for the year ended December 31, 1992.

Capital Gains and Losses

A corporation is not permitted to use net capital losses to offset ordinary income. Net capital losses can only be used to offset past or future capital gains. Any excess losses may be carried back to the preceding three years, and any remaining unused capital losses may then be carried over for a period of five years.

Solved Problem 16.12. Calculating the Taxable Income of a Corporation That Has a Capital Loss

The Beanbag Toy Corporation had the following items of income and expenses for the tax year 1992:

Income	$8,000,000
Cost of goods sold	2,000,000
Long-term capital gains	400,000
Long-term capital losses	840,000
Salaries paid	1,600,000
Operating costs (rents, electricity)	1,400,000
Payroll and other taxes	300,000

Calculate Beanbag's 1992 taxable income.

Solution 16.12

Income		$8,000,000
Less: Cost of goods sold		2,000,000
Gross profit		$6,000,000
Less: Operating expenses		
Salaries paid	$1,600,000	
Operating costs (rents, electricity)	1,400,000	
Payroll and other taxes	300,000	3,300,000
Taxable income		$2,700,000

The net long-term capital loss of $440,000 ($400,000 – $840,000) cannot be used to offset corporate ordinary income but may be carried back three years. Any remaining unused loss may then be carried forward for five years.

Charitable Contributions

Corporations are not permitted an unlimited charitable contribution. A charitable contribution made by a corporation may not exceed 10% of a corporation's taxable income before deducting the charitable contribution. Any excess unallowable contribution may be carried over to the next five tax years.

Solved Problem 16.13. Calculating the Charitable Deduction Limitation For a Corporation

The Markoe Coal Corporation had the following items of income and expenses for the tax year 1992:

Income	$7,500,000
Cost of goods sold	3,000,000
Salaries paid	1,500,000
Operating costs (rents, electricity)	1,600,000
Payroll and other taxes	300,000
Charitable contributions	200,000

Calculate Markoe's 1992 taxable income.

Solution 16.13

Income		$7,500,000
Less: Cost of goods sold		3,000,000
Gross profit		$4,500,000
Less: Operating expenses		
Salaries paid	1,500,000	
Operating costs (rents, electricity)	1,600,000	
Payroll and other taxes	300,000	3,400,000
Net income before deduction for charitable contribution		$1,100,000
Less: Charitable limitation (10% × $1,100,000)		110,000
Taxable income		$ 990,000

The remaining $90,000 ($200,000 – $110,000) of unused charitable contributions is carried over to the next five tax years.

The Tax-Free Incorporation of a Business

The creation of a new corporation is essentially a non-recognition transaction. Under a tax-free incorporation, certain assets are transferred to the newly formed corporation in return for stock. Recognition of gain or loss on the property transferred is deferred based on the theory that the new entity is merely a change in the form of doing business.

80% CONTROL REQUIREMENT

In order to achieve tax-free incorporation, a control requirement must be met. This means that the person or persons transferring property to a corporation must be in control of the corporation after the transaction is completed. Control is defined as having at least 80% of the combined voting power of all classes of stock entitled to vote and at least 80% of the total number of shares of all other classes of stock of the corporation.

Solved Problem 16.14. Formulating a Tax-Free Incorporation

Karl owns a patent right worth $500,000 and Marks owns a manufacturing plant worth $1,500,000. Karl and Marks decide to organize the Jomo Textile Corporation, with an authorized common stock of $2,000,000. Karl transfers his patent right to the newly formed corporation in return for $500,000 of its common stock, and Marks transfers her plant to the corporation in return for the remaining $1,500,000 of stock. Is any gain or loss recorded based upon the transaction?

Solution 16.14

No gain or loss is recognized to either Karl or Marks, since immediately after the transfer they own more than 80% of the combined voting power of all classes of stock entitled to vote.

TAX TREATMENT OF CORPORATE DISTRIBUTIONS

Any distribution made by a corporation of money or property, other than its own stock, will be taxed to the distributed as follows:

(1)   ordinary income to the shareholder to the extent of the corporation's earnings and profits;

(2)   that portion of the corporate distribution that is not taxed as a dividend will be treated as a return on the stockholder's investment.

Dividend Defined

A dividend is any distribution of property made by a corporation to its shareholders out of its earnings and profits accumulated after February 28, 1913, or out of its earnings and profits for the current taxable year, computed at the close of the current taxable year.

Solved Problem 16.15. Determining the Taxability of a Cash Dividend

The Zenon Copper Mining Corporation was incorporated on January 1, 1988, and for each of its first 4 years of operation it earned $2,000, for a total earning of $8,000. At the end of the fourth year, it distributed a $10,000 cash dividend. (a) How does the Internal Revenue Code treat the first $8,000 of the $10,000 cash dividend? (b) How does the Code treat the remaining $2,000?

Solution 16.15

(a) The first $8,000 of the $10,000 cash dividend will be taxed as if it was ordinary income.

(b) The remaining $2,000 ($10,000 – $8,000) will be treated as a return on the taxpayer's investment and therefore nontaxable.

Stock Dividends

Stock dividends are not taxable if they are pro rata distributions of stock, or stock rights, on common stock. The shareholder has merely received additional shares to represent the same total investment. The additional shares received lower the original cost basis of each share of stock held by the shareholder.

Solved Problem 16.16. Determining the Cost Basis and Taxability of a Stock Dividend

The Fenton Steel Fabricator Corporation issued a 10% stock dividend to all of its common stockholders. Wallace Anther owned 10,000 common shares issued by Anther that originally cost $10,000. (a) How many shares did Wallace receive? (b) What is the new cost basis of each share? (c) Is the stock dividend taxable?

Solution 16.16

(a) Wallace received an additional 1,000 shares (10,000 × 10%).
(b) The new cost basis of each share is $0.91 a share ($10,000 ÷ 11,000 shares, (10,000 + 1,000 additional shares).
(c) Stock dividends are generally not taxable.

Property Dividends

When a corporation distributes property rather than cash to the shareholder, the amount distributed is measured by the fair market value on the date of the distribution.

Solved Problem 16.17. Determining the Taxability of a Property Dividend

The Phelan Appliance Corporation distributes land with a fair market value of $75,000 to Wendell Cork, the corporation's sole shareholder. To what extent, if any, is the dividend taxable to Wendell?

Solution 16.17

Wendell has a taxable dividend of $75,000, the fair market value of the property.

THE SMALL BUSINESS CORPORATION (S CORPORATION)

Definition of a Small Business Corporation

A small, closely held corporation may elect to be treated in a manner similar to that of a partnership. In effect, all the earnings or losses of the electing corporation are passed through to the shareholders. The result is no tax liability at the corporate level. Instead, the shareholders are individually taxed on their share of the corporate earnings, whether or not the corporation actually distributes the earnings to them.

Qualifications Necessary to Be an S Corporation

In order to qualify as a small business corporation, the following requirements must be met:

(1) The entity must be a domestic corporation (i.e., incorporated or organized in the United States).
(2) There cannot be more than 35 shareholders, and they generally must all be individuals, estates, or certain trusts. A husband and wife who own stock jointly are treated as a single shareholder.
(3) None of its shareholders are nonresident aliens.
(4) Only one class of stock has been issued.
(5) An S corporation cannot own 80% or more of the stock of another corporation.

When the Election Must Be Made

To be effective for the following tax year, the election can be made at any time during the current year. If the election is sought for the current year, it must be made on or before the fifteenth day of the third month of that current year.

Solved Problem 16.18. Determining the Due Date for an S Corporation Election

In 1991, the Thornton Cooler Corporation, a calendar year corporation, decided to become an S corporation for the year beginning January 1, 1992. A timely election was made during 1992 to accomplish this objective. If, however, the election is to be applicable to 1992, when must the election be filed?

Solution 16.18

The election must be filed on or before March 15, 1992. An election after this date will not permit Thornton to operate as an S corporation until January 1, 1993.

An election to be treated as an S corporation must be filed on Form 2553 and signed by *all* of the shareholders.

Solved Problem 16.19. Calculating the Effect of an S Corporation's Net Income on Adjusted Gross Income (AGI)

The Dickens Tool Corporation, an S corporation, earned $500,000 and recorded tax deductible operating expenses of $300,000. For 1992 the corporation made no cash distributions of profits to its shareholders. Hector Peters, a shareholder who owned 100 of the 1,000 common shares outstanding, also had dividend income of $50,000 from another corporation and royalty income of $60,000. (a) What is the corporation's 1992 distributable taxable income? (b) What is Hector's 1992 AGI?

Solution 16.19

(a)

Corporate income	$500,000
Less: Operating expenses	300,000
Corporation distributable taxable income	$200,000

(b)

Hector must pick up 10% (100/1,000 shares) of the corporation's taxable income whether or not actually distributed. Thus, Hector's 1992 AGI would be $130,000, calculated as follows:

S corporation income ($200,000 × 10%)	$ 20,000
Dividend income	50,000
Royalty income	60,000
AGI	$130,000

RECONCILIATION OF TAXABLE INCOME AND ACCOUNTING INCOME

Taxable income and book net income are seldom the same amount. Many items of book income, such as the proceeds from a life insurance policy due to the death of a corporate officer and municipal bond interest, must be included in calculating book income but are not taxable. In addition, net capital losses and the federal corporate tax liability are deductible for book purposes but are not deductible for tax purposes. Form 1120 (the corporate tax return) contains schedules that reconcile a corporation's book income with its taxable income.

Solved Problem 16.20. Reconciling a Corporation's Taxable Income with Its Book Income

During 1992 the Melvin Leather Corporation reported the following transactions:

Net income per financial statements after tax	$70,000
Federal tax liability ($40,000 × 15%)	6,000
Taxable income	50,000
Interest income from municipal bonds	5,000
Net capital losses	29,000
Life insurance proceeds due to death of Sidney Olin, the president of Melvin Corporation	50,000

Prepare a schedule reconciling book net income with taxable income.

Solution 16.20

Net income per financial statements after tax		$ 70,000
Add: Nondeductible amounts		
Federal tax liability	$ 6,000	
Net capital losses	29,000	35,000
		$105,000
Less: Nontaxable amounts		
Interest income from municipal bonds	$ 5,000	
Life insurance proceeds	50,000	55,000
Corporate taxable income		$ 50,000

*T*he decision whether to operate as a partnership or in the corporate form when conducting a trade or business must be carefully considered. When doing business as a partnership, the partners, and not the partnership, are subject to tax. A partner must take into account his or her share partnership income, losses, capital gains and losses, and other separate items of income and deductions. A partner can deduct partnership losses directly against his or her *other personal income. Each partner must determine the basis of his or her partnership interest upon admission to the partnership. No gain or loss will be recognized to a partnership or to any of its partners where property is contributed. Operating in the corporate form subjects the corporate-source income to double taxation—once at the corporate level and again when cash or property dividends are distributed to the shareholders. In addition, corporate operating and stock losses cannot be passed along to the shareholders. The election of S status generally avoids tax at the corporate level and permits corporate distributions to be taxed only once, at the individual income tax level.*

Index